Changing Lives through Redecision Therapy

by
Mary McClure Goulding
and
Robert L. Goulding

*Western Institute for Group
and Family Therapy*

With a Foreword by
VIRGINIA M. SATIR

Grove Press, Inc.
New York

First Evergreen Edition 1982
First Printing 1982
ISBN: 0-394-17980-3
Library of Congress Catalog Card Number: 81-48537

Library of Congress Cataloging in Publication Data

Goulding, Mary McClure, 1925–
  Changing lives through redecision therapy.

  Originally published: New York: Brunner/Mazel, c1979.
  Bibliography: p. 291
  Includes index.
  1. Psychotherapy.   2. Transactional analysis.
I. Goulding, Robert L., 1917–   . II. Title.
RC480.5.G663   1982   616.89′14   81-48537
ISBN 0-394-17980-3 (pbk.)   AACR2

Manufactured in the United States of America
GROVE PRESS, INC., 196 West Houston Street,
New York, N.Y. 10014

Changing
Lives
through
Redecision
Therapy

To

"Nan" and "Zach"

and all the other participants in and out of this book,

with love and respect.

FOREWORD

The content, spirit and direction expressed in this book is the flowering resulting from rudimentary beginnings occasioned by survival necessity during World War II, 1941-1945.

In brief, the world had been outraged at the incomprehensible human atrocities perpetrated by one group upon another.

The energy of every man and woman involved was essential to stopping this scourge. In the armed forces, this meant that when service personnel were psychologically injured, they needed to be restored to duty as soon as possible.

There was no time to waste. Up to this time the techniques and philosophy relating to treating psychological impairment were slow, often with disappointing results. These approaches were centered more on the pathology.

There had to be a more immediate and successful approach. This turned out to be focusing on strengthening health with a view to quick results. Here the approach was made directly to the individual and to his capacity to be restored with the conviction that it could be done.

The new focus was how to achieve function as quickly as possible. The trite phrase that "necessity is the mother of invention" applied here, as it was soon discovered that people had far more potential for recreating themselves than had ever before been thought. New possibilities began to loom.

The effect of these efforts were slow to manifest themselves in the private and civilian psychotherapeutic sector. However, within a few years following the end of the war, therapies that focused on integration and hope for change and a conviction that people could "get well" began to surface. They teased and eventually began to reroute and transform established psychological approaches. Gestalt therapy, transactional analysis, rational-emotive therapy, bioenergetics, Rolfing and other body therapies, family therapy, and brief therapy were among these.

Without going into detail about the various "ups and downs" encountered by the leaders of these new therapies, now enough evidence has accumulated to show that human beings *can* grow and change and they can be "responsible" for their own well-being.

All children are born little. Their instructors for becoming fully functioning people are the adults already there who shepherd them from the time when they are born, when no child can take care of him or herself, to the time when they can.

These instructors (parents) can present only what they have learned. If their learning for how to be fully human is incomplete or distorted, that is all they have to pass on.

These instructors do the best they can. Since very little attention has been paid to developing fully functioning human beings, most of us build ourselves on non-credentialled staff. The curriculum has been focused largely on conformity and obedience, which is a fertile soil for developing decisions and conclusions about oneself that are often detrimental. Furthermore, these decisions and conclusions often *feel* genetic.

The need for hope among people is crucial. Among therapists the need is critical.

A philosophy of hope, an understanding of how growth and change process works in humans, techniques and approaches to make it happen, and an absolute "bone" conviction that people can change, can transform the threat of "burn-out" in therapists to a feeling of hope and conviction that they can really help.

I think Mary and Bob Goulding understand this thoroughly. This enables them to come to every person with compassion, hope, and certainty that each person can become fully human. They show in simple, straightforward ways how to accomplish this.

VIRGINIA M. SATIR

ACKNOWLEDGMENTS

When Bob first joined Eric Berne's San Francisco Social Psychiatry Seminars in 1961, the membership of the Seminars did not exceed 20 people, most of whom were on the Board of Directors! Since then, its successor, the International Transactional Analysis Association, has grown to over 10,000 members in over 50 countries around the world. The organization sets standards for TA therapists and for those members who use their knowledge of TA in special fields, as in business and education. Oral and written exams must be passed for certification in advanced membership. We want to acknowledge, first, friends from the very early days of TA: Joseph Concannon, Franklin Ernst, Kenneth Everts, Viola Litt Callaghan, Ray Poindexter, Mel Boyce, Frances Matson, Myra Schapps, Claude Steiner, Herb Courland, Anne Garrett, Paul McCormick, Tom and Amy Harris; and just a little later, a whole host of people: Jean Fowler, Jeanne Kanevski, Jack Dusay, Muriel James, Dorothy Jongeward, Stephen Karpman, Hedges Capers, H. D. Johns, Elizabeth Palms, Sol Samuels, Gordon Haiberg, Mary Michelson, Bill Collins,

Herb Enos, Gordon Gritter, Ben Lewis, Bob Hodges, Margaret Frings Keyes. Then, as time went on, many other good friends became clinical teaching members: John Daley, Len Campos, Tom Frazier, Jerry White, Treva Sudhalter, Jon and Laurie Weiss, Natalie and Morris Haimowitz, Fanita English, Richard Abell, Charles Tuggle, David Steere, Shulamit Peck, Kristyn Huige, Lois Johnson, Bill and Tracy Wolfson, Stanley Woollams, Harris Peck, John Anderson, Louis Forman, John O'Hearne, Lillian O'Hearne, Graham Barnes, Vann Joines, Marty Holloway, Barbara and Jim Allen, Harry Boyd, John Gladfelter, Martin Haykin, Martin Groder, Jack Kaufman, Dorothy Hellman, Vince Gilpin, Paul Ware, Curtis Steele and Nancy Porter, Barbara Hibner Gonzales, Rudi Rogoll, Gisela Kottwitz, Mike Reddy, and Carol Solomon. We could add most of the other TM's on the list, as well as more than half of the other 10,000 members whom we have taught over the years, and from whom we have also learned.

We wish to thank our associates: Ruth McClendon, Les Kadis, Bob Drye, Gene Kerfoot, George McClendon, Bill Holloway, Jim Heenan, George Thomson, John McNeel and Ellyn Bader, and our part time faculty, Ed Frost, Will Baumker, Liladee Bellinger and Joan Minninger and our former associates, Charles Elias, Virginia Satir, and Anita Plummer.

We thank our Gestalt friends: Jim Simkin, Miriam and Erv Polster, Joen Fagan, and Irma Shepherd. We have learned much from each of them, as well as from many of our other friends in our American Academy of Psychotherapists family.

And of course, we thank posthumously Eric, and Fritz, and Dave Kupfer.

For reading early versions of this book and discussing them with us, our special thanks go to the participants in the four-week workshops in 1977 and 1978, and to the Doctoral Candidates from the Fielding Institute who attended a May, 1978, workshop here.

And for his magnificent job of editing, and his encouragement, most especially I (Bob) want to thank my oldest and dearest friend, my brother Phil G. Goulding, whose patience, wit, and skill kept us out of jargon and into good, plain English. Mary, of course, thanks him too.

CONTENTS

Foreword vii
    Virginia M. Satir

Acknowledgments xi

1. INTRODUCTION TO REDECISION THERAPY 3

2. OVERVIEW OF TRANSACTIONAL ANALYSIS 11
    Ego States 12
    Child Ego State 12
    Parent Ego State 21
    Adult Ego State 23
    Transactions 26
    Strokes 29
    Time Structure 29

Games 30
Rackets 33
Injunctions and Counter-Injunctions 34
Decisions 39
Scripts 42

3. IMPASSES AND REDECISIONS 44

4. CONTRACTS 50

The Contractual Process 50
No-Suicide and No-Homicide Contracts 55
No-Psychosis Contracts 61
Contracts with Reluctant or Involuntary Clients 69
Changing Unacceptable Contracts 71
Therapy Without a Contract 82
Ulterior Contracts 85

5. STROKING 94

Giving Strokes 96
Accepting Strokes 99
Seeking Strokes 102
Self-Stroking 103

6. EMOTIONS 110

Anger 117
Suppressed Anger 127
Blame 133
Sadness 135
Suppressed Sadness 147
Fear and Anxiety 150
Suppressed Fear 155
Shame 157
Guilt 160
Regret 171

7. GOODBYES 171

8. Redecisions 185

    The Redecision Scene 185
    Recent Scene 189
    Early Scenes 190
    Imaginary Scenes 194
    Combination of Scenes 197
    Context, Other, and Client 202

9. The Curing of Depression 215

    If Things Get Too Bad, I'll Kill Myself 218
    If You Don't Change, I'll Kill Myself 221
    I'll Kill Myself and Then You'll Be Sorry
      (or Love Me) 228
    I'll Almost Die and Then You'll Be Sorry
      (or Love Me) 229
    I'll Get You to Kill Me 230
    I'll Show You Even If It Kills Me 231
    I'll Get You Even If It Kills Me 238
    Summary 239

10. Obsession-Compulsion: A Case History 241

11. Phobias: One Wednesday Afternoon 258

12. After Redecision 280

    Notes 287

    General Bibliography 291

    Index 295

Changing
Lives
through
Redecision
Therapy

CHAPTER 1

Introduction to Redecision Therapy

This book is written to teach psychotherapists how to cure people.

It is also written to help people cure themselves.

The authors see no contradictions in these two purposes. Our primary audience is psychotherapists, but we view them as being endowed with no magical powers which are not also available to the people they seek to cure. Indeed, if the outcome depended solely on the magical powers of therapists, there would be no cures.

For more than 15 years our chief activity has been teaching therapists how to cure people. Our methods combine many approaches, including (but not exclusively) transactional analysis, gestalt, interactive group psychotherapy, and desensitization. We are interested in, and have taught, whatever works—whatever works to aid people to stop being phobic, to turn their anxiety into enthusiasm, to stop being compulsive or depressed, and to *enjoy life* instead. We have helped couples stop fighting and we have helped them start making love. We have helped other couples look for joy elsewhere when they were unwilling to find it together. We have taught people how to *manage their own feelings* instead of deceiving themselves that other people *made* them angry, sad, depressed, anxious, enraged, confused, bored, or worried.

Eric Berne, the genius who fathered transactional analysis, wrote the million-copy book *Games People Play,* and founded the 10,000-member International Transactional Analysis Association (ITAA), wrote and talked about *curing* people, rather than "making progress." He talked about pausing before entering a group, to ask himself the question: "How can I cure everyone in this room *today?*" That has been our question for these 15 years, and that is what this book is all about.

The methods we use are simple, clear, and concise. In teaching, however, that is not enough: They also are *communicable.* Psychotherapy has been called an art, not a science, but it can be a science as well as an art, and the science can be taught; so can artistry. Our methods do not require the therapist to be all-powerful or all-knowing. They do require that the therapist listen carefully, observe carefully, and confront carefully.

Our approach is creative, as we constantly look for new methods. We do not blame the patient when there are failures, or make lists of "untreatable patients" to present to the Annual Meeting of the American Psychiatric Association. Rather, we search within ourselves . . . and within others . . . to find a method, a way of creating an environment that will facilitate change. The method of therapy we use to bring about change we call *redecision therapy.* This book describes this method, starting with the theoretical framework of transactional analysis as we have refined it, and then giving detailed examples of our work.

When we first make contact with a patient, we listen and look for a series of connections: What is the chief complaint? What was this patient doing to himself at the time he decided to seek assistance? What are his feelings? What behavior does he dislike in himself? Is he obsessing instead of thinking? Is he depressed? Is he angry most of the time, or bored, or phobic? Is he unhappy in his marriage? In his work? There is some *specific* feeling or thinking or behavior about which the patient is unhappy; otherwise, he would not now be sitting before us. What does he want to change? This specific change, desired by the patient, becomes the *contract*.

Having identified the specific complaint and formulated with the client his specific contract, we are now interested in his emotions. How does he generally feel about himself and his environment? What kinds of games does he play to maintain his unhappy feelings? What beliefs and fantasies does he cling to in order to stay unhappy? For instance, does he lie awake at night, anxiously obsessing about the future? Does he obsess about what the President is doing in order to maintain angry feelings? In sum, does he ignore the "here and now" in order to be unhappy?

As we listen to a patient, we ask him to stay in the present tense. When he gives information about the past, we ask him to pretend that he is in that past scene right now, and to tell it as if it were happening at this moment. When he wants to talk about someone, we ask him to pretend the person is in the therapy room and to fantasize talking to the person right here. In this way, we keep our therapy focused on the *here* and *now*. By being in a scene rather than talking about it, the patient connects memory with affect and can deal more directly with his internal struggles.

We ask the client to claim his own autonomy whenever he gives it up. For instance, he might say, "A thought came to me." Now how in the world can a thought "come"? Who does the thinking? So we ask him to say this another way, claiming credit for his own thoughts. If he starts a sentence with "it," as when he speaks of being anxious or depressed and says, "It comes over me," which is both impossible and a cop-out, we ask him to start his sentence with "I." "I scare me" and "I sadden and depress myself" are statements that acknowledge what the patient is actually doing to himself. We ask the patient to be aware that he is responsible for his own feelings. We teach that he makes himself anxious. There are no uncontrollable emotional clouds that descend upon us, even though we may speak as if there were. We also teach that each person makes himself feel and that no one makes another person feel.

People don't "make him angry"; he chooses anger in response to the stimulus of another person . . . it is *his* anger. This is one of the most significant statements in this book. The notion that we are in charge of our own feelings is counter to our literature, our songs, and our upbringing. "You made me love you, I didn't want to do it," says the song. "The world situation worries us all," says the commentator. "You make me so worried I can't sleep," says mother to daughter. Therapists who ask patients, "How does that make you feel?" reinforce the patient's own delusion that he is a helpless victim unable to cope even with his own emotions.

We explore what kinds of early decisions the patient made in order to get along in the home of his childhood. What kinds of decisions satisfied overt and covert instructions to him? What is his life-style? Is he heroic or banal, winner or loser? How are these early decisions still being used in his life today? And, again, how does he choose to change? How does he want to feel differently? Behave differently? Think differently?

We are interested in his "stuck" spots . . . which in gestalt therapy are called "impasses." We are interested in how his impasses relate both to his recent past and his archaic past, and how we can help him resolve these impasses.

For instance, the person who says, "I want to stop smoking," while lighting a cigarette, is in an obvious impasse. A part of him says, "I don't want to smoke" while another part says, "I want to smoke." Until he resolves this, he will smoke and harass himself or not smoke and be miserable. This impasse, like most impasses, may well relate to an early decision that he still maintains outside his awareness . . . a decision about hurting himself, for instance.

In our experience most good therapy is centered on assisting the patient to break through a series of impasses, which had their origins in messages he received in childhood and decisions he made about these messages.

As the patient works through his impasses, we offer cognitive understanding of how his archaic patterns of thinking, feeling, and doing fit together and affect his life in the present. Pure gestaltists may not give such cognitive feedback; pure TA therapists seldom allow the highly emotional work which leads to impasse breakthrough. Research done by Lieberman, Yalom, and Miles[1] indicates the importance of both affect and cognition. They state that those therapists who give maximum cognitive feedback with moderate affective stimulation get the best results.

We work only in groups and for the most part in intense groups in which people stay with us for three days, a week, two weeks, or four weeks. We have found that the process taking place in a group of people living together is far more effective for change than ongoing groups that meet for an hour or two, once or twice a week. We work in groups for many reasons, one of which is the support and encouragement participants give each other. The group can be used by the patient for experiments in being different. For instance, a client may have had a traumatic experience in second grade, decided never to recite again, and remained phobic. He now has trouble giving public speeches, or even lecturing to his own students. After some important impasse work is done, he may use the group as enthusiastic audience for his first "public speech."

Group therapy allows the therapist more leeway in stopping work when it is to the patient's advantage to stop. If a patient breaks through an important impasse in the first few minutes of work, for example, we like him to be able to relish the feeling of victory before he does any more work. This is difficult to do if we have another 40 minutes left in an hour's individual therapy. With a group, we can go on to someone else, while the patient enjoys his victory.

Another advantage of group therapy is the use of the time by other members of the group while one patient is working. Each, reminded of something similar—or different—in his life, may do silent work and make silent resolutions. As one patient makes a breakthrough for himself, others are encouraged by the change and become more confident that they, too, can effect changes for themselves.

The group spirit is entirely different from the environment which exists when individual patients do not even see one another in a waiting room; one goes out the back door before the next one comes in the front. Although much good therapy is done by individual therapists doing individual therapy, our experience indicates that *for us* group therapy is more effective and (extremely important for us) more fun.

Our method of therapy is not complicated. It is tricky, but not complicated . . . and the tricks are not against the patient nor in any way hidden from him. We can cure most height phobias in 10 minutes and water phobias in less than half an hour, as is described in the chapter on phobias. Other problems may take longer, but people do make changes that seem very quick to therapists who believe therapy is a complicated, long-term process. Certainly, in our early experience as therapists, when we worked within the classical system, therapy did take longer . . . sometimes forever . . . and it was too complicated.

We teach our redecision methods at meetings and workshops for the American Group Psychotherapy Association, American Academy of Psychotherapists, American Psychiatric Association, and the International Transactional Analysis Association, and at workshops and professional meetings all over the world. Often therapists are skeptical. People challenge us . . . and come to study with us. Bill Holloway, formerly treasurer of AGPA, listened to us for five years with skepticism and then came to California to see for himself. He learned our methods, which he added to his own methods and skills, passed the clinical and teaching membership examinations in TA, became president of ITAA, joined our faculty at the Western Institute for Group and Family Therapy (WIGFT) and is now training and treating in Southern California. In many parts of the world, training institutes have been established by therapists who learned our methods.

What is a redecision? A man attended one of our lectures and afterwards complained to his therapist that she never did "any of that redecision work" with him. She reminded him that he was no longer suicidal, was making friends instead of staying alone, and was functioning with increased effectiveness at work. To do all this, he must have made redecisions. "Oh," he said, disappointed. "Somehow, I thought redecisions would be fancier."

Redecisions are not always "fancy," if fancy means either dramatic or complicated. When a child is no longer afraid, he'll go into the basement to explore. He may be proud of his new bravery or may not even remember that he used to be afraid. Either way, he has redecided.

Redecisions cannot be made solely by learning the "facts." If the child attempts to talk himself into going into the basement by reminding himself that, "The facts are, there is nothing in this basement that will hurt me," he may react like the little boy in the kreplach story, which is often told to graduate students of psychotherapy: A little boy is afraid of kreplachs (a three-corner pancake filled with meat), so his family sends him to a psychiatrist. The psychiatrist devises a fine treatment plan. She takes the little boy with her to buy the ingredients for kreplachs. Then, together, they chop and cook the meat, add the other ingredients, and prepare the dough. He is interested and unafraid. They roll the dough, cut it, add the meat, and fold the first corner of the first kreplach. He remains unafraid. They fold the second corner. As they fold the third and last corner, the little boy screams, "Oy, kreplach!" and runs from the room. Adult reasoning is not enough.

Nor will adaptation achieve redecision. If the child is shamed, spanked, or told to stand in a corner until he is ready to do as he is told, he may go to the basement because he is more afraid of parents than of basements. In this case, he'll probably remain fearful and will also add other pathological decisions. He may never trust parents again. He may decide never again to let anyone know when he is afraid. He may squelch the childlike part of himself, believing his "childishness" caused the problem. If he is loved for being brave and good enough to conquer his fear of basements, he may go into the basement in order to be loved. Again, he may make additional decisions, this time involving the price of being loved.

In redecision therapy the client experiences the child part of self, enjoys his childlike qualities, and creates fantasy scenes in which he can safely give up the constricting decisions he made in childhood. He recreates the basement scene and this time *does the scene the way he wants to do it.*

Jay, who had feared being alone in the dark ever since seeing *The Wizard of Oz* when he was a child, is creating such a scene.[2] He pretends he is in his present home at night and is holding a flashlight. He will turn the flashlight on whenever he scares himself about the dark and will turn it off when he stops scaring himself. When he reaches the cellar door, in fantasy, he turns on the flashlight and reports being afraid. The therapist suggests he call out, "Hey. I'm not going into this cellar because the Wicked Witch may be there!" As he does this, he laughs delightedly, recognizing that he is no longer afraid of witches.

Peggy pretends to be the goblins in her basement and tries to scare the other "kids" in the group. As she becomes the one who scares people, she stops scaring herself. Elaine, reenacting an early scene with mother, realizes that she is not really afraid of basements; she's afraid of her sadistic mother, who used to put her in the basement for punishment. She affirms that she can now protect herself from such mothers . . . and, spontaneously, is not afraid.

A depressed client fantasizes picking up self as a newborn baby, loving self, and promising self, "I'll take care of you." Then the client fantasizes self as the newborn baby being loved and cared for. Over and over, in angry or sad or funny or exciting scenes, clients "become as little children" in order to shed the pathology of the past. This is what we mean by redecision therapy.

In this introductory chapter, we have highlighted some aspects of redecision therapy. In the chapters that follow, we will first outline the fundamentals of transactional analysis (TA) and describe how we use these fundamentals to get redecisions. Then, in the remainder of the book, we will discuss in detail the methods we use, with transcriptions from our work with patients.

CHAPTER 2

Overview of Transactional Analysis

Transactional analysis is a theory of behavior development which is not complex. This is one of its primary advantages for both therapist and patient. Like other systems, however, it has both a jargon and a basic framework of its own. In this early chapter we will give a brief overview of that framework as a precursor to detailed presentation of our work and will define some . . . by no means all . . . of the jargon. Included will be a short discussion of: ego states (Child, Parent and Adult), transactions, strokes, games, rackets, injunctions, counter-injunctions, decisions and scripts.

The fundamental TA theory was written by Eric Berne and many other therapists, as well as by a few non-therapists. It is published in books, in the *TA Bulletins* and the *TA Journal,* in *Voices* and in other publications.* Our concept of TA is not always in agreement with the fundamental theory written about and practiced by others. We will come to some of our differences in this chapter, and from time to time throughout the book we will discuss other differences.

The building blocks of TA are the ego states, which are by Berne's definition psychological positions the individual takes which are phenomenologically observable. They are drawn simply in the familiar three ego states shown in Figure 1. Our complete ego state drawing is shown in Figure 2. The Parent ego state is made up of incorporations from real parents and parental figures plus what the individual has learned and accepted about parenting from any source. People behave outwardly in ways similar to those of these parental figures, and also give themselves messages inside their heads about behavior, thinking and feeling . . . messages they took from someone else, as well as messages made up when parenting was lacking. The Child ego state is the part of people that thinks, feels and behaves as they did in the past . . . particularly as children, but sometimes as grown-ups. The Adult ego state is the part that thinks, stores and retrieves data, and behaves in a non-feeling way.

THE CHILD EGO STATE

Early Child

In order to more easily understand the development of ego states, it is helpful to think first of the little preverbal child and how he develops his primary ego states: early Child, early Adult and early Parent.

The baby is born with a functioning body and a set of impulses: he gets hungry, he drinks, he makes appropriate use of his diaper, he has other behaviors which seem to be fairly constant for all babies. Without outside information and modeling to guide him, he has basic impulses which lead to observable behavior. Here TA and psychoanalytic theory are somewhat similar. Psychoanalytic theory states that there are impulses which are called "id." In TA, there are cer-

---

* See the General Bibliography for list of general references.

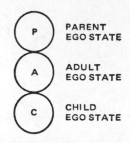

SIMPLE EGO STATE DIAGRAM
Fig. 1

tain phenomenological characteristics of the small infant that we call the early Child ego state . . . a state of being at infant level. At any given time in a child's development, when he behaves as an infant behaves, we say he is in his early Child. (In TA writing, capitalizing the Child, Adult or Parent indicates we are writing about ego states, not a real child or adult or parent.) If, at age five, in response to trauma, he cries in the manner of a very young baby, sucks, wets, and doesn't relate to others, we say he is in this early ego state. This ego state is represented in Figure 3, in which the large circle represents the total Child, and the inner circle represents the infant in the Child, which TA therapists label C_1. The total Child is labeled C_2.

This early Child is the source, the well-spring, of feelings. If an infant is raised lovingly and zestfully, the C_1 becomes more than just basic impulses; it becomes the joyous, enthusiastic stimulus for life and life processes.

Early Adult

. The infant begins to make observations about his environment and himself, and begins to develop the early Adult (which Berne labeled "Little Professor" because of its intuitiveness). This developing Adult is labeled A_1. (See Figure 3.) The infant learns, for instance, that the breast or bottle is not part of self, but comes and goes; he learns that his fingers and toes are part of himself, and under his control. He is now developing his little storehouse of in-

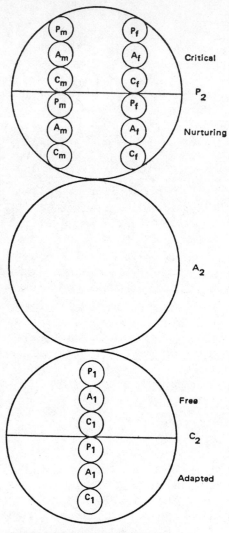

COMPLEX EGO STATE DIAGRAM
Fig. 2

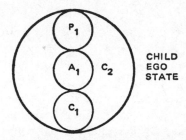

CHILD
EGO
STATE

THIS DIAGRAM SHOWS THE STRUC-
TURE OF THE CHILD EGO STATE. IT
DOES NOT YET SHOW ADULT AND
PARENT EGO STATES, BUT ONLY THE
DEVELOPMENT OF EARLY CHILD,
EARLY ADULT and EARLY PARENT.

Fig. 3

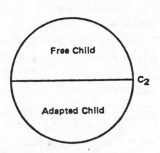

This diagram shows the
FUNCTIONAL division of the
Child Ego State.

Fig. 4

formation. He processes that information and makes decisions based upon it. This information is preverbal and consists of experiential, possibly pictorial, processes. Bob has treated schizophrenics who have early memories of infantile years, remember them pictorially, and, if they regress in therapy, have to struggle to find words to describe their experiences. They often need to come back (in the therapy scene) to a later age to describe what they had experienced in the earlier scene.

As the infant begins to "think," to observe and store data and to act on the observation or storage of data, this primitive, nonverbal Adult remains within the Child ego state. Some call it the little Adult or the intuitive Adult. As mentioned above, Berne called it, affectionately, the Little Professor, because the young child often appears almost miraculously wise and intuitive in his observations and responses to the world. Though he may be remarkably wise at times, as he uses nonverbal cues to make sense of his surroundings, he also stores faulty information and acts on this misinformation. For instance, Mary's grandson Brian insisted on crawling downstairs first and would raise a tremendous fuss if we turned him around so that he was crawling feet first. At that time in his young life, his early Adult (A_1) had processed the head first method . . . possibly in order to see where he was going.

Early Parent

The young child also develops a rudimentary Parent ego state, labeled P_1. (See Figure 3.) When Brian (Mary's grandson) was three months old and Bob's grandson Robert was 13 months old, young Robert held Brian's head lovingly against his chest, just as his mother held him. This was the first indication we had seen of Robert's early Parent. Within moments, however, Robert returned to early Child, C_1, as he snatched away Brian's rattle. Then, when the grown-ups complained, he used his early Adult, A_1, to figure out that he could keep the rattle if he handed Brian a substitute toy.

The early Parent, then, is the incorporation of the real parents by the nonverbal child, and is comprised of the child's early *perception* of his parents' behavior and feelings, prior to the recognition of language. Thus, when mother and father are critical, as when they scold the infant for sucking his thumb, the child may incorporate their scolding behavior and emotion into his early Parent ego state. From this position he may later scold himself, in an irrational, affective, largely nonverbal way, and feel self-disgust. When he is a parent, if he hasn't changed, he may be repulsed, without knowing why, when his own children suck their thumbs, and may give them irrationally exaggerated messages about thumb-sucking.

It is this irrational, destructive element in the early Parent that some TA therapists consider to be the totality of P_1. They may call this early ego state the Witch mother, the Ogre father and the Pig parent. *We object to this nomenclature.* It is pejorative, and we object to pejorative terms in scientific literature. Also, such labeling ignores the part of P_1 that is nurturing as well as the part that is the incorporation of joyful, excited messages from the Child ego state of father and mother.

Little has been written in TA literature about the permission for fun and joy that the child receives from joyful parents. Usually happiness and playfulness are seen as the natural conditions of childhood. We won't quarrel with this position that the child naturally develops playfulness and a free spirit. However, we think parents are blamed too much for the negatives in a child's life and are not appreciated enough for the joy they model for their offspring. This joy, this zest for life, which many parents feel, is incorporated as part of the early Parent ego state of the child, and becomes permission to be joyous. We remember the young son of a psychiatrist friend, who enthusiastically ducked his head under the garage doorway when following father, who was so tall he had to duck his head. Son was copying father . . . and at the same time incorporating father's joy in life.

One afternoon grandson Robert was moving back and forth from the little pool to the big pool at our home, while his mother and Bob watched him. After several trips from the little pool to the shallow water in the big pool, Robert popped into the deep water and started to go under. Had his mother been phobic or frightened, she might have screamed and carried on, and Robert might then have incorporated, from her frightened Child ego state, a frightened little Parent, which he would experience later as a fear that translates "Don't go near the water!" He would also have had an experience of water being scary, which he might store in his early Adult ego state. Without a corrective experience, he could grow up to be phobic of water.

What actually happened was that Bob grabbed Robert immediately and pulled him out. Robert started to screw up his face, as if he were about to cry, and Bob shouted, "Wow, Robert swims! What a great swimmer you are. You are great!" while laughing and looking pleased. Robert quickly changed his face, joined the laughter, and incorporated into his Child ego state a memory from Bob to put into his early Adult and Parent. His mother then took him back into the pool and played with him, holding him afloat while he kicked and swung his arms around, laughing with him, and supporting his conversion of the experience into a joyful one.

We disagree with some TA theoreticians on two grounds regarding P_1. First, we disagree with the concept that P_1 is totally negative, and second, we disagree with the concept, spelled out by Berne, of the formation of P_1. He believed that P_1 is the *automatic* depository for all the negative messages given by parents. On page 116 of the *What Do You Say After You Say Hello?* Berne states:[1] "The come-on originates from the Child in the father or mother and is inserted into the Parent of the Child. . . . There it acts like a positive electrode, giving an automatic response." According to Berne, then, the child is a complete victim in that his P_1 is inserted into his head automatically. He is a victim of whatever the parents say or do: "When the Parent in his head pushes the button, Jeder (a patient's name) jumps to it, whether the rest of him wants to or not. He says something stupid, acts clumsy, has another drink or puts it all on the next race, ha ha ha." Thus the parent's distortions, rage, loud voices, become automatically part of the child's introjection and part of the P_1 ego state forever and ever.

We believe, on the contrary, that the child *does* filter, select, make decisions for himself in response to such messages, and that he has some control over what he takes in. Young Robert might have continued to be afraid of water, despite his mother's and Bob's actions. Another child, frightened by a parent's fear, might redecide later that water is not frightening, and decide to learn to swim.

We know patients who obviously have filtered such messages and talk about them objectively, without much affect. One says, for instance, "Of course, I didn't pay much attention to her, because she always said things like that when she was drunk. I'd just split and go play." Therefore, we say that the child takes part in the creation of his own early Parent—by accepting the messages or by using his early Child and early Adult to barricade against accepting them.

Free and Adapted Child

The growing child makes decisions based on his own needs and wants. He also makes decisions based on his perception of what others want him to decide. For instance, if he is stroked positively for going to the potty and/or negatively for wetting his pants, he will learn to use the potty in order to please others. If he learns to use the potty simply because he doesn't like the feeling of wet pants, then he is toilet training himself in response to his own desires. When young Robert grabbed the rattle away from Brian, he was behaving spontaneously. He judged the rattle to be a toy, wanted it, and took it. No adaptation . . . yet . . . to parental rules about self-ishness, possession, or be-nice-to-little-children nonsense for him! However, he immediately discovered that the grown-ups did not like the way he acted. He heard their scolding voices and saw their frowns —and figured out right away how to satisfy *them* by giving Brian a

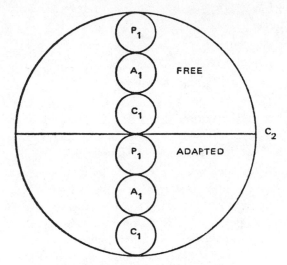

**THIS DIAGRAM SHOWS THE STRUCTURE OF
ADAPTED AND FREE CHILD EGO STATES.**

Fig. 5

second toy. Imagine his delight when he discovered he could adapt in such a way as to satisfy both himself and others. That is true sophistication at age 13 months.

The differentiation between the original "free" Child and the "adapted" Child is a *functional* division, as compared to the structural division into P, A, C that we have referred to previously. The structural division is represented in Figure 3. Figure 4 is the pictorial representation of the functional Child ego state, as divided into free and adapted Child. Mary has modified this, as demonstrated in Figure 5, showing that the three early ego states are present in the functional diagram. This *functional* diagram with its *structural* components explains pictorially the redecision theory that is the core of this book. The adaptive Child decides to go along with parental messages early in life, overruling the free or natural Child for survival purposes. Later, in redecision therapy, the early Adult in the Child makes a new decision—to overrule the pathological adaption and function freely.

Summary of Child Ego State

Some TA therapists believe that the Child ego state stops developing at an early age. We see the Child as ever growing and ever developing, as the sum total of the experiences he has had and is having in the present. A man of 45 may be behaving in a perfectly appropriate way until he sees a person who looks like the torturer who held him in captivity in Viet Nam; he may suddenly curl up in terror, or feel his heart pound and his hands sweat, and be overcome with fear. A woman of 50 may drive with comfort in a large, heavy car, but when she is riding in a small, light subcompact, she behaves as if she is about to be struck by an approaching truck, as she relives again the time when she was hit by a truck at age 40. Her Adult knows it is not the same, but nonetheless she *feels* as if she were back in that other car just before the accident.

The Child develops. We have stressed that the *Child* does the work. The Child both experiences and copies, and then incorporates. No one does anything to him without his having something to do with what he stores and what he experiences. Therefore, if he takes in originally, and if he continues to take in as he grows, matures, and ages, he can change, reexperience, and realign—from his own decisions and redecisions. This is tremendously important from a practical, therapeutic position.

For instance, if you, the reader, decided to be afraid of the water, because of your experiences, real or imaginary, then you can decide today not to be afraid of the water. It might be, and probably is, helpful for Bob to teach you that you really can float, but even that you can learn for yourself if you are willing to put yourself in the water and find out that when you just lie there with your lungs full of air, and with your hands and arms extended over your head, you float. You don't need to be reparented or analyzed for ten years; you can learn for yourself that your body can't sink—and can decide not to be afraid any longer. You can get an exciting, invigorating awakening, an experiencing in your Child, and an understanding in your Adult, that your body floats, that you simply *cannot* and will not drown as long as you keep some air in your lungs—whatever air it takes you to stay afloat.

PARENT EGO STATE

We view the Parent as the sum total of beliefs, emotions, and behaviors that a person *chooses* to incorporate on a remembered, verbal level, plus the Parent he or she creates for self and continues to create throughout life. The Parent ego state is more than a series of introjected "tapes in the head." It is made up of chosen incorporations plus the creative processes of the person's Child and Adult. Here again we differ from Berne, who saw the introjection of the Parent ego state as automatic rather than a choice made by the developing person. We think that the person filters and chooses what to listen to, depending upon where he is psychologically and physically, and what kinds of other support systems are available (such as siblings, grandparents, close friends). People incorporate parents all their lives, from real parents and from important figures in their lives, and even from the figures they create. One young man, who had never met his father, fantasized a kind, loving, caring person, incorporated his fantasy, and grew to have these same qualities in his own Parent ego state. The process of creating never stops. We often see people building up their own Parent from the data that their Adult collects to correct previous distortions; in natural development and/or in therapy they create the kind of Parent they want in their head. In the chapter on depression, we relate in detail how patient Nan developed her own loving Parent during the therapeutic process.

To compare, the child develops his nonverbal, pre-verbal early Parent ego state (P_1) from the incorporation of people around him. This ego state is made up of images, sounds and his interpretation of the meaning of those sounds and images. Later they are translated into words . . . critical, nurturing, demanding, as well as joyful, playful, loving. The verbal Parent (P_2) is, in our opinion, developed later, and includes, besides copied behavior and feeling, parental beliefs and rules for living. Religion, philosophy and morality are all part of the Parent.

Structurally, the Parent ego state is divided into three parts: the Parent, the Adult, and the Child of the real parents. For example, a client listening to a tape of his voice when he was being parental may immediately recognize the voice, the inflection, as being the

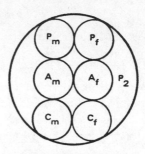

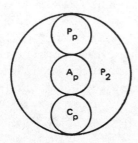

STRUCTURAL DIAGRAM
OF THE PARENT EGO STATE

Fig. 6

Structural diagram of Parent Ego
State, showing the incorporation
of TWO parents.
P_m is Mother's Parent, P_f is Father's
Parent, A_m is Mother's Adult, A_f is
Father's Adult, C_m is Mother's Child,
C_f is Father's Child.
Obviously one could also draw in all
surrogate parents, such as teachers,
psychoanalysts, etc.

Fig. 7

same as mother's Parental scolding and later hear himself sounding
like father's weary Child scolding, when father came home tired
from work. Thus, there is differentiation between Child and Parent
of the real parent, as shown in Figure 6, showing *one* parent, and
Figure 7, showing *two* parents. In redecision therapy, this differentiation and recognition of the different ego states within the Parent become very important in resolving impasses.

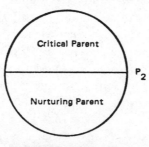

FUNCTIONAL DIVISION
OF PARENT EGO STATE

Fig. 8

Just as we divide the Child into structure and function, so we divide the Parent into structure and function. Functionally the Parent is divided into nurturing and critical (see Figure 8). The terms are self-explanatory. Mary also divides the Parent into internal and external components; the internal Parent nurtures and criticizes self, while the external Parent nurtures and criticizes others.

ADULT EGO STATE

When we lecture, a common question from the audience is "How is the Adult different from the ego?" The Adult is a concept, just as ego is a concept; the Adult, however, is an observable phenomenological entity. When you, the reader, are reading this book, storing the data, separating what is real for you from what doesn't fit for you, without any feelings, you are in your Adult. If you become angry, saying, "Those guys don't know what they are talking about," you have moved from Adult into critical Parent or angry Child. Listening to an engineer designing a project, a judge interpreting the law, or a doctor making a differential diagnosis, we hear and see clearly what an Adult ego state is. It is a state of being, observable, without feeling, in which we store data, retrieve data, and act upon data. The difference between the Little Professor, or A_1, and the Adult, A_2, is that the Adult has the ability in words to test out the data, to prove it, to discern what is reality in terms of both his own and other's experience and tested information.

Adult ego state pathology may be due to lack of adequate information, as when educated people based their calculations on the "fact" that the earth was flat. Usually, the problem is contamination. This term is used to explain the intrusion of one ego state into another. The person accepts as Adult what is in reality Parent or Child. Think about the sayings: "All men want is sex," or "Women are never practical." One man may only want sex, one woman may be impractical, but the beliefs are treated as Adult *fact* in order to support prejudice (see Figure 9). In the case of the Child intrusion into Adult (see Figure 10) a fear may be treated as fact: A person afraid of planes remembers every accident, forgets about planes that fly safely, land safely, and says, "If I fly I'll get killed." Illusions are also Child contaminations, in which a Child, in fear, transposes some-

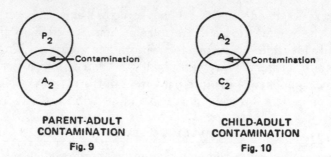

PARENT-ADULT
CONTAMINATION
Fig. 9

CHILD-ADULT
CONTAMINATION
Fig. 10

thing really there, as a shadow, into something not there, as a spider in the DT's of acute alcoholism.

Eric Berne didn't write about complicated contaminations, such as illustrated in Figure 11. Here all ego states are contaminated, including Parent intruding into Child. This is frequently seen in schizophrenic clients, as when the patient from his Child experiences hearing a parent's voice in his head, believes it is really his father down in the next bowling alley, saying, "You are a queer." He may at the same time hear the psychiatrist's voice in his head saying, "That is a hallucination when you hear your father talking to you, because, after all, he is dead," and go on bowling as if nothing had happened. At this point, he is not yet functioning from his Adult, but from the recently incorporated Parent (the psychiatrist). Later he will begin to decontaminate, as we work with him to determine

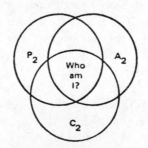

CONTAMINATION
BETWEEN ALL EGO STATES
Fig. 11

for himself whether the "fact" is truly fact or fantasy. In this way, we assist the client in sorting out his own ego states. Jack Dusay's book. *Egograms,*[2] is useful in clarifying these issues. We also occasionally use Stuntz's[3] five-chair technique, in which the client uses five chairs to represent Adult, free and adapted Child, and nurturing and critical Parent. Much of gestalt work is in the service of decontamination, as we will illustrate and demonstrate in the tape samples in future chapters.

In the old days of TA, much therapy time was spent on identifying ego states. Berne wrote in *Principles of Group Treatment*[4] that treatment must be analysis of ego states, transactions, games, and scripts, in that order. We are more likely to use ego state concepts in drawing diagrams after the work has been done, to add cognitive understanding to the affective work. We don't routinely ask the question *"which ego state are you in?"* or say *"that's your Parent talking."* However, we do listen for changes in ego states. During a workshop we heard a psychiatrist say, at the beginning before we had even started working, "I'm so tired; *you* work hard and *you* don't have any fun." He reported his experience, tiredness. He then gave the Parental messages "Work hard" and "Don't have fun." Rather than ask him cognitively to identify these messages, we asked if he was ready to talk back successfully against them. He did so, by redeciding that it was all right to have fun and to work only as hard as he chooses to work.

It is usually more therapeutic to use the changes in ego states as is done in the above example, than to simply identify them. However, in order to make use of ego states, identification may first be necessary. Changes are indicated by changes in vocabulary, tone, pitch, volume, and/or rapidity of speech, by changes in body position, or by familiar gestures.

Using video or audio equipment, we may play back to the client what he has just said, for the client to identify his own ego states. "Be an unprejudiced outside observer and listen to that man. As you listen, decide how old that person seems to be." The voice of a 60-year-old man may sound like a six-year-old. When someone leans his head over on his shoulder, he is probably in his Child, probably adapting. Asking him to take that position and then to "put his head on straight and talk" (which has a double meaning, of course) usually brings out more awareness and often a change from adaptive to non-adaptive thinking, behavior and feeling. As patients learn to be more aware of the ego state they are in, they learn to better handle their feelings, to better recognize their position in their life script, to be more aware that they have been, or are, game playing. They become much more aware of their adaptive behavior, adaptive both to their internal Parent and to the outside world. After becoming aware, they can knowingly choose to adapt or not to adapt.

TRANSACTIONS

In the beginning, Berne stated that the basis of transactional analysis, in addition to ego states, was the study of transactions—hence the name, transactional analysis. Berne divided transactions into complementary, crossed, and ulterior transactions. *Complementary transactions* are parallel, as in Figure 12, and may be from any ego state of one person to any ego state of the other, and return, as hus-

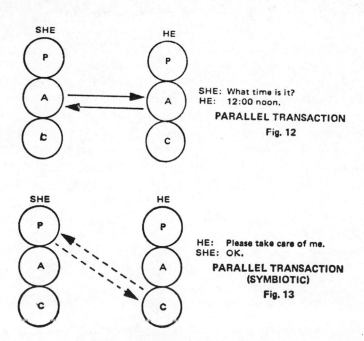

SHE: What time is it?
HE: 12:00 noon.

PARALLEL TRANSACTION

Fig. 12

HE: Please take care of me.
SHE: OK.

PARALLEL TRANSACTION (SYMBIOTIC)

Fig. 13

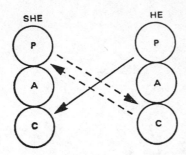

SHE   HE

HE: Please take care of me.
SHE: OK. I'll take care of you.
HE: Don't boss me.

CROSSED TRANSACTION

Fig. 14

band and wife in symbiosis (Figure 13). She is nurturing and parental, while he is submissive and childlike. They both like this and remain in such a relationship much of the time. When he suddenly switches and comes on from his Parent, there is a *crossed transaction* (Figure 14) and trouble begins, with a loss of communication until they get into complementary transactions again.

Ulterior transactions are secret, at least secret from the Adult ego state. In Berne's old example, the cowboy asked the girl if she would like to take a look at the barn. His secret, ulterior transaction is, *"Let's go for a toss in the hay."* She responds with, *"OK, I've always loved barns"* . . . and if she agrees to the ulterior transaction, her secret response is *"Wow."* They then enjoy sex together—their only purpose in using ulterior transactions was to keep their own Parent ego states from knowing what they were up to. If she doesn't understand his ulterior message, she is surprised, and perhaps angry, that he attempts sex with her. He is confused and unhappy at her response, as well as being surprised. They are then involved in a game. (Games are described later in this chapter.) In Figure 15, in order to avoid the sexism implicit in this typical description of the game of "Rapo," we have the girl making the overture, rather than the cowboy.

In addition to complementary, crossed, and ulterior transactions, there are also direct, indirect, and diluted transactions. *Direct* ones are I-Thou transactions, in which one person speaks directly to another. *Indirect* are I-He/She, in which someone speaks to someone *about* someone else. *Diluted* transactions are I-You All, in which an

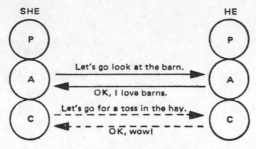

ULTERIOR TRANSACTION

Fig. 15

individual speaks generally to an entire group of people.

Ordinarily, we use *only* direct transactions when doing psychotherapy, and we ask the patients to keep their transactions direct. Many couples will start their work with indirect transactions, playing a game of "courtroom": *"He never does anything around the house," "She won't cook anything I like."* We are supposed to be judge and jury, and are expected to become caught up in the game. When we ask the couple to tell each other, their courtroom game is blocked, and they become more accessible to treatment. So long as they are talking *about* each other, it is difficult for them to be intimate—yet their professed goal is to stop fighting and increase their intimacy. As they talk *to* each other, they recognize that many of the things they say to each other are really related to unfinished business with their parents, and then we ask them to address their comments "directly" to the parent, in fantasy.

We ask patients to fantasize that mother or father is sitting in the chair in front of them, and to tell that parent what they are telling us, thereby making the transaction direct, in the "here and now," and I-Thou. Immediately, the patient will begin to move into his Child ego state and deal with the situation from his Child, rather than relating about it from his Adult. As he talks to the parent and moves to the other chair to respond as parent, he has a flood of memories, both of the scene and of the affect connected with the scene, and experiences himself as being in that scene in the "here and now." From this Child position he is then able to make affective changes in early decisions (redecisions), as he relives *in* the scene and closes old unfinished business. (These changes, or redecisions, are explained in detail in Chapter 8.)

Although we seldon use diluted transactions (I-You All) in doing therapy, we frequently use them to provide administrative information: "Do you all know that there is a seminar tonight?" or "Let's eat!" However, many therapists do use diluted transactions in what we consider an inappropriate way. For instance, it is common for a process group therapist to ask, after a patient has said something, "How does the group feel about that?" or even worse, "How does that make the group feel?" The problem with the first statement is that the "group" doesn't feel anything, since the group is not an experiencing unit but a social one. One member may feel angry, another sad, another hurt, another confused, and another bored. The additional problem with the second question is that no one *makes* anyone feel anything; each of us is in charge of our own feelings.

STROKES

Although we have a complete chapter on strokes later, a definition is included here inasmuch as we use the term so frequently. A stroke is a unit of recognition. There are three kinds of strokes: *physical* (touching), *verbal* (talking) *and nonverbal* (waving, winking, nodding, gesturing, etc.). Strokes are given for "being" (*unconditional*) and for "doing" (*conditional*). They may be *positive,* as warm physical touches, warm words, and friendly gestures, or they may be *negative,* as slaps, scolds, and scowls.

TIME STRUCTURE

Berne believed there are six ways people structure time: withdrawal (sleeping, day dreaming), ritual behavior (reciting a litany in church), pastimes (talking about the weather), activities (working, building a house), game playing (see section on games), and intimacy (loving sexual intercourse or other experiences of closeness between two or more people). We write "loving sexual intercourse" for intimacy, because one could fit sex into any one of the six time structures: withdrawal (masturbation), ritual (obsessive sexual rites as sado-masochistic play), pastimes (it's raining outside, so let's go to bed), activities (prostitution), game playing (Rapo, for example, as in the cowboy story told in the section on transactions), and, of course, true, intimate sex.

GAMES

Berne wrote about games in his first book on TA, *Transactional Analysis in Psychotherapy*,[5] and the term became widely popular with his *Games People Play*.[6] Unfortunately, since then there have been so many different definitions of games, many people are confused. For us, a game is a series of transactions that ends in at least one player feeling badly or being injured in some way. The game begins with an ostensibly straight stimulus. However, this stimulus also includes a secret or covert message. This secret message is responded to in an overt fashion. At the end of the game, the player experiences a payoff—he is unhappy or hurt. The entire series of transactions is not within his Adult awareness.

1. Ostensibly straight stimulus. (*"I'll paint the back porch for you."*)

2. Secret message. (As person procrastinates, *"Keep nagging me."*)

3. Response to secret message. (*"Why don't you get the porch painted?"*)

4. Payoff. Person feels angry, sad, anxious, or guilty, and so makes silent statements to himself about self and other, that solidify his existential position in terms of *"I'm OK"* or *"I'm not OK"* and *"You're OK"* or *"You're not OK."* (*"I'm angry. She always criticizes me. I never seem to be able to please her."*)

Jack Kaufman[7] enlarges on this definition by emphasizing that a game represents a repetitive pattern of behavior. An individual plays the same type of game many times. Kaufman suggests that the therapist not confront a game until he has evidence that the player has played it three times, unless, of course, the game is one in which the payoff includes real damage to the players. The first time may be an accident, the second a coincidence, but the third is evidence of a game.

Mary teaches that each person derives his own unique payoff and that this payoff is a repetition of important unfinished business in the past. Gary, George, and Gem each play exactly the same game; they come late to dinner parties and are criticized. Gary feels sad and says to himself, "Others manage so much better than I," and "I never do anything right." George is angry and says to himself, "What kind of friends are they, anyway, to be so critical," and "I'd rather be by myself." Gem is anxious and says, "They must think I am perfectly terrible," and "I'm always getting mixed up. . . . I wonder what I'll do wrong next!"

The late arrival or the explanation for being late is the ostensibly straight stimulus. The secret message is "Criticize me." The others criticize. The payoff is what each feels and believes about self and others. All of this is outside of Adult awareness. This means that the three players do not know that they arrive late in order to be criticized and to feel as they felt. They don't know that they are recreating scenes in the present that are repetitions of unfinished scenes in the past. Gary played the same game with his father, Gem with her mother, and George plays the game that his father played with George's mother.

Stephen Karpman[8] devised the drama triangle for explaining games. He suggests that games are dramatic and require the players to assume roles of persecutor, rescuer, and victim. The "action" occurs when the players switch roles.

The Berne formula, as written in his last book, *What Do You Say After You Say Hello?* is given as: Con plus gimmick lead to a response, a switch, a surprise, and a payoff. Berne doesn't indicate that the game is outside of the player's Adult awareness, nor does he believe that all games include negative payoffs. He defines "con" as the bait a player uses to "hook" another. The "gimmick" is the psychological flaw in the person who allows himself to be "hooked." He is "hooked" when he responds to the "con." The "switch" is a switch in ego states or, more likely, a switch in position on the drama triangle. The "surprise" is described by Berne as similar to the look on the faces of the villains in the old TV show "Mission Impossible" when they think they have won and suddenly recognize that they are about to lose everything.

Although the game rules of many TA therapists call for at least two players, in a strict sense that is not necessary. For instance, the Lost Car-Key game: The player hurries to his car as the blizzard is about to bury him, and suddenly . . . panic! The keys are in the car and the door is locked. "You stupid S.O.B.," he says to himself, "You are always doing something stupid!" He feels angry and confused, as he continues to call himself names from his Parent. No one else is involved in the game, although, of course, the person did play "Stupid" with parents or someone in the past. This a one-handed, or solitaire, game.

Some games are dangerous (third degree games), ending in injury, incarceration, or death. If we suspect such a game, we will not let it go on to completion. For example, a therapist/client in a workshop talks of the joys of open sexual contracts or says that he tells his clients of his open marriage agreement with his wife. We immediately ask whether he is having sexual intercourse with his clients. We believe that this is anti-therapeutic for clients, but instead of taking this ethical and moral stance (at first) we prefer to hook his Child into becoming aware of the game. We ask him to fantasize what will happen if someday someone turns him in to the Board of Medical Examiners or sues him for malpractice. If he states that he does not have sex with clients, but clients know that he engages in sexual intercourse with more than one person, we ask him to pretend he is in court, attempting to defend himself against an untrue accusation from a vindictive client, who might be willing to lie in order to win a malpractice suit. Recognizing the payoff helps this therapist/client to understand the true nature of his game, and he is more likely to stop than if we first confront him with our moral, ethical position, which he would probably respond to with "justified" Child anger.

In this game, the ostensible straight transaction is: *"I am having sex with other women besides my wife."* (This sounds straight, as if it were pure information.) The secret message to the Rapo artist is *"Please tell on me"* or *"Please sue me."* The response from the Rapo player is to tell her attorney that the therapist had sex with her. The payoff includes his feelings plus his statement about self and other. He may be angry, hurt, mortified. He may say about himself, "Just when I am about to be successful, I fail," or "I am so rotten I should kill myself," or whatever statement fits his negative existential belief about himself. About her he may say, "She failed me" or "She did me in," and both statements would confirm an existential belief, "You can't trust any woman!" The entire series of transactions is, of course, outside his Adult awareness. He thought he did what he did in order to be "honest" or because he loves women so much!

RACKETS

The unpleasant feelings that people experience following a game are called rackets. Like games, there are many definitions of rackets. Berne defined them as "the sexualization and transactional seeking and exploitation of unpleasant feelings." That is a complicated sentence and we don't know why he added the "sexualization," unless he was trying to make TA fit psychoanalysis. We also are uncertain what he meant by "transactional seeking." Presumably, he was suggesting that a series of transactions is followed in order to get the payoff, or racket, but his statement has led to confusion in TA literature and many different definitions. Some TA therapists define racket as the process that ends in the person feeling unhappy. To us the process is the pastime, fantasy, or game—the racket is simply the chronic, stereotyped unpleasant feeling.

These feelings are used to attempt to change others. At times, of course, people do what we want, if we suffer enough. All of us have had the experience of being sad or angry at someone—spouse, child, parent, boss—and of that person then changing his behavior. Extortion is the term we give to the use of rackets in an attempt to modify someone else's behavior.

Parents teach children about rackets. Mother or father says, "You make me so angry when you slam the door," "You make me so nervous with that whistling," "You make me so anxious when you don't get home early," or "You make me so happy when you pee-pee in the toilet." The child is thus told that he is responsible for the parental feelings. He grows up believing that he makes people feel. Does he ever ask himself what they were angry or nervous or anxious about before he entered the scene?

Rackets are used in other ways also. If someone is in a suicidal script, for instance, and has at one time decided he can always kill himself "if things get too bad," he'll save up his bad feelings, collecting them as if they were trading stamps so that, when he has "enough" stamps, he can kill himself. Such stamps can be produced in a number of ways. He can play games in which he ends up being kicked and feeling sad. He can look around to see what the bad news is today, such as the war in Lebanon or the rising inflation. He can lie in bed at night, remembering all the sad things that ever happened to him. He remembers that Mother never loved him or Father never played with him. He can spend his therapy hours dredging up sadder and sadder memories. In order to feel sad enough, he may even fantasize that things are happening to him. For example, he may fantasize that his wife is unfaithful even when there is no evidence for believing this.

One of the goals of TA-gestalt therapy is to help the patient drop his rackets and substitute good feelings. Chronically anxious people learn to change their anxiety into enthusiasm. Chronically guilty people learn to drop guilt and enjoy life. Chronically angry people use anger to motivate them to take action, and then drop the anger. Bob used his anger to write hundreds of letters to senators, congressmen, and others in high office when he used to wake up every morning angry at Richard Nixon!

INJUNCTIONS AND COUNTER-INJUNCTIONS

Each system of psychology contains its own explanation for the development of psychopathology. We do not suggest other systems are wrong and we use what we have learned from other systems. Freud's sexual development theory, Erik Erikson's zonal-modal model of ego development, the learning theory of the behaviorists, systems theories—all explain child development and offer treatment potentialities. We emphasize certain pathological messages from parents to their children which, if believed by the child, may result in chronic life problems for that child. We call these messages injunctions and counter-injunctions.

Injunctions

Injunctions are messages from the Child ego state of parents, given out of the circumstances of the parent's own pains: unhappiness, anxiety, disappointment, anger, frustration, secret desires. While these messages are irrational in terms of the child, they may seem perfectly rational to the parent who gives them.

We have drawn up a list of these injunctions and have written several articles about them in the past ten years.[9] We have been teaching them in lectures, seminars, and workshops all over the world. Our list does not exhaust all possibilities; undoubtedly there are many other messages that parents give, and upon which children act or do not act. However, this short list of general injunctions enables the therapist to listen better to what the patient says and thus to improve his treatment plan.

Here is our basic list: *Don't. Don't be. Don't be close. Don't be important. Don't be a child. Don't grow. Don't succeed. Don't be you. Don't be sane. Don't be well. Don't belong.*

Don't: This injunction is given by parents who are afraid. Out of their fear, they don't allow the child to do many normal things: Don't go near the steps (to toddlers); don't climb trees; don't roller skate, etc. Sometimes such parents hadn't wanted the child, recognized their primitive desires that the child not exist, and, feeling guilty and panicked by their own thoughts, became overprotective. Other times the parent is phobic, psychotic, or overprotective after having lost older children through disease or accidents. As the child grows, the parent will be concerned about each action the child proposes and say, "But perhaps it would be better if you thought about that more." The child believes that nothing he does is right or is safe, doesn't know what to do, and looks around for someone to tell him. Such a child will have great difficulty making decisions in later life.

Don't be: This is the most lethal of the messages—and the one we focus on first in treatment. It may be given in subtle ways, as "If it weren't for you children, I'd divorce your father." Less subtle, "I wish you had never been born . . . then I wouldn't have had to marry your father." The message may be delivered nonverbally, in the way the parent holds the child without cuddling, frowns and scowls during eating and bathing, screams when the child wants something, or is physically abusive. There are a multitude of ways the message is given.

This injunction may be given by mother, father, nurses and governesses, and by older siblings. A parent may be depressed because the child is conceived before marriage or after the parents no longer want more children. The pregnancy may end in maternal death and the father or grandparents blame the child for the death. The delivery may have been difficult and the child blamed for being too large at birth: "You tore me up when you were born." These messages, told many times in the presence of the child, become the "birth myth" that says, "If you hadn't been, our lives would be better."

Don't be close: If a parent discourages a child from becoming close, that child will interpret this as the message, *"Don't be close."* Lack of physical touching, and lack of positive stroking lead to such an interpretation by the child. Also, if a child loses a parent to whom he felt close, through death or divorce, the child may give himself this injunction by saying such things as, *"What's the use of getting close, they just die anyway,"* and decide never to be close again.

Don't be important: If, for instance, a child is not allowed to talk at the dinner table, is told, *"Children are to be seen, not heard,"* or is discounted in some other way, he may experience the message as *"Don't be important."* He may also receive such a message in school. In California, Spanish-American children have in the past had a hard time with importance, because the other children who speak only one language taunt them for trying to speak English as well as Spanish, and for doing so inaccurately at first. Certainly, Blacks receive this message from Whites, as well as from many Black mothers who didn't want them to be important enough to get into trouble with the Whites.

Don't be a child: This message is given by parents who ask the older children to take care of the younger. It is also given by parents who try to bowel train early, make "little men" or "little women" out of their toddlers, stroke them for being polite before they learn what politeness means, tell them—when they are still babies—that only babies cry.

Don't grow: This injunction is often given by mother to her last child, whether the second or the tenth. It is also given frequently by father to a pre-puberty or pubescent girl when he starts to feel some sexual arousal and becomes frightened. He may then keep the girl from doing the things that this girl's friends all do—using makeup, wearing clothes appropriate to the age, or dating. Also, father may stop physical stroking as soon as the girl begins to mature, and she interprets this as, *"Don't grow up or I won't love you.'*

Don't succeed: If father has been beating son at ping-pong and then stops playing when son beats him, this can be interpreted by son as, *"Don't win or I won't like you,"* which gets converted into, *"Don't succeed."* Constant criticism by a perfectionistic parent gives the message "You can't do anything right," which translates "Don't succeed."

Don't be you: This is most frequently given to the child who is the "wrong" sex. If mother has three boys, wants a girl, and gets a boy, she may make this last son her "daughter." If a son sees that the girls get the goodies, he may take this as, *"Don't be a boy or you won't get anything,"* and have difficulty with his sexual identification. Father may give up after four girls and teach the fifth to do "boy" and "man" things, such as playing football. (We realize that this is a sexist statement, but are pointing out what has happened in our culture.)

Don't be sane and *Don't be well*: If parents give children strokes for being sick and give none when the children are well, this is tantamount to telling them, *"Don't be well."* If crazy behavior is rewarded, or if crazy behavior is modeled and not corrected, the modeling itself becomes the message, *"Don't be sane."* We have seen many children of schizophrenics who have difficulty in testing reality, even though they are not actually psychotic. They act crazy, and are frequently treated as if they are psychotic.

Don't belong: If parents constantly act as if they should be some-where else, such as Russia, Ireland, Italy, Israel, England (in the case of some ex-English persons living in Australia and New Zea-land), it is difficult for the child to know where he belongs. He may always feel that he, too, doesn't belong—even though he was born in the United States, or Australia, or New Zealand.

Counter-Injunctions

Counter-injunctions are messages from the Parent ego state of parents which are restrictive and, if adhered to, may also prevent growth and flexibility. These include the "drivers" listed by Taibi Kahler,[10] *"Be strong," "try hard," "be perfect," "hurry up,"* and *"please me."* All of these, of course, are impossible to evaluate: When has one been strong enough, pleasing enough, tried hard enough, or hurried fast enough? There is no way to be perfect. Mary adds to Kahler's list the counter-injunction that accompanies the injunction, *"Don't"*: *"Be careful."*

Counter-injunctions also include religious, racial, and sexual stereotypes which are handed down from generation to generation. Even women who believe themselves to be emancipated often do the cooking and cleaning in addition to their regular employment, be-cause they still believe the counter-injunction that woman's place is in the home.

Counter-injunctions are obvious, given in words, and are not sec-ret. The giver of the counter-injunction believes that what he says is right and will defend his position. *"Of course women belong at home. What would happen to children if women didn't accept their responsibility!"* This is quite different from the response of the givers of injunctions, who give them secretly and without awareness of the impact of their words. If a parent is told that he told his child not to exist, he would be indignant and disbelieving, saying that he had no such intention at any time.

The Parental messages are called counter-injunctions because Eric Berne first believed that they *countered* the injunction. Therefore, if the client obeyed the counter-injunction, he would not have to obey the injunction. If, for example, the injunction is *"Don't exist"* and the counter-injunction is *"Work hard,"* the client can save his own life by working hard and ignoring his suicidal impulses. However, clients are more apt to obey injunctions than counter-injunctions, so they remain depressed while "working hard." Such messages as the counter-injunction *"Work hard"* and the injunction *"Don't grow up"* are impossible to follow. And imagine the plight of the boy who accepts the injunction *"Don't be a boy,"* does feminine things to please his parent and then is told by the same parent to go out and play football with the boys and to stop mooning around the house and acting like a sissy. At other times, both counter-injunction and injunction are the same. From all ego states, a parent may tell a child not to exist, not to be important, not to grow. In such cases, the child has an especially difficult time rejecting the messages.

Mixed Messages

Some messages are given from either the Parent or the Child of the parents, particularly those about thinking and feeling. Injunctions and counter-injunctions against thinking are: *"Don't think,"* *"Don't think that"* (some specific thought), or *"Don't think what you think—think what I think"* (*"Don't disagree with me"*). Feeling messages are the same: *"Don't feel,"* *"Don't feel that"* (a specific emotion), or *"Don't feel what you feel—feel what I feel"* (*"I'm cold, put on your sweater"* or *"You don't hate your little brother; you are just tired"*).

DECISIONS

Again, although injunctions and counter-injunctions are given, in order for them to be important in the child's development the child must *accept* them. He has the power to accept or reject. No injunction is "inserted in the child like an electrode," as Berne[1] believed. Furthermore, we believe that many injunctions were never even given! The child fantasizes, invents, and misinterprets, thereby giving himself his own injunctions. When a brother dies, a child may believe his own jealousy of brother magically caused the death, because the child does not understand pneumonia. Then, in guilt, he may give himself a *"Don't be"* injunction. If a beloved father dies, a child may decide never to be close to anyone again. He gives himself a *"Don't be close"* injunction in an effort to avoid reexperiencing the pain he experienced at father's death. In effect, he says, "*I'll never love again and then I won't ever have to be hurt again.*"

We have listed a limited number of injunctions; however, there are almost limitless decisions that a child can make in response to the injunctions. Here we suggest a few of these decisions. First, a child may simply not believe the injunction and therefore reject it. He may do this by recognizing the pathology of the giver ("*My mother is sick and doesn't mean what she says*") or by finding someone who opposes the injunction and believing him ("*My parents don't want me but my teacher does*"). We list a few of the many possible pathological decisions made in response to injunctions:

"*Don't Be*": "*I'll die and then you'll love me,*" "*I'll get you even if it kills me,*" and others listed in Chapter 9.

The decisions possible for the child to make in response to "*Don't*" are: "*I can't decide.*" "*I need someone to decide for me.*" "*The world is scary . . . I might make a mistake.*" "*I'm weaker than other people.*" "*I'm never going to decide anything on my own again.*"

"*Don't grow up*": "*OK, I'll stay little,*" or "*helpless*" or "*non-thinking*" or "*non-sexual.*" This decision is often seen in body, tone of voice, and mannerisms, as well as behavior.

"*Don't be a child*": Possible decisions are: "*I won't ever ask for anything again; I'll take care of myself.*" "*I'll always take care of them.*" "*I'll never have any fun.*" "*I'll never do anything childish again.*"

"*Don't make it*": The child may decide: "*I'll never do anything right.*" "*I'm stupid.*" "*I'll never win.*" "*I'll beat you if it kills me.*" "*I'll show you if it kills me.*" "*No matter how good I am, I should have done better, so I'll feel frustrated (ashamed, guilty).*"

"*Don't be close*": Decisions made in response to this injunction are: "*I'll never trust anyone again.*" "*I'll never get close to anyone again.*" "*I'll never be sexual,*" (plus all the restrictions on telling feelings or physical closeness).

"*Don't be well*" or "*sane*": Decisions are: "*I'm crazy.*" "*My sick-*

ness is the worst there is and I might die of it," (plus prohibitions on using body or thought processes).

"Don't be you" (the sex you are) : In response, the child may decide: *"I'll show them I'm as good as any boy/girl." "No matter how hard I try, I con never please." "I'm really a girl with a boy's penis." "I'm really a boy even though I look like a girl." "I'll pretend I'm a boy/girl." "I'll never be happy like this." "I'll always be ashamed."*

"Don't be important": The child may decide: *"No one ever lets me say or do anything." "Everyone else counts first around here." "I'll never amount to anything." "I may become important but I can never let anyone know it."*

"Don't belong": Decisions may be: *"I'll never belong to anyone"* or *"any group"* or *"any country,"* or *"Nobody will ever like me because I don't belong."*

For the mixed messages about thinking and feeling:

"Don't think": Possible decisions: *"I'm stupid." "I can't think for myself." "I can never concentrate."*

"Don't think about that": *"It's bad to have sexy thoughts, so I had better think about something else"* (this person may become obsessive). *"I'd better never mention that* (whatever 'that' is, as being adopted, or 'father is not my real father') *or think about that again."* Or *"I'm no good at math"* (or science or cooking or football, depending upon the kind of messages with the injunction).

"Don't think what you think—think what I think": *"I'm always wrong," "I won't open my mouth until I find out what other people think."*

The decisions in response to the feeling injunctions are similar.

"Don't feel": The child may respond: *"Emotions are a waste of time." "I don't feel anything."*

"Don't feel that": *"I'll never cry again." "I'm never angry . . . anger can kill."*

"Don't feel what you feel—feel what I feel": *"I don't know how I feel."* This person asks therapists and group members, *"How should I feel? How would you feel, if you were me?"*

SCRIPTS

We do not use scripts in the detailed way that many TA therapists do, who have elaborate script checklists for diagnosis and see treatment as including understanding the intricacies of the total script. We prefer short-term therapy and therefore find it more advantageous to go straight to the injunction-decision-racket complex while for the most part ignoring the client's script. However, we advise beginning TA therapists to use script checklists and to understand script theory. Later they can decide what parts of script theory they prefer to accent in their own work.

According to script theory, when a child makes an early decision about himself, he begins to plan out his life based on the decision, using as a model a fairy tale or other story. For instance, a 40-year-old woman, still unmarried and not pursuing a satisfactory career, says she is "waiting for something to happen." Her favorite story in childhood was "Sleeping Beauty." Another woman spends her life working hard in an attempt to satisfy her ungrateful husband and children. She remembers her favorite story to have been "Cinderella." Many young men in the California Youth Authority use TV programs such as "Rifleman" for their model. Then, throughout life, the person may make additional decisions and amplify the basic story. We work with people to permit themselves to live autonomously rather than to be bound to past Child plans, whether these plans are embodied in "winning" or "losing" scripts.

Berne believed, as do TA reparenters and others, that children are "scripted" and that they need a strong Parent in the therapist to change the scripts. We don't believe in "scripting" any more than we believe in the electrode theory. We believe that the individual writes his own script and can rewrite it with the help of a strong Parent he builds himself, rather than incorporates from a therapist. It may be gratifying for a therapist to think he is needed for parenting purposes, but except for the young and the psychotic, the patient can do it better himself.

George McClendon,[11] in his work with families, deals with family as well as individual scripts. He believes that families must know their scripts, which he calls "myths," in order for each member to free self from the past and to put energy into living today.

For therapists who want to learn how to recognize scripts, we suggest a thorough reading of TA literature and practice using script check lists, such as those devised by William Holloway[12] and Paul McCormick.[13]

CHAPTER 3

Impasses and Redecisions

An impasse is a point at which two or more opposing forces meet—a stuck place. A person is poised on the railing of the Golden Gate bridge. He stops and says to himself, "But I don't really want to die." Another part of him says, "Yes, I do." As long as he stays poised on the bridge, conflicted, he is in an impasse. If he jumps, he has broken through the impasse. If he backs off, deciding not to die, he has broken through the impasse on the side of surviving, at least temporarily. He may face the same impasse in the future, but for now he has resolved it. (We are not satisfied with such temporary resolutions, which are usually made by the Adult ego state. We work to get a redecision from the Child not to kill self now or in the future.)

Bob categorizes impasses into three types or degrees.[1] The *first degree impasse* is between the Parent ego state of the individual and his Child ego state and is based on the counter-injunctions. The living parent, as we have explained earlier, gives messages from his Parent, such as *"Work hard."* Father tells son, *"Any job worth doing is worth doing well." "Always give an extra ten percent."* The little boy, wanting to please his father and get his approval, decides from his Little Professor (A_1) to work hard to please Daddy. He works hard until he is 55 and is still, outside of his awareness, pleasing parents. At 55 he decides that he wants to slow down a little, so he makes plans from his Adult to work only 8 hours a day, 5 days a week, and to take a month off every year. It appears that he has broken through this impasse. However, the decision from his "thinking" Adult is usually not enough. He begins to get headaches as soon as he slows down or, when he starts to play golf, he finds that he exhausts himself by playing 36 holes a day. He goes fishing and, instead of relaxing, is up at dawn at Yellowstone Park, rushing around all day trying to catch all the fish in the Park. He is still listening to the old Parent message, the counter-injunction, and working hard, succeeding, *"doing the job well."* He is still at the impasse, because he has not gotten down into his guts and made a REDECISION from the early Adult in his Child.

The therapy must be of a nature that he connects up a scene from childhood, in which he is confronting his parent (in fantasy, of course), seeing Daddy and telling Daddy that he is not going to be working hard anymore. Usually, a person does remember a real scene and experiences his feelings in that scene. For instance, one participant in one of our marathons remembers when he wanted to sign up for Little League baseball, but his father, a small-farm farmer, wouldn't let him because he had to pick berries. The patient went back into that scene and told father he was going to play baseball no matter what father said. He wasn't going to work so hard anymore.

The first time he said this to father, he tensed up his shoulders as if father was going to hit him. We asked him to say it again in a different way and then be father and respond as he thought father would respond. Sitting in father's chair he (as father) said, *"Don't you talk back to me like that. Get your ass out there in the truck."*

Then switching to his own chair, he again told father that he was playing baseball, not working, and that father could not hurt him anymore. Then he asked father how come father never let him play when he wanted to, and as father answered, *"Because we have to eat, and I can't do all the work myself, and if you don't help, we won't eat."* Then, as himself, he said, *"That's the way it was, and it's not that way anymore. I make enough money at my job, I don't have to work extra all the time."* After his Child redecision, he successfully made Adult plans: *"I am going to Fielding"* (a graduate school offering an external degree program) *"and I'll cut down my hours of private practice so that I won't be working day and night. I can afford this by moving into a less expensive apartment and trading my expensive car for a less expensive model."*

To repeat, the first degree impasse is in response to the counter-injunction. The child originally decides to do what the parent asks, such as working hard, and may feel OK about that as long as he gets strokes for working and doesn't experience the work as interfering with other desires in his life. At the point that he wants to change, to work less, but feels stuck and "unable" to change, he is in an impasse. To break through the impasse, he redecides from the Adult in his free Child—the same Little Professor that made the original decision to work hard.

In the *second degree impasse,* the Little Professor had made a decision in response to an injunction rather than a counter-injunction. For instance, the Parent ego state of the parent may have given the message *"Work hard"* (first degree impasse) and the Child of the parent gave the injunction, *"Don't be a child."* The decision might then have been, *"I will never do childlike things again."* Many therapists we train and treat are in this bag. They work hard, take very little time for play, and when they do play, their play is not as spontaneous, as free, as childlike as is the play of those who have not accepted such an injunction. They even use their vacation time to come here for a month's training!

These therapists can decide from Adult not to work so hard and decide from Adult to play more, but the play remains programmed rather than free. The resolution of this impasse, between the early Adult in the Child (A_1) and the parent's Child, now part of the early Parent (P_1), is more emotional than the resolution of a first degree impasse. For successful resolution, the patient involves himself in his memory of his real parents and how they sounded, how they looked, how they felt. Often the difference is in the intensity of the parent's feelings, which may not be so affect-laden in first degree work. The therapist creates an environment in which the patient feels intensely the same feelings he had when he made the original decision. The patient *must* be in his Child rather than Adult ego state! Usually this is done in an archaic scene, in which the patient reexperiences vividly not only the place and the participants but also the feelings he and all the other original players experienced.

A dialogue is set up, with the patient stating his goal, *"I am OK if I play. If I am doing childlike things, I am OK. If I laugh and am joyful and excited, I am OK."*

The dialogue continues, with the patient taking the part of the parent who gave the injunction and then being himself, as he works through the impasse. Sometimes his introjected parent holds fast, and the patient has to go ahead and make the redecision in the face of disapproval from his own other part, the Parent in his Child; other times he finds support from somewhere inside himself, as an introjected different parent or grandparent—or a psychotherapist. Sometimes he has to make up a new Parent for himself, so that both his Child's Adult and his Child's Parent finally agree to the redecision. Finally he says, believes, and experiences, *"I am playing, doing childlike things, I am laughing, I'm joyous and excited! I am OK being childlike!"*

This work is not easy. It takes careful listening on the part of the therapist and careful setting up of the environment. It is extremely difficult when the therapist is seeing a patient individually for an hour or two a week, but less so in groups or in weekend, one-week or one-month workshops.

The *third degree impasse* is one in which the patient experiences himself as *always* having been whatever it is he experiences. For instance, the depressed patient who successfully works through a second degree impasse and redecides not to murder himself may—and probably will—give up his depression. However, he may still experience himself as not being worthwhile, and state that he has *always* felt worthless. He doesn't experience his feelings as being the result of parental injunctions and a decision to adapt, but rather as his natural state of being. He was "born" that way, he states. In these cases of third degree impasses, the injunctions were given so early and/or so nonverbally that the patient is not aware they were ever given. Therefore, the second-degree impasse work between patient's Child and the fantasized Child of his original parent fails to get to the root of the impasse. Even though we know the patient had an injunction and made a decision, he doesn't experience this. The crucial work, then, will be between the two sides of his own Little Professor—the Little Professor who adapted and the Little Professor of the free Child, who can intuit a new way to be. The work is strictly between two sides of Child and is carried on in an "I-I" double monologue rather than the I-Thou dialogue usually used in first and second degree impasse work.

To repeat, in third degree impasses, the client believes he has always been stubborn, angry, worthless, or unable to play; he's really the opposite sex, tragically born into the wrong body. To work through such impasses, the patient needs to take both sides—"I am the male me" as well as "I am the female me" or "I am the playful me" as well as "I am the me who never plays"—and to be each side in turn until he experiences energy in the free Child part of self. As the person experiences this, experiences himself as being worthwhile, for example, he knows the excitement of beginning to change. This is a powerful, moving experience—as the client makes a redecision to give up a seeming life-long attribute and to experience his own freedom and personal autonomy.

SUMMARY

So far we have discussed general principles of TA, beginning with the basic concept of the three ego states—the Adult who stores and processes data, and behaves according to that data; the Child who is a sum collection of child experiences, real and imagined; and the Parent who behaves in a self-parenting or other-parenting way, as he learned to do from parents, surrogate parents, or from his own Child and Adult powers to create a Parent.

We have written about transactions, strokes, and games. We have explained rackets, chronic stereotyped emotions, as well as injunctions, counter-injunctions, and decisions. In this chapter we have focused on impasses and begun the subject of redecisions.

What is our objective? It is not to foster the development of a new language or even to persuade others to use our language. There is no magic in the jargon; other terms could be substituted. The words are no more than handy labels for understanding a theory of behavior development. They are useful only as they help people live happier lives.

Our objective is to establish an environment for change. We create an intensive, rather than extensive, environment, encouraging the patient to change himself in a short period of time—a weekend, a week, two weeks, or a month—and then go out and practice his changes without further therapy. We discourage negative or positive transference. We have no objection to patients' liking us for ourselves. In all the ways we know, we encourage the patient to take charge of his own behavior, own thoughts, and own feelings. We discourage dependence. We are interested in intrapsychic change rather than the analysis of transactions, group process, and interpersonal relationships. We are not interested in the process of the group and rarely talk about it, although we, of course, encourage "process" during workshops. This real "process" takes place 24 hours a day as people eat together, play together, and sleep in rooms accommodating two to four persons. We do primarily one-to-one therapy in the group, because it is easier for a patient to remain in the Child ego state, and thereby to make redecisions, if the scene is kept simple and the number of real participants is kept to a minimum. After redecision work, the patient practices what he has learned—at the swimming pool, the dinner table, and during the evenings of guitar-playing and quiet conversations.

CHAPTER 4

Contracts

THE CONTRACTUAL PROCESS

The therapeutic contract sets the focus for treatment. The client decides specifically, in terms of beliefs, emotions, and behavior, what she plans to change about herself in order to reach self-designated goals. She works with the therapist to determine the contract and makes the contract with herself. The therapist serves as witness and facilitator.

Some clients know exactly what they want:

Don: Hi, I'm Don. I'm here because I got a promotion and that means I have to do some teaching to the sales force. I heard you cure public speaking phobias and I'm . . . terrified of speaking in public.

Other clients are vague:

Ral: I want to work on . . . I try to get along with my boss. Along with that, it's related somehow, we end up arguing.
Bob: Give an example. A recent time when you wanted to get along with your boss and ended up arguing.
Ral: Well, just last week. We were in my office. . . .
Mary: Good. Will you pretend right now that you are in the office and tell the scene as if it were happening now. And here's an extra chair. When you are your boss, move to that chair and say what your boss said.

We have to know what the client is talking about before we ask what he wants to change. When Ral says he wants to get along better, therapist and client need common information. Our way of obtaining the information is to get an example, ask the client to bring the scene into the here and now, and to play the roles of each person in the scene. We encourage I-Thou dialogue even when the "Thou" is present only in the client's fantasy. Such work is richer and more real than a past-tense recital of "what happened." Also, the client, immersed in a scene, is more apt to allow himself to feel as well as report.

Ann: I get all tight inside whenever I like a man, whenever I want to tell a man I would like . . . to be friends.
Mary: Think of a specific recent man you wanted to be friends with. Like, "I am at a party and . . ."
Ann: I should say, I'm only this way with men I think are available. Not married men.
Mary: OK. Pick a man and a scene.
Ann: OK. Yeah. Last Friday. I'm . . . John is my instructor. I'm having coffee with him after class. I think of telling him I enjoy him, I fantasize asking if we can meet again, and instead I'm suddenly telling him I have to go. And I leave.
Bob: Pretend you've finished therapy. Do the scene the way you do

it when you've changed yourself and are the way you want to be.
Ann: I'm enjoying myself, telling him about my work. I fantasize meeting him again. Instead of running, . . . (*pause*) . . . I am saying, "*I've enjoyed having coffee with you. This has been a delightful treat. Can we meet again?*" I'm happy. This is what I want. Yes!

Ann, creating the new scene, experiences thinking and feeling simultaneously. She looks lively and her example is clear to everyone.

Much pseudo-understanding occurs when clients use words that are not explicit: "*I want to feel OK about myself*"; "*I want to be closer to people*"; "*I want to communicate better.*" In each instance, a specific example expedites contract-setting.

Tom: I want to give up a tape . . . a feeling . . . a script. (His words tell us that he knows and is misusing TA.)
Bob: A what?
Mary: Tape, script, feeling? See how you get into being confused? And if we said OK, we would be confused with you.
Tom: That's true. When you were working with Barry, and he said "*I'd want to kill myself,*" I felt sad. And then I thought about my parents, and I had this crazy thought, "*I'd never kill myself but I am going to end up like my parents. I'm going to die an unhappy death.*"
Bob: What do you mean by "die unhappily"?
Tom: They never got what they wanted.
Mary: So they lived unhappily and then died. Now what do you want for you, so, when you are dying, you can say "*I lived happily*"? Be explicit.

We don't know what Tom wants. He rambles vaguely, refusing to give examples, and finally explains that he works very hard, hassles himself about work instead of enjoying his work, has no hobbies, and his wife does not enjoy sex with him. He is depressed and feels worthless. His first contract is not to kill himself. His second contract is to feel worthwhile. His third contract is to have fun.

Rog, like Tom, is difficult to understand. Another method for im-

proving communication between therapist and client is to ask clients
to speak in child language.

Rog: I want to fulfill myself and own myself.
Bob: Say that in kid language.
Rog: I always have this feeling that something is wrong with me.
Bob: Yeah, like what? (Bob, too, is using "kid" language.)
Rog: (*Pause*) That I'm dumb and nasty and that I don't like people.
Bob: Are you all those things? (If the answer is "yes," we'd ask for
      an example, a time and place when Rog is what he calls "dumb
      and nasty" and believes there is "something wrong with me.")
Rog: No, I am not. That's it. I want to stop all this downing of
      myself.

Judy, also, does not know, when she begins, what she wants to
change about herself.

Judy: I get this wiped-out feeling. . . . I . . . I'm feeling it right now.
       Afraid and shaky.
Bob: And what do you say in your head so that you feel afraid and
      shaky? (Bob emphasizes that she gives herself these feelings; she
      doesn't "get" them.)
Judy: Umm. I have got something hard to do and I don't want to
       do it. (*Very soft, low voice*)
Mary: What?
Judy: I don't know. I am shaking.

At this point we have the options of concentrating on Judy's fear
and "shaking" or of asking her to ignore her fear in order to discover what she wants for herself.

Mary: So, if you weren't shaking, what would you be working on?
Judy: On being heard, being counted.
Bob: Good. Say that with an "I."
Judy: Being counted? I want to be counted. I want to be heard.
Bob: Again. Loud enough to be heard.
Judy: I want to be counted. I WANT TO BE COUNTED.

Bob: (*laughing*) I hear you. OK. So your goal is to stop scaring yourself and to be heard. Great.

Mae also demonstrated her problem in the present therapy situation. She reacted to the therapist as she reacted to her parents long ago.

Mae: I feel good. I want to feel good even when I don't do everything right.

Mary: Example? A recent time when you didn't feel good because you didn't do everything right?

Mae: (*Long pause*) I can't think of one.

Mary: And what do you feel right now?

Mae: Stupid.

Mary: Stupid is a judgment. When you call yourself stupid, what do you feel?

Mae: I don't know. (*Pause*) Sad.

Mary: OK. So in this scene with me right now, you don't think of a time, which means you don't do everything right, you call yourself stupid, and you feel sad. Is that a familiar pattern?

Mae: Yes. (*Sigh*) It's sort of the story of my life. My mother is a great deal brighter than I am . . . and I always feel stupid . . . and sad.

Mary: You just made an astute evaluation . . . that you were reacting to me as if I were your mother. So I am certain you are not stupid. In this example, you don't think of something, you call yourself stupid, and you feel sad. Is there anything you want to change?

Mae: Stop thinking I'm stupid.

Mary: Great!

These first contracts for change may not have been the most important contracts these clients could make for themselves. In fact, often clients begin with a contract that is relatively innocuous, so that they won't expose themselves until they feel safe in the group. At any time during the therapeutic process, clients may change their contracts or the therapist, hearing new material, may propose a different contract.

However, before the end of the first session, we want to know enough about the client to be as certain as possible that she is not suicidal, homicidal, or becoming psychotic.

NO-SUICIDE AND NO-HOMICIDE CONTRACTS

No-suicide and no-homicide contracts take precedence over any other contracts that a potentially suicidal or homicidal client desires. The contract is a statement by the Adult of the client that he will monitor himself in order to stand guard successfully over his own self-murderous or other-murderous impulses. He guarantees not to kill, for his own sake, for a day, a week, a month, and continues in treatment during that time. A new temporal contract must be made before the expiration of the old contract, if the client has not re-decided to live. If the client is willing to stay alive for one day, then the therapist must schedule an appointment before the day is over . . . and also make arrangements with the client to see some-one else if the therapist, for any reason, misses the appointment. Throughout this chapter, what we say about no-suicide contracts applies equally to no-homicide contracts.

When a client is suicidal, we ask first about facts in his current life. What is going on, what unsolved problems is he using as jus-tification for murdering self? The problems may be divorce, bank-ruptcy, lack of a job, alienation from friends, loneliness, death of a loved person. These become problems to solve *after* he redecides to live in spite of these problems.

Some suicidal clients have no specific reality problems. They de-cided early in childhood, as they recognized their own unhappiness, *"When I am older and successful, I'll be happy."* In kindergarten they believed they'd be happy when they got to second grade and in second grade they believed they'd be happy when they graduated from grade school. If they could be valedictorian, they'd be happy, and then, if they could get into medical school, they'd finally feel good about themselves. So they successfully pass hurdle after hurdle and come to us, saying, *"I have a fine practice, make more money than I can spend, and I'm suicidal. There's no challenge and in spite of everything I've done, I've never been happy."* The contract is the same as for clients with serious current problems: to stay alive while redeciding never to kill self. Then, when the client has redecided, the belief that there is no challenge and no way to be happy becomes the problem to be solved.

Ted is a middle-aged man, recently divorced. He is underweight because he has not been eating. He made a serious suicide attempt two months ago and remains depressed. We discuss with him his problems: loneliness, lack of friends, no lovers except occasional "one night stands," and increasing irritation with his job, which he used to enjoy. We ask him to go, in fantasy, through a typical workday and then a typical weekend day, and we learn that he spends most of his time alone, ruminating about the past.

We then bring in two chairs and ask him to experience two parts of himself, the part he wishes to murder and the part that he wishes to keep alive. In the first chair, he is the part of self that he wants to murder.

Ted: My miserable little-old-man part. . . . I've been a little old man all my life. The part that never has fun, never knows how to deal with people. That's why I am lonely. Frankly, I am not worth knowing. (This is said very slowly, over a 10-minute period.)

We ask about the other part, the part worth saving.

Ted: I don't think that part exists.
Bob: Yes, it does. You brought you here instead of killing you. Start there. *"I brought Ted here . . ."*

After considerable hesitation, Ted is in touch with liking his ability to work, his brain, and his compassion for others.

Ted: I haven't much faith in therapy.
Bob: OK, I hear that. I also know I can't cure a corpse. Are you willing to keep yourself alive while we work?
Ted: Frankly, I don't know. (*Pause*) I don't know.

Ted talks about his depression, not understanding that he depresses himself, and feels as if he is in the grip of an incurable disease.

He gives some history, some very sad early memories, while we keep reiterating the importance of his making a contract to keep himself alive.

Bob: Again take the side of you that wants to stay alive. That's the side that is compassionate and bright, and wants some joy in life. The side that brought you here today.

Ted: I don't really know that side.

Mary: Get to know it. Start with, *"I want to live . . ."*

Ted: I want to live. I don't believe in life after death and, frankly, that may be just as well. If I did, I'd die.

Bob: Stay with the side that wants to live.

Ted: I know there is more to life than I have. I want to know more. I came here . . . yes, there is the part of me that hopes . . . or I wouldn't be here. I was told you are especially good with people like me, and, yes, I do know I have hope. I brought myself here to be less miserable . . . to decide once and for all, actually. Yes, I'll live for one week

Ted did stay alive that week. He attended all 10 of our therapy groups and had several individual appointments as well. On the sixth day he extended for a second week his contract to keep himself alive. Before the beginning of the third week, Ted had redecided, "I'll never kill myself accidentally or on purpose." He continued attending two groups a week in order to overcome his prohibitions against getting close to people and having fun. Six months later, when a family tragedy occurred, Ted again was depressed and thought of suicide. He re-contracted, allowed himself to mourn, and returned to his decision to live and care for himself.

With a client as depressed as Ted, we suggest that the contract always be short-term. This way we keep the client focused on the key issue—his own life. Contracts that extend for several months can be dangerous, because therapist and client may be lulled into working on non-vital issues, or the client may "run out of steam," quietly abandon therapy, and kill himself. Should a suicidal client abandon therapy by missing even one appointment, we would contact him immediately and work with him to reaffirm his contract or hospitalize himself.

While a no-suicide contract is being established, we watch for signs that a person might not keep the contract. Body language may be incongruent, as when a client shakes his head negatively while speaking positively or pushes with his hands as if to keep the therapist at a distance. The client may use ambivalent language, such as, *"I think I can say I won't kill myself."* A psychotically depressed client may agree and then increase his agitation, or may flatly repeat whatever the therapist asks him to say without making real contact.

When a person knows he will not kill himself during the contract period, he usually reports and demonstrates a change in his feelings. He may report immediate relief that he has a period of rest from his anguished obsession of "to be or not to be." He may report despair, knowing that he has blocked off an escape from his problems before he has solved the problems. Either way, his voice usually strengthens and his gestures become congruent.

If we have any doubt about his intentions or capabilities, we ask him to pretend he has just left the office and to fantasize aloud, in the present tense, what he is doing, thinking, and feeling from the moment he leaves the office until he returns for his next appointment. We stop him any time he reports depression or thinks of suicide, and ask what he will do to stay alive. We want him to plan ahead whom he can count on for support and what he will do if that support is not available.

A seriously suicidal client, like Ted, should be seen daily if he is to be treated without hospitalization. Some clients must be hospitalized, or otherwise protected, because their thinking processes are not sufficiently intact for them to make firm "no-suicide" or "no-homicide" contracts. They may be psychotic, brain-damaged, or decommissioned by alcohol or drugs. Clients who become more depressed and suicidal with use of alcohol or marijuana need to decide to abstain until they are no longer suicidal or homicidal. Hysterical characters, if they refuse to think on their own behalf, may be too impulsive to maintain their contracts. Clients who might otherwise be good candidates for outpatient treatment may be living in such difficult social or economic circumstances that their environment is seen to be overwhelmingly supporting suicide or homicide; therefore, temporary hospitalization may be the best choice. The therapist and client assess each client's ability to contract and any client who cannot or will not make a firm no-suicide or no-homicide contract should be hospitalized until he has made such a contract.

Depressed clients may ruminate about suicide without telling the therapist that they are suicidal. Whenever a client says she is lonely, sad, depressed, or presents material that indicates a lack of interest in life, we ask, *"Are you suicidal?"*

Alice: I want to change what I am doing to my daughter.
Mary: How old is she?
Alice: Thirteen.
Mary: Tell her. See her in front of you. And tell her specific ways you want to change what you are doing with her.

Again, this procedure establishes an example, told in I-Thou in the present, so that the client and therapist understand the client's reality and how the client wants to change herself within her reality.

Alice: Susan is my daughter. Susan, I want to listen to you. I want to listen more and be more available. I want you to be popular and go off and enjoy yourself. I think you hang around me because I am lonely.
Bob: Are you lonely?
Alice: Yes.
Bob: Suicidal?
Alice: I have thoughts but I wouldn't do it. My daughter needs me.
Mary: Right now your depression is more important than your behavior with your daughter. Will you stay alive this week while you work on deciding to live for *your* sake?
Alice: Yes.
Bob: Fine. I guess that the real reason you came here was to stop being depressed.
Alice: It is.

In order to test the strength of a person to maintain a contract, we ask what, if anything, "could happen" that would cause the client to change her mind about the contract.

Bob: You have said you will stay alive this week. Is there anything that could happen . . . anything at all . . . that you'd use as an excuse for suicide?

Alice: I can't think of anything . . . nothing will happen to my daughter this week. . . .

Bob: Think about this. Take your time. Will you decide that you will stay alive this week no matter what happens to your daughter? To anyone?

Alice: One week? Yes. Yes, I will.

Bob: Sure?

Alice: Yes.

Bob: Is there anything else you think of that might be used by you to get you to commit suicide this week?

Alice: No. No, I will stay alive this week.

We also use no-suicide contracts for clients who are not clinically depressed but who are a danger to themselves because they drive or fly recklessly, take risks in mountain climbing or scuba diving, or give a history of being "accident-prone." We offer the same contract to people who do not take good physical care of themselves: diabetics who "cheat" on their diets, clients who maintain high blood pressure, and all who kill themselves slowly with drugs, nicotine, alcohol, or overeating. (See Chapter 9.)

No-homicide contracts and redecisions are necessary for clients who fantasize murder or behave violently. They contract not to hurt or kill anyone no matter what the provocation. We use the same format and techniques described in no-suicide contracts, plus appeals to the client's Child to avoid murder in order to avoid punishment for murder. If the client cannot or will not make such a contract, we want the client in custody.

A no-homicide contract can be vastly relieving to a paranoid client. During a one-week workshop a participant became acutely paranoid, believing that another participant was arranging to have him killed in order to marry his wife. At the time deer season had just begun, so there was considerable rifle fire in the hills surrounding our property. The man used this fact to believe that his would-be murderer had hired killers to shoot him. We worked first with the "other man," easily obtaining from him a no-homicide contract since the man was not in love with the wife nor in any way homicidal. We then did exactly the same work with the paranoid participant. After several sessions, he stated firmly that he would not kill . . . he would not kill the other participant, his own wife, Bob, Mary, or anyone else, no matter what the real or imaginary provocation. When he firmly believed himself, his paranoid symptoms diminished and he was able to recognize and deal with his angers and jealousies. After the workshop he remained in ongoing therapy for several years, without further acute paranoid episodes.

Sometimes therapists think of potential murderers only as those who are criminals or insane and forget the importance of no-homicide contracts for clients who might kill accidentally. We get no-homicide contracts from clients who drive while drunk, to impress upon them that their behavior is potentially murderous. With this contract they stop drunk driving. Once we initiated the same contract with a sweet, seemingly harmless older woman who had been driving with severely impaired vision.

NO-PSYCHOSIS CONTRACTS

Clients with histories of brief, acute psychotic episodes sometimes can contract successfully not to become psychotic in reaction to future stress. We explore with them their present problems and their alternative ways of solving them, and also look at what they may choose to do in the future if problems arise similar to those they experienced prior to an acute psychotic episode. They make themselves aware of danger signals in themselves and use these to remind themselves to return to medication or to whatever is appropriate to ward off psychosis.

Chronically psychotic clients may monitor their behavior in order to remain out of the hospital. Jan had been a back-ward patient almost continuously from age 18 to age 43 and had received many series of shock treatments. When she joined two of our therapy groups, each of which met once weekly, she had been out of the hospital only a week and already her relatives were clamoring for her re-admission. Her contract was simply to change whatever she had to change about herself in order to stay out of the hospital. To implement her contract, she fired the practical nurse hired by her aunt;

stopped telephoning her relatives, who fortunately did not live nearby; and finally went by herself to Superior Court and obtained a change of guardianship. All of this she did while still hallucinating from time to time and still showing signs of organic impairment in her thinking.

In the group, she was often disruptive, as she spoke of the British poisoning the water supply and accused group members of being insane. We confronted her psychotic talk by saying, *"Hey, Jan, you're talking crazy again,"* and stroked her when she deconfused. Gradually she let herself recognize that she became "crazy" in order not to listen to group members talk about anger or sex. She then gave herself permission to leave a group session, if she chose, to avoid these topics. Later, she tolerated all subjects, made astute observations of group members, and achieved a degree of closeness with them. She terminated after two years and is still—10 years later—living in the community.

Borderline clients are asked to make no-psychosis contracts before we work with other issues in their lives. Carl, a borderline client, is attending a weekend workshop. Usually, we screen out such clients because they need a long-term group and because the intensity of work done by others may be quite upsetting. Carl slipped by our screening procedure.

Carl: I have been withdrawing my attention and then bringing it back. I am learning more about people and their eyes. I at times would like to work here. I am not sure what to do. Because of the fact that when I start to work I lose contact. (There are long pauses between each of his sentences.) I end up choosing what someone else would like or taking their suggestion. And following suggestions. So now what I do is withdraw.
Bob: Either way you withdraw.
Carl: There is some value in that, too. I would be willing . . . to . . . um . . . spend time . . . um . . . today . . . exploring.

Carl's statement about what happens when he starts to work has not occurred here inasmuch as this is the first time he has spoken in the workshop. During breaks, he speaks continuously, doesn't listen, and displays evidence of considerable confusion.

Carl: I would like . . . I do not want to feel violated.

Bob: Good.

Carl: The question remains. . . .

Mary: I am not willing to spend time exploring unless I know what it is you want to change about you.

Carl: That is what I was saying. (*Long pause*) I would like to . . . For me, I don't know what I would like to do. I do not get past that point. . . . I can't start thinking.

Mary: You sure discount yourself. Like, what degree have you got?

Carl: What degree?

Mary: Yeah. You are smart enough to have gotten through college, right?

Carl: Yeah.

Mary: You discount both your strength and your brain.

Carl: (*Long pause*) I don't think you understand.

Mary: Tell me.

Carl: Where I am, OK? My experience is a little difficult for me to describe, because I haven't the language to describe it.

Bob: Bullshit. I experience you as saying a lot and doing very little.

Carl: Yeah!

Bob: Want to change that or stay in that same bag?

Carl: I have two options?

Bob: No, you have lots of options.

Carl: I think the thing I am resenting right now is that you are jumping to a conclusion about what I am.

Bob: I said I experience you. You do a great deal of talking, during the breaks, very little of which I undertand. I hear you talking about doing something, and not doing it. What is inside your head, what you know about yourself, I don't know. I do know what I experience.

Carl: Umm.

Bob: And I guess that what goes on inside your head is obsessing, not thinking.

Carl: (*Long pause*) I would like to consider that. I can consider that. I had a flash of thought, too. Actually, I would like. . . . The opposite is also very true.

Mary: Opposite of what?

Carl: The opposite of not wanting to be violated. I can consider wanting . . . to put myself . . . open ended into going wherever you choose to go with me.

Bob: I wouldn't consider doing that.

Carl: What troubles me right now is. . . . Am I in contact? I don't want to. . . .

Mary: Again, listen to your discounts about yourself. You are discounting your brain, you are discounting that you know what you want to do, discounting that you are strong enough to say "No" to me, which you really are saying, since you have been saying "No" in your own way since we began. Therefore, after all your discounts, I'm supposed to think for you.

Carl: What would you want me to say?

Mary: I wouldn't. As Bob said, I won't lead you because that would be discounting your brain.

Carl: Actually, I put thinking off.

Mary: Is there something you want to change about you?

Carl: I would like to explore the idea in terms of. . . .

Mary: I surrender. I give up. (*Waves white flag*)

Carl: It isn't as bad as that in my experience.

Mary: I am the one giving up. I give up. You win.

Carl: (*Long pause*) What happened? I am not . . . I respect you can quit.

Mary: Do you understand?

Carl: I think you mean I have to come further out for you to work with me.

Mary: No. I want to hear what you want to change about you. I will not explore an idea with you.

Carl: I want two things. One is this. (*Pause*) Have faith.

Bob: What?

Carl: Have faith that I will think. I need to slow down. I want to share with you what's on my mind. Trade in desperation (*pause*) for fighting back.

Mary: What is your desperation about?

Carl: I heard you. One sec. Don't block off. Punishment. Like a . . . (*not distinguishable*)

Mary: What are you desperate about in your life?

Carl: What it's for. I need something right away. Um. . . . I know. Um. . . . You move too fast. (*Tone is angry*) I am aware all this is a defense, OK? Sticking your hand out. My experience is of reaching out and going through the pain of being cut off.

Mary: I am willing to go slower. I'd also like facts, rather than fantasies. I would like to know what goes on in your daily living that you are desperate about.

Carl: I am withdrawn from it most of the time. Let's see. I involve myself with four or five different areas, most of the time trying to effect, trying to find enjoyment in it.

Mary: Give me an example of one of your areas.

So far, we have had great difficulty in making Adult-Adult transactions. The client gives tangential responses. We want the client in Adult rather than confused Child.

Carl: Sure. (*Sigh*) In relating to . . . I have a fascination for painting.

Bob: Do you paint?

Carl: No. I have done two . . . long ago. I am fascinated with feeling for a sense of flow. . . .

Mary: I want you to be concrete. What do you do for a living?

Carl: Sorry. What I do for a living is (names a civil service job). I don't have any friends. And I don't . . . I don't feel I am doing anything. I don't feel hope. I am doing nothing at work. I sit at my desk. I don't communicate.

Mary: And do you live with anybody?

Carl: I feel frustrated. Not knowing how to reach others. I have a girl friend and that extends the complexity of the problems. So I guess I need to do something for myself.

Bob: Are you depressed?

Carl: I don't know.

Bob: Suicidal?

Carl: No. I am not conscious of where I am.

Bob: Do you contemplate suicide, in your desperation?

Carl: I keep banging my head up against it. . . . I think about it. And I . . . I won't kill myself.

Mary: Now you are talking clearly. Have you also decided that you won't cop-out by going crazy?

Carl: (*Long pause*) That isn't a thought to me. I am not aware of thinking of going crazy.

Mary: I asked you that because you were talking tangentially. You were discounting, and acting as if you couldn't think. (*Pause*) Will you keep you from going crazy?

Carl: I experience overwhelming helplessness in trying to achieve this myself, and a sense of being humiliated if I have to ask for help.

Mary: And now? Now that you have indicated where you need help? What do you feel now?

Carl: Ashamed.

Mary: Really?

Carl: I suddenly become aware of all the people in the room.

Mary: All of whom are in perfect mental health and wouldn't consider asking for help. (*Laughter*)

Carl: Well, it sounds facetious, but actually that thought gives me some support. (*Starts crying*)

Bob: J, would you pass him the Kleenex, please? (*Bob*: On hearing this tape, I am surprised that I was taken in by his helplessness. Usually, I do not give Kleenex unless the patient requests it.)

Carl: I don't need it.

Bob: OK. It's available to you.

Carl: I'm all right now.

Mary: You know, I really like your straightness.

Bob: I do too.

Carl: You do?

Mary: Yeah. You may make it harder on yourself, having to do without Kleenex, but I admire you . . . like you don't take the Kleenex and pretend to use it.

Carl: I don't understand the word "pretend."

Mary: You don't pretend to use Kleenex just because Bob says "pass the Kleenex."

Carl: OK. Yeah. And I waste time being the way I am.

Bob: Yeah.

Carl: Where have we gotten? I am confused right now.

Bob: I have found out some facts about you. I have found out that you have a girl friend, and you have some complications about that. You are not doing your job and you feel desperate. That is a lot more than I knew about you 15 minutes ago. And my hunch is that you need to do a lot of work around the area that it is OK for you to make it even though someone else wants you to. That it is OK to make it even if they want you to.

Carl: Even *if* they do?

Bob: Yeah. Because you are stubborn enough, like with the Kleenex, that if someone else wants you to do something, like make it or use the Kleenex, you might say, "Fuck you," just to get back at them.

Carl: That could be a danger.

Bob: Yeah. Does it fit?

Carl: Yeah. The word "surrendering." Rendering. It is a magical feeling . . . trying to render somebody impotent by not cooperating.

Bob: Yup.

(*Long pause.*)

Mary: Where are your parents in your life at the present time?

Carl: My family are back in the South. Both my mother and father are alive. My father is about 50, my mother is 45. She is remarried to a physician, and my father is still single. And he works in the "x" business. I had contact with him recently. I became aware that I needed to contact my father. I have been needing to do that for a long time. So I called him on the phone. No introduction. I said, *"Pop, it's me. I really care about you a lot."* He did what I have been doing . . . nothing clear. Like grasping and there's nothing. No sense. I withdrew. And said OK. The contact with my mother . . . the most recent thing was when I was in college. I sent her some poems. . . . I can't tie myself down to writing. . . .

Bob: You won't.

Carl: I can't and then. . . .

Bob: Won't.

Carl: And. . . .

Bob: (*Yells*) WON'T!

Carl: I get you. (*Everyone laughs*)

Mary: See, you have met someone equally stubborn. (*Group laughs*)

Carl: I do not have the ability . . . that is a "can't."

Bob: You have the ability to stick with it . . . you won't. And that is OK as long as you don't say "can't." It is perfectly OK to choose to write or not choose to write.

Carl: I hear you. So I wrote the poems. It is an interesting problem. She sent them back to me completely rewritten and xeroxed. She had sent them to all her friends and mine, rewritten. So I called her up. I was very angry.

Group member: She changed *your* words?

Carl: Yeah.

Group member: That is awful.

Bob: No wonder it is hard for you to put your hand out.

Carl: I had to explain to her what I meant. She didn't understand why I was angry. So that didn't work either. So . . . the next contact with my father, he comes out and sees me. The man is nuts. He is crazy . . . paranoid. Obsessive. Infantile behavior. An alcoholic. And he did his trip. We took him around, and he brought a woman with him. To whom he was rude and vile and violent. He vomited on people. Umm. I go hug him when he arrives and his response is uncomfortableness, as if he was in his underwear. . . . This uncomfortableness continued throughout the whole visit. And my girl friend got really scared and anxious. (*Voice continues without emotion throughout this recital*)

Mary: It was a sad visit.

Carl: It ended with, well, I sat down with him and I said . . . I was like I am now, shaking. I said, *"You can't do this when you are in my house. You are going to have to be decent with people and you will have to cut it out."* (*Fights against sobbing*) He said to me. . . . (*Sobs, pounding on chair arms*)⋅ As you see, what he said hurt me. Hurts. Then he said . . . (*Sobs*) He didn't understand what I was trying to say. And his response was *"I'm shocked. I don't believe it. I spent three weeks of my life to hear this."* I told him, *"Dad, I really care about you."* He said, *"That's a lie. You never even called me 'Dad.'"* I had to remind him that I just did. That's the part that really hurts, when you have to remind your own father that you love him. So I, ahh, severed ties with him. Except for the hurt. He is one person I would like to kill.

Bob: And you won't?

Carl: As I am talking, the feeling is pretty strong. I don't imagine I will go back down South and do it. No, I won't.

Bob: You have some kooky parents.

Carl: I think so.

Bob: I do, too. They are both nuts. Congratulations on making it, without being crazy.

Carl: Thanks.

Mary: I see how you want to find some other way of being grown up.

Carl: Yes, Mary. (*Sobs, again*)

Mary: And you have already found another way . . . the way you told your father—no violence and nothing vile in your house.

Carl: Yes, Mary. I want to thank you for not interfering.

Mary: I want to thank you for telling me when I am. And when I am going too fast.

Carl: I need time. I can't work fast.

Bob: You can and you did.

   (*General laughter*)

Bob: I want you to know that in the beginning you talked in a crazy manner. You were what we call tangential, which means that ·you'd move away from a subject in ways that didn't make sense. Then you stopped talking crazy and you were completely clear.

Carl: (*Laughs delightedly*)

   (*Group applauds.*)

During this interview we honored Carl by insisting that he talk in non-psychotic fashion. We addressed ourselves to his health rather than his pathology. He has a distance still to go before he clarifies sufficiently his differences from his parents to be capable of saying firmly that he is not going to be crazy no matter how lonely or desperate or angry he becomes. He needs continued stroking for his astute thinking as well as for allowing himself to think and feel simultaneously.

CONTRACTS WITH RELUCTANT OR INVOLUNTARY CLIENTS

The major problem in dealing with reluctant and involuntary clients is that they assume that others, who exert some form of power over them, are in charge of the contract. Often this is true. Parents and therapists discuss what symptoms in the child need to be "cured." Therapists in welfare and probation, in jails and in hospitals, often do choose their clients' goals. The man who refuses to join his wife's therapy group believes he is in exactly the same spot . . . that the therapist and the group have already determined what is wrong with him and what he should change.

With a reluctant client we begin with questions about what "the others" in his life want him to change about himself. We explain that we want to know this in order that we avoid aligning ourselves on the side of these people . . . even if their contracts are in the client's best interest.

Mary: OK, your wife wants you to quit drinking. She's probably right, you know. The stuff is poison and eventually you may be brain-damaged or die of liver problems. Anyway, that's what she wants. If you could change yourself in any way you choose, what would be your wish?

or

Bob: I hear that your welfare worker wants to get you off welfare and you want to stay home and play with your kids and raise vegetables. So . . . they are willing to pay for six group sessions for you. During those six sessions what are you going to change about you that would please *you*?

Many years ago Mary was asked to treat a young man on probation who professed to want exactly what the judge wanted for him . . . to strop truanting, get good grades, and become a "good citizen." Mary said she didn't believe that he wanted to go to school regularly or he would go. She then explained the rules: *"You have to come here once a week for six weeks or be returned to Juvenile Hall. That's what the judge told you and me. If you don't come, I call your proba- tion officer. If you do come, I'm not into getting you to be the way the judge wants you to be. I'm into you deciding how you want to be."* During the third session, he confessed, half-challengingly and half-yearningly, that he wished he could stop blushing. *"To stop blushing or to stop caring about blushing"* became the contract. Six months later he was not concerned about blushing and was back in school on a work-study program, which he was handling very well. By his own choice, he continued in treatment beyond the required six sessions.

With hospitalized or imprisoned clients, we want to know what the client wants that is obtainable. Obviously, the first response is, *"I want out of here."* That is fine! We ask what are the rules of the place . . . how does a person get out? If the patient doesn't know, gathering of information is important. Then, is the client doing what is necessary to get out? If attending occupational therapy and "socializing with other patients" are requirements, non-attendance at O.T. and refusal to socialize means that some part of the patient is invested in remaining in the institution. After exploring this, the contract may be to do exactly what is required for discharge.

For prisoners, behavioral change may not hasten "getting out of here." Then the question is, *"Granted that you changing you will not shorten your sentence, how can you change you in order to make your life better here?"* Prisoners at Marion penitentiary, who were in the therapeutic community, became interested in becoming therapists, studied hard, and certainly had far more creative, happy moments than most prisoners experience.

CHANGING UNACCEPTABLE CONTRACTS

Parent Contracts

A Parent contract is a contract that a client *should* want to fulfill. We accept such a contract only if the client has some Child investment in achieving it. All contracts to stop eating, smoking, drinking, and using drugs are primarily Parent contracts . . . and probably will not be accomplished until the Child redecides to live and be healthy. Therefore, from the beginning the Child must be involved in the contract.

Some Parent contracts are difficult to diagnose, because what is Parent for one person may not be for another. Geoff wants to stop being angry, a Child contract, because his use of anger keeps him from achieving intimacy. Gordon also wants to stop being angry—his is a Parent contract. He recently married for the first time and is harassing himself for his anger at his stepsons, who don't pick up their belongings, tease his dog, and in general behave as one would expect of two young boys with a new stepfather. In his own childhood, Gordon obeyed his parents, repressed his anger, and learned to feel guilty instead. Now, each time he feels mild to moderate irritation at the boys, he experiences guilt. We don't accept his contract to suppress anger and instead suggest that he get acquainted with his angry self and then learn to be assertive in order to get his own wishes met.

Ann suggests a contract she has no intention of keeping, as can be seen by her words, *"I should. . . ."*

Ann: My problem is keeping the house clean. (*Pause*) I *should* keep it clean.

Mary: Why? ("Why" is a question asked sparingly in our therapy. We tend to restrict its use to occasions when clients consider the reasons to be self-evident.)

Ann: Because it's filthy.

Mary: So? When my kids were little and I was staying home with them, I always left the vacuum cleaner beside the front door. That way, if anyone came to call, I could grab it fast and pretend I was starting to clean.

Ann: (*Laughing*) Well, I *should*. . . .

Mary: Of course, you should. Such a nice person as you . . . the very least you can do, if you aren't going to clean your house, is feel guilty. Will you at least do that?

Ann: You are very funny.

Mary: I know. And funny people are excused from doing dumb things like cleaning houses.

Ann: Well, if you don't accept my honorable contract, I don't know what I have to work on this week.

Mary: Oh, shit! Then you'll have wasted the money you spent to come here. If you don't clean up your house, you should at least clean up your psyche.

Ann: Never mind. I am going to sit here very happily and I am not going to feel guilty.

Bob was offered a similar Parent contract and took a different approach. During a one-day workshop for psychiatrists, held in the South, Bob was lecturing to a large audience when a member of the audience asked him to demonstrate his techniques in contract-setting. The man volunteered to be the patient and came to the front of the room. (*Because the session was not taped, this is written from memory.*)

Bob: What do you want to change about yourself today?
Psy: What!

To the classical therapist the notion of "change today" is startling, as most training prepares therapists for long, ongoing work with patients. The question, however, is most important. It alerts the patient that change is possible, that it is possible now, not next week or next year, and it also alerts the patient to the fact that he will be in charge of his change. Some therapists ask, *"What do you want to work on?"* Bob likes *"change"* because otherwise patients may elect to work and work and work and work and work and never change.

Psy: I think perhaps I might like to. . . .
Bob: Think . . . perhaps . . . might (*Bob emphasizes the cop-out words*).
Psy: (*Laughing*) I want to stop putting things off. (*He gives, as an example, that he puts off writing for publication.*)
Bob: What do you say to yourself about not writing?
Psy: I bawl myself out, of course. I feel sad and angry at myself and guilty about putting off writing.

In our experience the problem is not procrastination but what people do to themselves about procrastinating. They criticize themselves, feel badly, promise to do better, and obsess about the unfinished product. We prefer a contract to stop harassment, which is a contract on behalf of the Child, before accepting a contract to finish something that the client has put off doing. Otherwise, if we are on the side of the Parent, the patient may "defeat" us, too, in order to criticize himself even more harshly and feel even more guilty.

Bob: Willing to first give up your bad feelings and stop harassing yourself?
    (*Laughter from psychiatrist and the audience.*)
Psy: Yes.

Bob: Good. Would you be willing, each time you start to bawl your-self out for procrastinating, to switch and have a sexual fantasy instead?
(*Again, patient and audience laugh.*)

Bob suggests substituting a sexual fantasy for harassment in order to prove to him that he is in charge of his own thoughts and that he doesn't have to think unpleasant thoughts, such as harassments.

Psy: Fine!
Bob: OK, so now that you have that settled, what is the title of the article you are going to write?
Psy: (*Thinks for a moment, and then gives a title.*)
Bob: Will you write your title on a piece of paper? (*Psy. does*) Will you now write the first sentence? (*Psy. does*) Now will you write the closing sentence? (*Psy. does*) OK, now you have a title, an opening sentence and a closing sentence. When will you put in the middle?
Psy: Before next spring.
Bob: And every time you harass yourself about this, will you have a sexual fantasy instead?

He may or may not write his paper. He'll write it if he wants to write it more than he wants not to write it. Whether he writes or doesn't write, Bob believes that the psychiatrist has learned to stop hassling himself about procrastinating.

Sometimes the difficulty in contract-setting occurs because the rebellious Child of the client sees the therapist only as a Parent to be fought. Whatever the contract, the client will turn it into a Parent contract as soon as the therapist accepts it. Our associate, Bob Drye,[1] suggests that the therapist, on recognizing this situation, immediately bring it to the client's attention and even stroke the client positively for the creativity, strength, and excitement in rebelliousness. Bob Drye gave us the following example:

Pat: I have lots of anger. In another group I saw people release anger while the therapist and group members held them down. That might be helpful. My breathing is tight.

Bob Drye: I'd like more information about your anger first. Let yourself breathe more deeply.

Pat: (*Not breathing deeply*) My anger is like a ball of fire. I am so angry at my mother I stand in the doorway thinking, "If she won't listen to me, I'll go crazy."

Bob: You're not breathing deeply.

Pat: If I think of breathing, I feel sad.

Bob: Like I want to take something away from you? You want to do an anger exercise and I ask you to breathe deeply.

Pat: Yes. (*Smiles*)

Bob: I'll bet your mother couldn't get you to do much. You are still not breathing deeply.

Pat: She had a terrible time with me. (*Laughs*)

Bob accepted one part of Pat's contract, to permit himself to breathe deeply, and immediately this became a Parent contract to be fought by Pat. When Pat does establish a contract, he may need to add, "*I'll succeed even if my success pleases my therapist, my group, and my mother.*"

Contracts to Change Others

Another unworkable contract is one that has within it the requirement that someone else change. John, in the guise of wanting to change himself, offers instead a Parent contract for his wife, Shelley. They are attending the workshop together.

John: I need to change something. (*Pause*) Oh, hell, I don't know where to start.

Mary: Start with "want," not "need." Need is for survival, and is said by people who don't know it is OK to want.

John: Well, it feels like a need. I . . . I want to and need to change the way I relate to Shelley.

Bob: Tell her.

John: I want to change the way I relate to you. That is my contract.

Bob: Say more to her, and be specific.

John: I want to be able to be free. . . .

Bob: You *are* able.

John: What?

Bob: You are able. (Even before we knew what he was talking about, we are attacking his victim position, by emphasizing the difference between "want" and "need," and the difference between "not able," "can't," and "won't.")

John: I want to find a way to be free.

Mary: Give her a specific. A specific behavior you want to change in you. Don't use labels like "free" because that's meaningless.

John: I don't know. I just feel controlled a lot. Example. On the plane. We ride in the smokers' section. If I want to be with you, I have to ride in the smokers' section.

Shelley: That's true. I want to smoke. I am willing to ride alone if that is your choice.

Mary: So this particular contract is to get your wife to change, right?

John: I want her to stop smoking.

Mary: So . . . back to the beginning. What do you choose to change about you so that you will feel free and relate better . . . those were goals you mentioned . . . whether your wife smokes or doesn't smoke?

Later, we may ask Shelley if she wants, for her sake, to stop smoking. If she does, we will accept that contract. We do not accept a contract for her to stop so that he can feel better. That is blackmail.

Often, each partner has an agenda for the other:

Russ: I want to be more nurturing to my wife and not critical. (This is a Parent contract . . . what he *should* want.) I don't like our arguments. (This may be Child.)

Bin: I don't agree with your definition of arguments. Many times I'm not arguing, I am excited. Like when I was talking about the Governor and you called it arguing. I was having fun and I don't like being told I am talking too loud. (Already she argues.)

Russ: I'd say that was accurate. I have had some difficulties being assertive and then permitting you to be assertive without my getting scared or angry. (He backs down in the argument, so his Child probably *is* afraid of arguments.)

Mary: (Missing the argument and capitulation) I am into *"permit."*

Bob: Of course. (*Laughs*)

Russ: I suppose that is my problem. (Capitulates again)

Bin: I don't like your saying, *"I'll allow you"* this and *"I'll permit you"* that. That is exactly when I do get mad. In some ways I'm responsible, too. I used to like it. But now, since I have gone back to school, am doing things on my own, and have been very creative, I no longer like or want that.

Group member: Hurray for you!

Group members discuss various aspects of Bin's and Russ' problems and state their own beliefs as well as some "Why don't you" suggestions for solutions.

Group member: So you are changing, Bin, and you (Russ) are not liking...

Russ: I'm liking, but ...

Bin: That is the main reason I wanted to come here, so that Russ would let go.

Group member: So you both came to change each other.

Mary: Great comment! You're right on target. OK, so let's get back to what does each of you want to change about self?

Bin: It's important. I want him to let go. What's wrong with that?

Bob: (*Giving them a belt*) Each of you grab an end. Now tell each other to let go.

Bin pulls hard, yelling, *"Let go!"* Russ lets go and Bin continues to clutch her end of the belt.

Bob: Bin, you are still holding on.

Bin: Oh. (*Pause*)

Mary: Understand?

Bin: Yeah, I got it. I got it. (*Throws belt down*) When I get angry that you are holding on, very often I am the one who won't let go. Thank you. I learned something.

Bob: You are welcome.

Mary: Neat. Another point. . . . Russ, did you come from a quiet home?

Russ: Very. I was an only child. A very quiet household.

Mary: Well, for practice and for fun, the next time your wife is noisy, pretend you are Zorba the Greek . . . a good noisy, gesticulating man . . . when you answer.

Russ: (*Laughs*) OK.

Mary: And have fun.

Russ: I'll do that.

Game Contracts

Game contracts are contracts in which the client asks the therapist's approval to do something which will end in the client's being hurt or unhappy. The client, of course, is not aware of this when she seeks to establish the contract.

Marg: I want to change my feeling vis-à-vis my Dad. That I am a failure. Specifically, I have been separated from my husband for a year and I haven't told Dad. He is 84.

Mary: Go on.

Marg: I am afraid this would be such a blow to him that I shouldn't. He'd be so disappointed that he might have a heart attack. He might because he is so old and frail.

Bob: Is there a reason why he should know?

Marg: For me.

Bob: Why?

Marg: I feel dishonest that I have not told him.

Mary: What reaction are you still wanting from your father . . . about you?

Marg: I want approval, and I don't want disapproval.

Mary: OK, so the way to insure that you can keep the old crap going . . . that he dies disapproving . . . is to tell him that you are separated from your husband. He can then say, "*Ah, one more piece of evidence for my disapproval box!*" And you can feel guilty.

Marg: Yes, I would feel guilty. What is your point? I have missed it.

Mary: Step one: "*I want you to approve of me and my separation from my husband.*" (Mary is writing the steps of the game on the black board and referring to the first step in the diagnosis

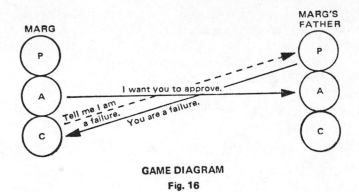

GAME DIAGRAM
Fig. 16

of a game, the ostensibly straight message. Next comes the secret message, then the response to the secret message, then the payoff. See Figure 16.)

Mary: Step 2: "*Tell me how bad I am.*"

Marg: No, it is not "bad"; it is, "*Tell me I am a failure.*"

Mary: OK. Step 2: "*Tell me I am a failure.*" Step 3: "*I certainly will tell you that you are a failure.*" And then you can be disapproved of again. And say whatever you say about yourself and about him. And feel what you feel. That is the payoff.

Marg: Which I don't want.

Bob: The only way you can win that way is if he changes. What are the odds of his changing? Of his approving of your separation?

Marg: Slim. Non-existent.

Mary: OK. So I don't accept your contract. Accepting it would only mean helping you play your game.

Marg: Where he feels bad and I feel worse. Yeah. In truth, I don't want that. That must be why I haven't told him.

Bob: Nice going.

Of course, another option would be for her to tell him and not "feel worse" whatever he does, but in view of his age and her belief that he might react poorly, it does seem rather pointless to tell him. He has been so convinced over the years that she can "make" him feel that he believes it . . . and he is not our patient.

When we suspect a game, we ask the client to go to the future, when the game is completed, and experience the "best" and "worst" possible outcomes. Because games are initiated by the Child or Parent ego states and are not monitored by the Adult, the client may block from awareness the "worst" outcome. If so, we give our fantasies of possible negative results.

Mary: OK, so you tell your boss you are quitting and you see no possible bad results. I don't understand. Aren't you managing to ignore that he may give you such bad references that you won't get another job?

or

Bob: A lot of open marriages fail. What do you feel if he decides he loves one of these partners more than he loves you?

Forever Contracts

Some clients work forever toward a future goal, with the secret agenda of remaining unhappy until they are perfectly cured. They may have experienced years of psychotherapy, because they believe they have to dredge up the last piece of psychopathology, understand the last clue to its origin, and ventilate the last drop of negative feeling before they can be happy. The original reason for therapy is forgotten or irrelevant. They continue in order to receive the same strokes they received in childhood, strokes for working hard and for suffering. From such clients we accept only one contract: to stop making self suffer about the past.

Irv: I have unfinished business with my father.
Bob: Father's dead?
Irv: Yeah.
Bob: And how does your unfinished business with your dead father affect your life today?
Irv: I'm angry at you. Angry that you didn't defend yourself . . . that you didn't fight to be yourself. . . . (He has immediately started a two-chair dialogue with father, ignoring Bob's question.)
Mary: Bob asked you to say, first, how holding on to your father affects your life today.

Irv: Uhh . . . What? What comes . . . I am stuck with him.

Bob: How?

Irv: Uh . . . what I am aware of is . . . if I don't get angry at him, I won't finish this business. It keeps coming up. . . .

Bob: *You* keep bringing it up for some reason or other, and you choose not to say what change you plan to make in yourself once you have done this work.

Irv: The connection I make is I have to learn to fight . . . to stand up for myself.

Bob: Go on with that.

Irv: I am mad at you because you didn't teach me to fight. You ran from emotional situations and I do the same because that is what you taught me. (Irv, the bit between his teeth, continues his diatribe. Bob and Mary wait, until he slows down.)

Bob: Now where are you?

Irv: I'm aware of sadness for my wife and child. My child is a cripple. (Amplifies about wife and child.)

Mary: I don't think father is the important issue. What I hear is you have all these dramatic sad stories you tell yourself and you tell them over and over. How much therapy have you had?

Irv: Ten years. More than 10 years.

Mary: Good heavens! So for more than 10 years you have been finding all these reasons for sadness.

Bob: You sure are willing to pay a pile of money to justify your sadness. Are you willing to drop your sad stance?

Irv: Yeah. '(*Looks up*)

Bob: (*Laughs*) You look as if the sky would fall.

Irv: Well, it might. If I drop my sadness, they may bounce up again.

Mary: Think of your big ball of sadness as a yo-yo. You can bounce it for another 10 years or you can cut the string.

Throughout the four-week workshop, we focus solely on Irv's accepting himself and enjoying himself as he is. We refuse to listen to any "change" contracts except self-acceptance and fun. He begins enjoying his time here and, after he returned to his own therapy practice, he reported excitedly his good results in using short-term therapy for many of his own long-term clients.

THERAPY WITHOUT A CONTRACT

Pure gestalt therapists rarely seek contracts and instead make contact, exchange awarenesses with the client, and work with blocks or incongruities which may appear. Sometimes we begin in this fashion, although, unlike the purists, we do end with a contract.

Bob: What's happening?

Kay: What's happening? I go blank.

Bob: Say more.

Kay: I just stopped my breathing.

Bob: Say more.

Kay: I shouldn't be here at all. (*Pause*) OK, now I am saying I don't know what is going on.

Bob: You don't know what is going on with what?

Kay: I don't know.

Bob: You nodded. What does your nod say?

Kay: I am scared to tell you. I do know what is going on between us. I want to tell you that I am a good therapist.

Bob: Be aware of your head. Don't straighten it. Be aware of the angle of your head. Now put it on straight and repeat, "*I am a good therapist.*"

Kay: (*Head straight*) Yes. I am a good therapist. (*With tears*) That has a whole different feel to it.

Bob: Will you say "*I*" for "*It*"?

Kay: I am different. With my head straight I am competent. (*Cocks head*) It is hard to be a good therapist from here. (*Straightens head*) I'm finished. Thank you.

Following this work, Kay establishes her contract to claim her importance personally and professionally.

Joan finishes her work before her contract is clear:

Joan: I'm glad I am here. I am really feeling good, really alive. And then I feel bad and give up. I don't know why.

Mary: Example?

Joan: I don't think of one. My mother is in there telling me to practice and my father is hovering. And I feel like giving up. I never feel fine for long.

Bob: Does anyone praise you for being fine the way you are?

Joan: (*Long pause*) I am not sure I am fine the way I am. In my head I buy what you say, but I don't know where my guts are. My guts don't believe I am all right.

Mary: Hey, was your hero Joan of Arc? (Mary said this on a hunch because girls who are not "all right" probably were supposed to have been boys.)

Joan: Oh, yes!

Bob: Always doing more and more.

Joan: And always with the expectation of being burned at the stake. That's right. All my life I have said, "*I will fight just this one more battle.*"

Mary: What was wrong with you when you were born? (Obvious question)

Joan: I was a girl.

Mary: That was what was wrong with Joan of Arc. Hey, I hear the University of . . . Medical School has done some fine work on sex change operations for women. A true breakthrough. Not just cosmetology. What they do surgically. . . .

Joan: I'm not interested in that! I am fine the way I am! Wow! I AM FINE THE WAY I AM. Amazing . . . 'cause I am. I really feel it now.

Bob: Fine. Then your contract is to firm up your decision that you are fine the way you are . . . so you don't have to keep fighting battles unless you want to.

Joan: I like that. And I think just now I did the firming up.

Sometimes, though very seldom, we work without a contract because the client does not know what he wants. We would not do this beyond a session or two.

Mac: I don't know what I want. I keep myself too much away from other people. Sometimes, since I arrived at this workshop, I have really come out. More than ever in my life. Other times I cut myself off. I used to hassle about this and I don't anymore. I don't know that there is a change I want.

Mary: Pick someone in this room, someone you cut yourself off from, and talk to the person. I want to see and hear what goes on with you.

Mac: OK. I am cut off from you, Pete. (Pete is a friend of ours who is not part of this workshop. He's observing in exchange for lecturing and will be here only two days.) I'd feel a bit of a fool if I came up and started to talk to you.

Pete: Why is that?

Mac: You'll be gone tomorrow. So I have nothing I want from you.

Mary: Gone soon . . . so I don't want to know you. Does that fit when you were young?

Mac: No, no one left me.

Bob: Did you leave, move around?

Mac: Whew. I was the new kid every year. We never stayed anywhere more than two years at most. (He describes difficulties making friends.) I just get a vague feeling of what it is. It's just a . . . last night I was talking with you, mate (*addresses another participant*), and in the middle I thought, God, do I really want to get into this, do I want to be stuck talking with you? And I stayed and after a time I was enjoying. Sharing time together. It is that, sharing time together . . . I don't know.

Bob: Yes, you do. Finish your sentence. "It's that, sharing time together. . . ."

Mac: (*Weeping*) That I keep missing out on.

Bob: Yeah. Say it again.

Mac: Just sharing time together, that's what I miss out on.

Bob: Yeah. And then you say, *"Oh, what's the use, I'll be gone tomorrow."*

Mac: That is true.

Bob: That is what you miss in life and that is what life is all about. Life is today, not tomorrow. You act as if life is about tomorrow.

Mac: Yes, I . . . I hear you. And today is what is hard to get into.

Mary: So what do you want to say to Pete about today?

Mac: (*Weeping*) I would like to know you for today.

Mac does not need to spell out his contract. He has made an important contact with a person he had avoided and learned something about living in the here and now.

From time to time clients do not want to make contracts because they have more pressing issues than self-change. A woman has received word of acceptance into graduate school and shares her triumph. A man's son has been arrested for shoplifting and he shares his anger and grief with his friends in group. A relative dies and the client wants to speak her grief. At such times, we encourage other participants to respond with their thoughts and feelings, and we also respond.

ULTERIOR CONTRACTS

Every client wants to grow, to change, to have a better life . . . and every client, outside of Adult awareness, struggles against his therapeutic contract. *The ulterior contract is the pact between therapist and client to prevent the client's reaching his goals.* If the client restricts feelings, the therapist may analyze rather than set up an environment in which the client experiences his emotions. If the client restricts his thinking, the therapist gives advice. If the client does not take action, the therapist agrees that the client "can't" act on his own behalf. To the extent that therapist and client deny the client's power, the client is a victim. To the extent that they believe he has power which is not his, as in changing someone else, the client is both grandiose and a victim.

The easiest way to guard against an ulterior contract is to be aware of the therapist's and client's words that deny autonomy. We suggest that therapists tape their sessions in order to listen carefully to vocabulary. The therapist asks self, *"How did I reinforce lack of autonomy by my words?"*

"Would you *try* to tell me?"
"*Can* you describe your symptoms?"
"*Perhaps* you *could* say a *little* more?"
"How did that *make* you feel?"
"When did your *depression begin?*"

Try

When a client says, *"I will try to . . . ,"* we suspect that she is willing to put forth effort in such a way as to fail to accomplish. Children learn to say *"I'll try"* in order to get parents off their backs.

Parents, weary of the struggle, accept trying as a substitute for doing. Of course, there are legitimate uses of the word. We may try to swim faster than we are now capable of swimming, may try a new flavor experimentally, or try to influence others while knowing that the choice is theirs.

The therapist and client need to be aware of the "try" that is a Child plea for the therapist to join in a pact against accomplishment. The client "tries" to stop smoking, "tries" to arrive on time, or "tries" to enjoy a day at the beach. Parental therapists patronize clients by asking them to "try" or by offering advice designed to make the "trying" easier.

Bob has a cowbell, named "the try-bell," which he rings loudly whenever someone misuses "try." We ask the client to be in touch with how she plans to sabotage herself when she says "try" rather than "do."

Can't

"Can't," like "try," is a substitute for "won't" in families that forbid the autonomy of "won't." There are very few things we can't do, in terms of changing our thinking, feeling, and behavior. There are many things we won't do as long as we believe in "can't."

A client said, *"I can't talk about myself or write about myself. I have a very important letter to write and I have to write it to get a promotion. But I just can't."* Obviously, she can and she won't. As long as she believes her "can't," she remains a victim. Her work in therapy begins with the statement, "I won't write about me."

Therapists, like clients, use "can't" selectively in order to obey their own injunctions and counter-injunctions. Once, while explaining this, Mary noticed a social worker nodding vigorous agreement. However, at the coffee break, this same social worker said to a friend, *"If only I could hang up on my clients when they call at night!"* She obviously did not hear her own "can't." As long as this social worker does not acknowledge that her hand is capable of replacing the receiver on her telephone, she will probably not work successfully with others who are self-trapped by polite rules which they think they "cannot" break.

Make Feel

Children are taught to believe they are responsible for the feelings of others. Mary's grandmother, otherwise a grand, loving woman, used to serve a bacon-grease and lettuce salad, which Mary was required to eat "so as not to hurt Grandma's feelings." Why would Mary's food preference be used by Grandma to make herself feel hurt and why would she then blame Mary for the feelings she gave herself? Because, of course, she was taught that others made her feel. When a child misbehaves, an angry parent says, *"You make me mad"*; a sad parent says, *"You make me sad"*; and a guilty parent says, *"You make me feel guilty."* The child grows up to be a therapist who traps a client into victimhood by asking, *"How does that make you feel?"*

We watched a fine behaviorist desensitizing a phobic client and heard him say, *"When the plane scares you, raise the index finger of your left hand, and when you are comfortable, raise the index finger of your right hand."* His statement implies the client is a victim of the plane. We consider it crucial that the client recognize that *she scares herself* when she flies or imagines flying.

TA therapists who cling to the belief that others are in charge of their feelings write about *"making people not-OK"* and have appropriated the word *"discount"* to express the same belief. If someone asks you to pass the salt, you must hear her, acknowledge her request, and pass the salt; otherwise, they say, you discount her and she has the right to feel angry or sad and to blackmail you into acknowledging your guilt. Certainly, people need to know when they don't respond appropriately to others. However, each of us alone is in charge of whether we decide to consider ourselves discounted. The following client has had considerable therapy from a TA therapist who believes that discounts are responsible for making people feel:

Paul: There was something insidiously bad about seeing JoAnn. She did two things that were huge discounts of me, you know.

Mary: I don't know.

Paul: OK, I will make that clear. JoAnn did two things which were huge discounts and she didn't even sense it that way.

Bob: Put JoAnn in front of you and tell her exactly what she did.

Paul: (Explains to JoAnn that she forgot to mail some important material she had promised to mail and she returned to visit an old neighborhood, after promising not to go there.) JoAnn, I'm not going to be able to live with you if you discount me. You make me feel like a little boy.

Bob: She didn't make you feel anything. You chose to feel like a little boy.

Paul: That's how I feel, like a fucked-over little boy.

Bob: She didn't do what you wanted and what she said she would do, and you decided to feel like a little boy.

Paul: I feel like a little boy. You told me you were going to do something and you didn't. (He is very angry now.) If you tell me you are not going to do it, that's OK, but if you tell me you are going to do it and then don't, you make me not-OK. You discount . . . and I feel like a fucking little boy. (We work for about 15 minutes on the pattern he sets up to feel the way he felt as a child. We emphasize the fact that no one "makes" anyone "not-OK." This is a delusion.)

Mary: So. She does her thing. Maybe some game or other. I am not interested in what she does. You may decide to solve the problem by counting her assets instead of her liabilities or you may decide not to go on living with her. You decide about you. And only you decide whether to feel like a little boy because of her actions. Got it?

Paul: It's a new idea. I am thinking. And I am astonished at the importance of what I am learning now. I am feeling some freedom. I choose. This is a very new idea, the opposite of everything I learned in my old group. I need to think some more about this.

Mary: Good. "Discount" is a new word which the "make-feelers" have rushed to adopt.

Bob: We'll catch up to them yet.

Group: (*Laughter*)

1-It

"It" in place of "I" denies autonomy. Some clients refuse credit and accept blame, as when they say, "*It* (my speech) *was OK until*

I forgot what to say next." Others do the reverse and say, *"I was giving a fine speech and then everything got loused up."* If the client consistently uses "I" for persecution and "it" to diminish self-praise, we suspect depression. Persons with character disorders are more apt to use "it" to deny responsibility.

Clients speak as if their symptoms were beamed in from outer space . . . and so do their therapists. *"The depression comes on . . ."* is said instead of *"I depress or sadden me."* *"My anger gets the best of me"* is said rather than *"I anger me and then pretend I am not in control of what I choose to feel and do."* Phrases such as *"A thought passed through my mind"* deny that the client thinks. *"It feels that . . ."* denies that the client feels. *"It happened"* denies the client's autonomy of action.

Some TA therapists turn their ego states into "it" by saying, *"Let's take our Childs out for beer,"* *"My Adult is aware that . . . ,"* or *"My Parent wants to help you."* In our groups, although we acquaint clients with their ego states as part of treatment, we want them to recognize "the whole of my parts" by saying "I."

A client says, *"If I don't work very hard when I'm doing something, it doesn't count."* Mary asks him to change *"it"* to *"I."* *"Unless I work very hard, I don't count."* Immediately he begins to weep, remembering himself as the little boy who "didn't count" in his home and who therefore worked terribly hard in an attempt to be important. The focus of treatment for him becomes *"I count!"* A few sessions later, he tells of a new accomplishment and says, *"It is really exciting."* Again we ask for an *"I"* statement. As he says, *"I am exciting!"* he smiles and breathes deeply. *"I AM exciting."* *"I AM EXCITING."* By changing *"it"* to *"I"* he experiences a whole new range of power, importance, and excitement.

I-You

When a person switches *"I"* to *"you,"* the switch signals a change in ego state from Child to Parent. Beliefs, myths, family slogans, and parental instructions are repeated in this form. *"I'd like to get to know more people, but you can't just rush in"* is said by a young man who accepted the family injunctions of *"Don't be close"* and *"Don't."* *I feel wonderful, but you can't expect such a fast change to be lasting"* is stated by a woman whose previous therapist insisted that rapid personality change was impossible. We do not ask clients to substitute *"I"* for *"you"* since it is important that they understand the significance of both their *"you"* and *"I"* sides.

I-We

In family treatment, the client who says *"We"* for *"I"* is the self-designated spokesperson. In order for each member to be autonomous, the *"we"* statements are examined carefully to see if they do reflect the feelings and opinions of each member.

Maybe, Perhaps

These and other qualifying words need a questioning response from the therapist. Very often, when a therapist brings a tape of an interview in which she "felt stuck," we hear the client say *"maybe"* and the therapist race on, pretending that the client said *"yes."*

Client: I think maybe I . . . what I want is to have more friends.
Therapist: Fine!

Instead, the response should be *"Maybe?"* or *"Take both sides . . . you do want more friends and you don't want more friends."*

The First Con

The first con in each session is tremendously important because, if it is not confronted, the entire session may be devoted to acting out the con. A client said, *"I never do what I say I am going to do,"* and then settled for a contract to quit smoking. The trainee/therapist worked diligently and unsuccessfully for 30 minutes before we stopped the session to play back the con: *"I never do what I say I am going to do."* The therapist exclaimed, *"My God, I never even heard that!"*

A con, delivered in the first session, may set the stage for the entire course of treatment, if not confronted. When a client tells a therapist, *"I've seen 17 therapists and I hear you are good with cases like mine,"* watch out, Cowboy, you are about to get taken. The response is, *"And how are you going to defeat me?"* Then Bob says, *"For your sake, I'd like to see you achieve your goals in therapy. If you don't change, my life will go on just the same and I'll remember you for a few days as another guy who is stuck and who may or may not change someday."* Then, if the guy doesn't change, he may in the future remember our prediction and this memory may serve him when he next decides on therapy.

Gallows Laughter

People laugh at a comedian when he proves himself ignorant, naive, or incompetent, or when he in some way injures himself. When clients make fun of themselves, the laughter they elicit from therapists and group members reinforces their pathology and is called "gallows laughter." A young businessman in a marathon with his associates told a story of wrecking his motorboat while staring at a woman whose bikini top had fallen to her waist. Many participants laughed. Mary said, *"It's not funny to wreck your boat."* His associates then reminded him that he tells many favorite stories about himself that involve his spoiling his own fun. He refused to consider the implications of this, insisting that his stories "meant nothing." Bob asked him to conduct an experiment. *"For one month tell no stories to yourself or to anyone else that make fun of you for spoiling your good times and let us know the results."*

Six months later he wrote, *"I still think my way of joking is meaningless, but I do not like the same jokes. Even though I think this does not have psychological meaning, I am reporting that I have had more fun than ever in my life and I have had no troubles or accidents to joke about."*

Injunctions and decisions can be identified through gallows humor. Clients laugh at accidents when they are acting out *"I'll almost kill myself"*; at losing money when they are in a *"Don't make it"* money game; at not thinking, or not growing up, or not being childlike, when these injunctions-decisions apply. Whenever we hear gallows humor, we state, *"That is not funny for you."* Most people become irritated initially and insist that their laughter is *"just nervousness."* We ask them to let themselves be aware that they display this "nervous laughter" only in response to certain problems in their lives.

Bea often used "gallows laughter" during her work. Her contract for this session was to stop getting lost while driving.

Bob: Be in the car and you've taken the wrong turn. How long are you driving before you figure out it is the wrong turn?

Bea: Well, I (*giggle*) take a while before I begin to wonder.

Mary: You giggle. Getting lost isn't really funny for you.

Bea: No, it isn't. But my laughing is just nervousness.

Mary: You do a lot of *"Yes, butting"* about your smile and laugh. I think your laugh and smile have a meaning. I don't know what the meaning is.

Bob: Yep.

Bea: Oh . . . The thing that I remember . . . my association is that when we would go on long trips when I was a kid, when my father would drive, he was always getting lost. (*Giggles*) That wasn't funny either. I don't know why I am giggling. My mother always fell asleep in the car and then she'd wake up and we'd be lost. (*Grin*)

Bob: You grinned and giggled.

Bea: (*Laughs as she talks*) My mother would get really mad at him.

Mary: The last time you worked, you described him hitting you . . . being cruel. I'm guessing a part of you enjoyed his getting lost and getting bawled out by your mother.

Bea: Hmm. That's interesting. When I . . . when we would go on trips, I would help him read maps. Like I was on his side.

Bob: You helped him get lost?

Bea: (*Bursts into peals of Child-laughter*) I guess I did. Well, *I'm* not going to get lost anymore!

Often the gallows remark is so humorous that the therapist also laughs. Typical examples are the story dry-alcoholics tell about the things they did when drunk. As soon as a therapist recognizes her own laughter as a response to pathological humor, she can say, *"I take back my laugh. I will not laugh at something that is not funny for you."* Group members also learn to identify pathological humor rather than laugh at the jokes.

Body Language

A client may say *"yes"* while shaking his head *"no,"* pull at his wedding ring while insisting his marriage is happy, slump after stating, *"I want to work,"* or hold his hands in a barricading position while talking about his desire to be friends with other group members.

We don't interpret body language, but instead ask the client to experience his body and learn what his body is telling him. If he has difficulty doing this, we suggest that he increase and exaggerate his posture or gesture. Throughout treatment, we reinforce autonomous language, laughter that supports health rather than pathology, and congruent body movement.

CHAPTER 5

Stroking

Mary is watching her daughter Claudia play with her seven-month-old son, Brian. They are on the rug together, he sitting beside her, holding a large many-colored wooden bug. One antenna is in his mouth; the others whirl madly as he shakes his head. Claudia grabs an antenna in her mouth and they giggle as they topple together. Brian drops the toy, clutches her hair, and gazes intently as he licks her nose and she sniffs his tongue. He nuzzles her cheek; she moves, makes soft, then louder kisses against his belly. He shrieks, hiccoughs, she copies his hiccough exactly, and they both laugh. He hiccoughs again and they repeat. Then they hug silently.

Their contact is total, absorbed, uninhibited and beautifully pure. In the duller language of TA, they are exchanging physical and nonverbal positive unconditional strokes. Because most of us have learned to inhibit our stroke-giving and receiving, part of treatment is the changing and expanding of stroking patterns.

Al: I like physical contact but am blocked at public display of affection.

Bob: Blocked? (*Bob is responding to the passive words "am blocked."*)

Al: Yes.

Bob: So when you decide to unblock yourself, who in here do you want to make contact with?

Al: Probably any woman.

Mary: That's a sure way of not getting.

Bob: Pick one.

Al: (*Long pause*) Ann. (*He starts to walk toward her.*)

Mary: Wait a minute, Al. Tell her exactly what you want and ask her if she is agreeable.

Al: Whatever you want.

Mary: Nope. That won't do.

Al: I want to be able to. . . .

Bob: That won't do either. You are "able" now.

Al: I want to walk holding your hand. Without being conscious or embarrassed by it.

Mary: Oh, Al. If you are asking to hold her hand, you are not asking her to do something about your consciousness or embarrassment. Are you willing to hold her hand, whatever the hell you feel?

There are several important aspects to Bob's and Mary's comments to Al about his seeking and accepting strokes during this piece of work. They underline that the way to avoid getting what he wants is to generalize his requests: "Whatever you want (to give)" from "Probably any woman." He's asked to say to a particular woman exactly what he wants, without attaching conditions about how he is supposed to feel about getting what he wants. He is asked to find out if his chosen partner is agreeable, to avoid games in which he might attempt to force agreement and then be disappointed.

Al: Are you willing?
Ann: Yes.

Al and Ann walk slowly around the room, holding hands.

Al: I feel good. I feel warmth.
Ann: Good. I am enjoying you and I am excited. I am on parade
and all these other people can only sit and watch. I like your
smile.
Al: I like yours, too.
Ann: Shall we look at the others and talk to them or just walk?

Al begins chatting with others and continues to talk easily to Ann,
and she to him.

Al: (*To Mary*) I am finding I can stand like this and not be embarrassed. I think the underlying reason is. . . .
Mary: Are you going to enjoy your experience or clutter it with reasons?
Al: (*Laughing*) I'll enjoy the experience.

Al is happy and enthusiastic as he continues the contact which had
been difficult for him. Previously he didn't touch and dealt with
others primarily by discussing politics or psychological theory.

GIVING STROKES

Unconditional strokes are given, as to a baby, for the fact that she
is. Positive unconditional strokes are verbal: *"I love you"*; nonverbal
with gurgles, smiles, gestures; and physical, with touching, holding,
caressing. Negatively, a baby may be told, in effect, *"I don't love you
because you are,"* by words, grimaces, and painful or unpleasant
handling.

Conditional strokes are for doing rather than being. When the
baby first pulls herself erect, mothers and fathers talk to her excitedly, clap, smile, and kiss. When she spills or cries too long, she
may receive angry words, scowls, or slaps.

Learning how and when to give strokes is one of the most important aspects of becoming an effective therapist.

Reg holds the Kleenex in his lap and passes it, tissue by tissue, to a weeping woman. So long as she continues to weep and he continues to have a monopoly on the Kleenex supply, he will be needed. As he hands each piece, he smiles sympathetically, thus stroking her for her tears.

Tom is a rescue-by-ambulance type. He speeds for the Kleenex and races it to the victim before she is aware she needs it.

George, the comforter of Melancholy Babies, wants to hug everyone who cries.

Joan says to Ronald, *"I am so glad to hear your feeling. I'm so glad you have finally joined the group."*

June says to the group at large, *"I enjoy hearing about people, because then I know I am not the only person in the world with troubles."*

Ned tells Frank, *"I resent you. I just thought you'd want to know. I resent your attitude of not having problems. It keeps you outside the group."*

All of these participants, lovingly or resentfully or banally, are giving the injunctions *"Don't be well"* or *"Don't be happy"* or *"Don't be independent."* All except June are group therapists. We teach when to give and when to withhold strokes. Usually the best guide is the individual's contract. If the person is learning to be dependent, then asking for Kleenex rather than getting it herself is changed behavior to be stroked.

With clients who repress tears, we stroke when they first weep. With chronic weepers, we withhold when they weep and stroke for other qualities. We don't permit anyone to stroke a client physically for demonstrating her own typical, stereotyped negative feeling. When the hugger begins to hug, we say, *"Stop. Not now."* Afterwards we explain that stroking reinforces pathology and ask the rescuer if she is interested in finding new, healthier ways to make contact.

We rarely give negative verbal strokes to clients. We find the *"Let's all tell Johnny what we don't like about him"* approach to be destructive. When a client has "resentments" against other clients, we neither encourage nor discourage her telling her resentments the first time, knowing that she probably came from a family or a therapy group that prizes "honesty" so long as "honesty" equals negative stroking. If the client continues to stroke negatively, we ask if she'd like to learn new stroking patterns.

We never use negative physical strokes. We dislike a world in which human beings model violence in the guise of attempting to prevent violence. We ask for contracts from parents, teachers, and therapists that they will never hit, pinch, spank, or verbally humiliate children . . . and we believe grown-ups also have the right not to be hurt.

June: I have a phobia. I don't let my feet go off the ground. (She explains that she won't dive or water ski.)

Bob: What are you afraid will happen?

June: I don't know.

Bob: I want to stay with what you are afraid will happen. Pretend you are standing beside the pool. What do you experience? What scary story do you tell yourself?

June: My feet will go out from under me. I'll lose control.

Bob: And then?

June: I don't know. I'm too afraid. You see, my father used to grab me and hold me by my feet, hanging so I couldn't touch the ground. He did it in fun.

Mary: No, he didn't. He did it in sadism.

Group member: Why do you say that, just because he was teasing?

Mary: Tickling, teasing, putting snowballs down dresses, throwing into swimming pools and lakes, holding someone by her ankles . . . all are despicable acts when forced on a weaker person by a stronger person. They are rapes. Would you prefer I call her father a rapist?

G. M.: But if he was playing. . . .

Mary: She was violated. Where are you, June?

June: I hadn't realized. My mother was so terrible, I thought my father was perfect. He was kind, warm, and totally non-supporting. Besides the business of holding me upside down . . . (*Weeps*) I think I am crying for the young me who did not have a good life.

Bob: I'm not your father and I won't ask you to do anything you

don't want to do. I can teach you to dive in 10 minutes. Want
me to teach you to dive?

June: Yes.

Bob: I'll meet you by the pool after lunch.

At noon June learned to dive . . . and was no longer phobic. The
entire group watched and cheered. After each successful piece of
work, participants cheer. In this way, they all learn to give positive
strokes for growth. One month, four French Canadian participants
stood and sang *"Bravo, Bravissimo"* each time a participant worked
successfully. Workshops and therapy groups provide fine training
in new ways of giving strokes and thereby increasing intimacy.

One difficulty may arise from the good contact and closeness
among participants. They may decide that their workshop friends
are more interesting and exciting than people back home, and this
may be true. People who in the past did not stroke well may have
married in kind. We have three suggestions for avoiding estrange-
ment from spouses. The best plan for myriad reasons is to come to
workshops with spouses. If this hasn't been done, we create fantasied
home scenes during the workshops so that participants can, in fantasy, learn ways of using their new stroking talents to promote closeness at home. Also, during workshops, we ask participants not to have
sexual experiences with anyone except their own spouses. This rule
discourages "Rapo" games, in which the participant has sex in order
for self or other to be unhappy later. It also promotes non-sexual
intimacy during the workshop.

ACCEPTING STROKES

Sometimes, listening to friends, colleagues, and clients, we imagine
that each has a secret rule book, some tiny and some larger than an
unabridged dictionary, filled with all the rules for turning down
strokes. These rules are not based on logic: A woman who is a fine
cook may criticize her own cooking the minute she receives a compliment, yet accept a compliment on a hand-made dress that appears
quite ordinary. Some beautiful women reject appreciation of their
beauty; others love it. Some take no unconditional strokes; others
no conditional. These rule books are finely detailed and obviously
written long ago.

Bob: Good insight!

Hank: Thank you, I was telling my . . .

Mary: Did you hear Bob say you have good insight?

Hank: Yes. Yesterday when I . . .

Mary: Hey, did you believe him?

Hank: Not really, if you want to know the truth. I thought you were trying to bolster my confidence. (Hank continues on the subject of yesterday and his wife.)

Bob: A while back, Hank, I knocked on your door to deliver the message that you have good insight, and a part of you refused to hear the message. A part of you that refuses compliments about your intelligence.

Hank: I don't understand.

At this point it would be anti-therapeutic for anyone to "understand" for him. He is maneuvering to get strokes, positive or negative, for not thinking, to offset the stroke for thinking.

Bob: When you've got an idea what that part is like, let me know.

Hank: The part that shuts the door? (*Long pause*) I don't have good insight. That's what the part says. I'm not trained like the others here. They all know more than I do. *You* are stupid. (Here he switches from reporting from Adapted Child to accusing from his Parent, as he says *"You"* instead of *"I."*) You are . . . you'll never learn. You keep butting in where you aren't wanted. And nothing you say is worth hearing. Wow. That's my big brother.

Bob: Good insight.

Hank: (*Laughs*) Yeah, as a matter of fact, I hear you. I have demonstrated good insight twice in less than half an hour, and screw my brother.

Clients such as Hank are not helped by continued stroking or reassurance from the group, after they have turned down a stroke. In inept groups, the group would try to change his mind by urging him to agree that he is insightful. This group waited until Hank accepted his insightfulness, and then supported his change by giving him other examples of his creativity and insight.

Clients have many rationalizations for rejecting strokes: *"He only says that to bolster my confidence," "to be nice," "to try to change me,"* or *"to get something from me."* In effect, they blemish the stroker rather than accept the stroke, by suggesting that the stroker is either a liar, a manipulator, or an extortionist. We ask clients to recognize what they are doing, by telling the stroker, *"You are a liar"* and then *"You are not a liar"* and see which fits.

People are trained to eat grandmother's salad, not only so that she will be happy but also because *"She is always so good to you."* In families that regularly "bait the hook" with loving strokes, a child may stay distant, distrusting strokes, or, when stroke hungry, accept the strokes and with them minor and major martyrdoms. For this reason it is important to teach clients to take strokes and refuse any unwanted obligations that may accompany the strokes. *"I accept a birthday check from Father without believing I have to listen to him bad-mouth Mother." "I accept an invitation to dinner without agreeing to have sex with you afterwards."*

Another common excuse for rejecting strokes is, *"If they really knew me, they'd know I am not worthy."* A sound technique is to ask the client to play both sides, the "worthy" and "unworthy." The "unworthy" side rarely comes up with anything more significant than *"When I was little I was a bad girl because. . . ."*

Some clients, including many delinquents, wear an invisible coat of armor in order to ward off all strokes. Wards of the California Youth Authority call this "shining it on." If a client "shines you on," that means that nothing you say will have impact on him, although he may pretend to listen and may even respond with seeming appropriateness. This is a life-saving tactic for those in penal institutions, poor mental hospitals, and homes and neighborhoods where any sign of feeling response may bring injury or death. Black and Chicano young men have played versions of "Dirty Dozen" for many years, insulting each other in order to practice never showing feeling under any provocation. This is training for getting along in a White society—and in slums.

Therapists who don't understand the "shine-on" technique may condemn themselves to fruitless work with such clients. Instead, the therapist recognizes the stroke-refusal and compliments the person for using this method for personal safety. She may ask for a contract that the client tell her when he is not "shining her on," although she'll also reassure the client that she expects he'll try to fool her often enough to test her out. One treatment goal is that the client learn to be judicious in his use of stroke-rejecting.

SEEKING STROKES

We teach clients to ask for the strokes they want, rather than wait and hope that the right ones come along. Many people believe that it is impolite to ask and that asking somehow diminishes the value of the stroke. Mary's son and daughters know that it is their responsibility to remind others when their birthdays are approaching and to ask for the presents they want or ask to be "surprised." In some families, no one is reminded, and then guilt messages are sent to those who forget.

Al, who walked hand in hand with Ann, had been willing to settle for "whatever you want to give" from "anyone." With such a statement, he might have received even better strokes than hand-holding, but he'd have remained a victim who gives the initiative to others.

However, there are times when we choose for a client. We do this when we sense that a particular stroke is more important than the problem of asking or not asking.

Mary: Tell your father what you want from him.

Kay: I want you to say I can be me and do my own thing.

Mary: Tell him what you really want.

Kay: (*Long pause*) I guess I want him to say he accepts. . . .

Mary: I hear you speaking very fast. Running very fast. You've been running fast . . . boarding schools, medical school, all the time doing so well. . . . I don't hear there was anybody to say *"I love you."*

Kay: (*Shakes her head as she begins to weep*)

Mary: And you gave up asking.

Bob: And keep running to avoid your sadness.

Kay: There is no way, no way he'll say *"you are nice."* No way.

Bob: That's sad. That there was no one.

Mary: You needed praise and you need touching. Would you like someone to Daddy you? Would you allow that here?

Kay: (*Long pause*) Would you say that again?

Mary: I'm thinking that you need Daddying. You've been a lonely, hardworking, understroked little girl.

Kay: (*Another long pause*)

Bob: What are you doing?

Kay: I was thinking, "*I'd rather do it myself,*" and knowing that's the story of my life. I'm finding this difficult. I don't like the idea that I am looking for a Daddy.

Mary: I wasn't accusing you of that. I was saying quite the opposite. I was experiencing that you have needed for a long time some Daddying.

Kay: OK. I think I'd like that.

Mary: Want to pick someone?

Kay: Bob, are you in this?

Bob: Move over. (He picks her up, holds her against him, and she buries her face against him, sobbing. Bob, too, is weeping and they remain together for some time.)

Kay: Thank you.

Bob: A pleasure. A real pleasure. Anytime.

Group member: Kay, you look so pretty and soft.

Kay smiles, leans back in her chair. Her face is no longer strained and she continues to smile.

In this scene our technique was the opposite from that described in our work with Al. Kay, a very successful physician who takes care of everyone but herself, needed to accept being given to without asking. Her half-request, "*Bob, are you in this?*" was sufficient. In fact, had she said, "*I want Bob to hold me and I want to cry on his shoulder . . . ,*" one of us would have asked her to be willing to relax and not program what she would receive. And this is the difficulty of teaching therapy. Working with clients so that they learn to give and to receive requires from the therapist diagnostic acumen, a respect for differences, and the personal freedom to make contact in different ways.

SELF-STROKING

"*I celebrate myself and sing myself*" was not popular in Walt Whitman's day and is still considered not quite nice in spite of the encounter movement, Women's Lib, and Black is Beautiful. Our workshops and marathons begin with a quiet time, when we ask participants to get in touch with "what you like about yourself." We do this to counteract the belief that psychotherapy consists primarily of digging into pathology and exposing whatever secrets the client considers bad or sick. Our focus is on enhancing the strengths that the client already knows she possesses and creating an environment in which the client becomes aware of new or hitherto denied strengths. Whatever the therapeutic contract, the client will fulfill it more easily with self-love than self-hate.

Jack Dusay[1] invented the egogram to serve as an easily understood personality profile that can be drawn impressionistically by anyone who knows the individual. It shows the person how he is perceived. We see a "typical" nurturing therapist as drawn in Figure 17.

We see a "typical" intellectual therapist as drawn in Figure 18. In these profiles there is very little critical Parent, although slightly more in the intellectual therapists than in the nurturers. Nurturing Parent is high in the first and moderate in the second. Adult functioning is moderate in the first and high in the second. Free Child is rarely displayed in either, which is why therapists are astounded to

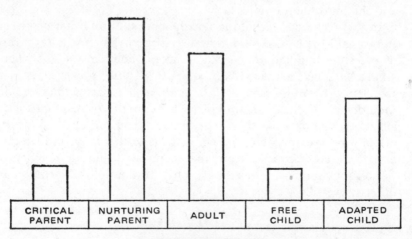

CRITICAL PARENT | NURTURING PARENT | ADULT | FREE CHILD | ADAPTED CHILD

A NURTURING THERAPIST

Fig. 17

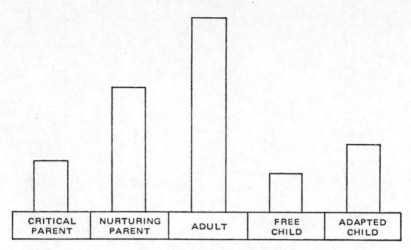

AN INTELLECTUAL THERAPIST

Fig. 18

hear us talk of curing while laughing and having fun. Adapted Child is moderate in both.

These are the profiles that the world sees. Over and over again we discover that these therapists' internal profiles differ markedly from the ones they show the world. (See Figure 19.) This internal diagram, hidden from others, is seen when the therapist is client. She reveals herself to be estranged from free Child and very low in self-nurture and self-praise. Instead of positive strokes, she gives herself harassment and persecution, demanding a level of perfection she would never dream of imposing on her clients. For these therapists, the major contract is to see themselves as lovable and to find ways of loving themselves.

The first step is for the therapist-client to recognize exactly what she says inside herself that is self-persecutory. *"You are dumb." "You don't seem to be able to help anybody!" "Why does John do so much better with that patient than I do—he's only a paraprofessional!"* The next step is to take charge of the persecuting, by admitting that this persecution is not "tapes in the head" or "pig parents" or an "ogre" or anything else outside the control of the self. *"I use these words to persecute me."* Then the client may go back into early scenes

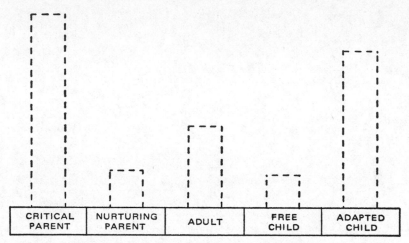

INTERNAL EGOGRAM OF SELF-CRITICAL THERAPISTS
Fig. 19

in order to recognize who said the words originally and to redecide that the words are not helpful or applicable.

After this, there are fun techniques for stopping self-persecution. A person may make her persecution ridiculous by exaggerating, by putting the persecution to music and singing the words, by turning the words into gobbledygook, or by acting out the persecution in exaggerated, nonverbal ways. Clients use these techniques in group. For example, one of our favorite psychologists spent two days, during a four-week workshop, singing his self-persecution to the tunes of famous arias. He began with *"This is all right for now, but they'll be tired of you soon, you bastard,"* in a beautiful baritone voice.

Others use Bob's favorite, *"When about to persecute, have a sexual fantasy instead."* Others do an awareness continuum, becoming open to whatever they see, feel, taste, or hear in the present.

John Howard[2] gave us an interesting technique for stopping persecution.

John Howard: Next time you give yourself a negative stroke, stand up and apologize to yourself.
Client: I don't understand.

John: Like this. (*Stands*) I apologize to me. I am very sorry I just
said that I am stupid. I apologize for everything I said. . . . I
don't treat anyone else as meanly as I treat me and I shouldn't
treat me that way. I am really a nice guy.

Client: That's what you want me to do when I criticize me?

John: Exactly.

We give assignments such as: "*Tonight, before you fall asleep,
wiggle your toes until you are aware of your toes as interesting and
lovable. Then say, 'Toes, I love you.' Next, move your ankles and
repeat. Do this for your whole body and then report back, if you
like.*"

Sometimes we use an exercise for the whole group: "*Look out the
window and see whatever you see.*" We give them a minute or two,
then ask them to report. Usually, they see our mountains, hills, trees,
flowers, birds, and cattle. Sometimes the hawks are soaring and the
fields are orange with poppies. Next we say, "*Now pretend you are
in a room of mirrors. You have taken off your clothing and are looking at yourselves. What do you see?*" Too often they report blemishes . . . unwanted fat, sagging posteriors or breasts, wrinkles, and
postural problems. We say, "*Look again at the scenery, this time
through the eyes that looked at you. See the kinds of blemishes you
reported.*" Finally, we say, "*Be in the room with mirrors and this
time look at you the way you first looked at the scenery. See what is
beautiful.*"

For clients who do not remember experiencing loving parents, we
devise an exercise in which we ask them to imagine that they are the
loving parents that they have always sought:

Abe: I'm in touch with a lot of sadness when others are in sad scenes,
especially when they were little boys. I don't know where to go
with that.

Mary: What's your hunch? It's not necessary for you to be perfectly
sure where to go with that. (Said because Abe is a perfectionist.)

Abe: Well . . . with my father, I never felt close. I think basically
he had no room for me in his life.

(Abe has already worked on aspects of his past, so Mary decides not to go back with him to specific scenes with father.)

Mary: Tell you what. Make up a new father.

Abe: What?

Mary: Stand up and talk to Abe. Be the kind of father you want now.

Abe: (*Stands*) He . . . I . . . ah . . . I care a lot about how you feel. I don't get angry with you. I'm not always looking to see what was wrong with whatever you are doing. I like what you are doing. You are really a very caring probation officer. And you do well. (*Turns to Mary and Bob*) This is embarrassing.

Bob: Keep on, you're a great new father.

Abe: I am interested in what you are interested in. I hear what you want to do and I approve. And when you start putting yourself down, I'll tell you to cut it out. That's the only time I'm going to criticize you. I . . . I enjoy you. That's it. I enjoy you. (*Begins to weep, and sits back in his own chair*)

Bob: Will you be father again, and tell Abe what you enjoy about him?

Abe: (*Standing*) I think you are a lot of fun.

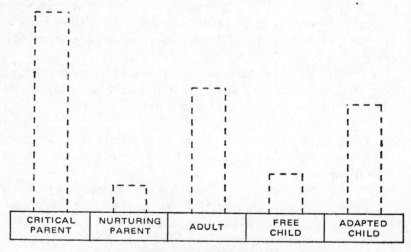

ABE'S INTERNAL EGOGRAM

Fig. 20

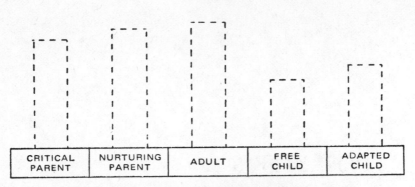

| CRITICAL PARENT | NURTURING PARENT | ADULT | FREE CHILD | ADAPTED CHILD |

ABE'S INTERNAL EGOGRAM AFTER PARENTING HIMSELF
GOULDING'S IMPRESSION

Fig. 21

Mary: Father, as you say that, you are backing away and putting your hands in your pockets.

Bob: How can you use your hands to say that, as well as your words?

Abe: (*Pantomimes hugging self*) I think you are neat. I've always wanted you. (*He is weeping*) I like you. I don't just like you, I love you. (*Returns to his own seat*) I didn't know how much I wanted that, how long I've wanted that. How much I hoped that some day, if I just got good enough . . . I feel solid. I feel loved.

Mary: Fine. And will you keep on treating you this way? Nurturing you, loving you.

Abe: I will. I am very satisfied.

Later Abe reports: *I realize what I did has another aspect. I have a son. I will also treat him the way I wanted to be treated. I'll treat us both this way.*

At this point, Abe's internal egogram is shifting from Figure 20 to Figure 21.

As the client shifts from self-harassing to self-nurturing, she learns to enjoy herself. She brings together stroke giving, stroke accepting, and self-stroking, and becomes increasingly aware of her own loveliness. "I am the only one of me there will ever be." This is the philosophical basis for the TA statement, "I'm OK."

CHAPTER 6

Emotions

Unhappiness and the quest for happiness are universal. Clients hire therapists primarily because they are not happy. Their therapists hire other therapists for the same reason. People marry, divorce, have and don't have children, buy or save, work hard, accept or repudiate religions, all in the hope that something will bring them happiness. Some yearn for happiness now, while others are willing to put up with unhappiness if they can be reassured that sometime in the future, either in this life or the next, they'll finally be happy.

In working with people from many different nationalities and cultures, we have observed that each believes her group to be the least happy. Some even take group pride in unhappiness, as when prejudiced Whites accuse Blacks of being happier and equate this with being childish, ignorant, or morally inferior. In Fundamentalist families the message is, *"Don't feel too good! If you feel too good, you must be sinning."* This message is delivered when a child is caught in sex play or even when he is laughing instead of working. In Jewish families we hear the message, *"Don't feel too good or something bad will happen."*

A psychologist from Israel was learning to float in our swimming pool. As she dropped her fear and enjoyed her accomplishment, she laughed delightedly . . . and then ran, sobbing, from the pool area. Bob followed her and asked, *"What's wrong?"* She said she was sud-denly remembering her nephew, who died in the war. Bob wondered aloud why she thought of her nephew at precisely the moment she experienced joy. Smiling sheepishly, she said, *"I believe I know. When he was killed, I was attending a convention in Denmark and was having a wonderful time. As I am now. It sounds silly, but I am afraid. I'm afraid that if I am too happy, something will happen to Israel."* In the magic of childhood, she was keeping Israel safe through her tears.

Babies are not born to be happy or unhappy. Internal and external factors dictate their periods of well-being and distress. During this period, the *"Don't be happy"* injunction is given by illness, neglect, deprivation, or abuse, but since our culture reinforces parent-baby love, most babies are loved. The world coos at them and they copy the happiness they see.

All this may change with horrifying suddenness during the toddler stage, when parents define the little person as being a "child" rather than a "baby" and therefore someone who must be punished. A child plays with her genitals, breaks a vase, or screeches momentary rage, and without warning she is punished. She is screamed at, pinched, or hit. The people she loves and needs have temporarily become monsters. This *"happens to her,"* *"comes out of the blue,"* and *"makes her frightened or sad."* All the words that adults use to deny autonomy are realities for the non-autonomous child. With-out words, she decides "in her guts" against happiness in order to stave off such pain in the future. As the child grows, she may remem-ber only the trauma, while forgetting the lesson that the trauma was expected to teach. *"I remember father beating me . . . I don't remem-*

ber why." She may repress the trauma as well, keeping it only in her muscles. She has no idea why she tightens against joy or sexual feeling, or why she sucks in when she laughs.

We believe children continue to be happy, in spite of occasional destructive parenting, if their parents teach them happiness by example. Babies and children need someone from whom to copy happiness and someone with whom to be happy. If their parents are caught up in their own unhappiness, unhappiness is modeled in the home. We use an exercise to increase awareness of how family stroking patterns reinforce happiness or unhappiness:

"Be little and see the house in which you lived. Put all the people in your family inside the house. You are outside. You are going to run into the house and tell them and show them how you feel.

"First, you've fallen and skinned your knee. One drop of blood is running down your leg. Even if you would never have done this, run into the house sobbing that your knee is hurt. Show them the drop of blood. Now see the expressions on each person's face. What are they feeling? What are they saying to you ... and to each other? What are they doing about you? About your knee? The next time you skin your knee, what do you guess you'll feel ... say ... do?"

We repeat the exercise, using different emotions.

"Run into the house crying. You are very sad, because you lost your pet snail."

"You are angry and shouting and you throw a tantrum. A big boy took your cookie."

"You are just as angry as before. This time you are angry at your mother. She forgot to put cookies in your lunch box."

"You race into the house and are very scared. You thought you saw a great big animal behind the tree."

"You say you are jealous of the girl next door because she got a new jump rope and you want one just like it."

"You whisper to them that you are ashamed. Something terrible happened. You wet your pants and the big kids laughed at you."

"You run in laughing and giggling. You are very happy because you have a gold star on your school paper."

"You run in giggling and happy and you don't know why. You just feel like giggling."

Most clients are still repressing the emotions that were unacceptable in their childhood homes. They use, as substitutes for happiness, the emotions that were rewarded or allowed. And some of them, happily, discover in their exercises that their happiness was enjoyed. Usually, these same clients know how to be happy.

Parents teach and model specific unhappy feelings. A son may be encouraged to be angry, as the family laughs and calls him "A chip off the old block" when he tantrums. When mother uses sadness to manipulate the family or to keep herself from thinking autonomously, daughter may grow into a weepy replica or become a sad caretaker of the mothers of the world, as she attempts to make them happy.

Men in our culture are expected to "come home exhausted" from a "hard day's work," even though their day consisted solely of their sitting behind a desk. They have copied "exhaustion" from their fathers, who copied their fathers, who copied their fathers who did exhaust themselves tearing down forests and planting the land without the aid of mules.

Once a child learns which unhappiness to demonstrate, she uses this racket to manipulate others:

Mary: Maybe pushing and being angry were important . . . served you well as a little kid?

Marta: Oh, it did. I got a lot of things I wanted. God knows, it was about the only way to get what I wanted. I couldn't just ask and get anything. Everything had to be fought through. Mom would go into a tizzie, but if I wanted it bad enough, like going to birthday parties, . . . and, God, when I was old enough to learn to drive! I had to throw honest-to-god tantrums for six months!

Bob: So that is why you now look for people to say, "No." So you can keep up your old anger and keep pushing at people. Well, you might as well know that you can tantrum all month and I am not going to change my rules about no smoking in bedrooms.

If a child demonstrates sufficient unhappiness, she may, like Marta, get to drive the family car. She may persuade her parents to stay home, stop quarreling, or even reconcile after a divorce. Although most children do not make such major impact by being unhappy, they continue to fantasize that if they are unhappy enough, they can change their parents or at least make them feel guilty.

Eighty-year-old parents and their 50-year-old sons and daughters continue to use unhappiness in attempts to change each other. They also continue to dwell on the past, as if they could somehow change it if they feel badly enough today. None of us need to care, once we are grown, what our childhoods were like, and yet clients may keep themselves stuck for years as they moan about what can't be changed. The magic wish to change the past is used to foment unhappiness in the present.

The child learns that if he feels badly enough, he is excused from doing what he doesn't want to do. If father comes home exhausted, he doesn't have to repair the washing machine, play with the children, or talk to his wife. The unhappy wife is excused from cooking dinner and instead is taken out to eat. The procrastinating psychiatrist, described in the previous chapter, does not have to write for publication so long as he keeps himself guilty about not writing.

Having accepted "Don't be happy" injunctions, our clients copied their parents' unhappiness, received strokes for being unhappy, learned precisely which unhappy feelings to experience, found they could manipulate others and excuse themselves when they used these feelings . . . and finally unhappiness becomes habitual.

Jane: I don't know if it's worth the struggle. Going back to work. I love to work, you know. I just hate the hassles.
Mary: Who are the hasslers and hasslees in your house?
Jane: Well, when I . . . if I go back to work, the kids have got to shape up. I can't do it all . . . I can't do it the way they are now.
Mary: See them in front of you and tell them.
Jane: (Alternating between anger and tearful sulking, she tells

them all the jobs she expects them to take over in order to free her to work outside the home.)

Mary: I don't understand. Your household will have how much more money a month, if and when you go back to work?

Jane: I'll have expenses. After expenses and taxes, I estimate about $800 a month.

Mary: Then why the hell aren't you planning to use the money to buy a clean house and cooked meals?

Mary knows why. Jane was taught early not to be happy. It's fair to say that in the beginning she was "made unhappy" by an angry mother. Jane whined because she was an unhappy little girl trapped in an unhappy home. Because she believed that being a mother meant being unhappy and an angry blamer, she grew to be a woman who alternates between parental anger and child whining. If she gives up being unhappy about staying home when she wants to work and gives up blaming her children for her plight, she will be "in danger" of getting what she wants most and has experienced least: happiness.

April, like Jane, has no current reality reason to be unhappy. She is attending a workshop at our Mt. Madonna home, where she has lovely surroundings and food and the company of some of the most exciting people one could imagine. Instead of enjoying herself, she reports on Monday morning that she had a *"terrible weekend"* and is *"disgusted with myself.... I ruined the weekend."*

Mary: OK. Take Sunday. And tell your day as you lived it.

April: I didn't accomplish anything. I started to write and put that down. I went over to swim, but didn't think I had time to swim, because I didn't do some other things. (*Talks rapidly in a clipped, angry tone and sighs frequently*) So I swam one or two laps and got out and jumped up and decided that I would like to make a contract on stroking. I got waylaid and forgot about it. And also I had wanted very much to use the time for going over the tapes I had done . . . and I didn't get to it. At the end of the day, I felt exhausted and thoroughly disgusted with myself.

We work for about 20 minutes, getting nowhere. April doesn't know what she wants to change, isn't sure how she got herself to be so unhappy, and her energy is primarily invested in haranguing herself.

Mary: Hey, how about doing something different? Pretend you are the happiest person you have ever met. And tell Sunday all over again . . . present tense . . . from happiest position. Doing exactly what you did.

April: (*Balks briefly, asks that the instructions be repeated, and then begins*) OK. Well, actually . . . I go to get a gestalt book and I start to read it and I read . . . but I decide I really don't want to read it. . . . (*Giggles*) It's a very boring book for a Sunday. . . . So I pop myself up and I walk around the place. I am with somebody and we have a fine talk. And then I see everybody swimming, and I realize I am hot, so I jump in the pool and feel really great. (*Laughs*) So I swim around and then I say to myself, oh, I think I will do something else again. There is so much to do. And it is so nice here when everyone's gone and the few of us left have it all to ourselves. So that whatever we do is fine. And . . . I did forget my tapes . . . that was too bad. . . .

Bob: How lucky I forgot my tapes and didn't ruin my day listening to the boring things.

April: You are right! If I'd had to stick myself in that room back there, all by myself, and nobody to talk to, and I . . . all the damned things I should have done. Instead I had a great day with a group of people who are awfully nice.

Group members: (*Laughter and cheers*)

April: I am incredulous. . . . I am utterly incredulous. I had a fine time, and I made myself feel bad most of that day. I had a fine time. I am staying with that. (*Laughs, shakes her head disbelievingly*)

We are glad she got the message. By the following weekend, she, had stopped self-hassling and was having exciting times. She began walking in a new, springy, young way and she talked with animation.

Our goal in therapy is for clients to experience the feelings they have long buried and then to use all feelings as a stimulus for thought and action. Our position is that clients want to be happy and therefore want to spend as little time as possible in misery. To do this, they need to drop their chronic, stereotyped unhappy feelings, which we call rackets.

ANGER

We remember with pleasure a bright, angry man in one of our New York workshops. Bill believes in the righteousness of his own anger and challenges anyone to dispute him. He is angry at the government, his ex-wife and, at the moment, he is particularly angry at our theory that people are in charge of their own feelings. As Bill says this, Mary falls to the floor, pretending to sob. *"My God, you are right. Look how you have made me feel!"* He laughs, and for the rest of the day is less argumentative.

The next day he explains that he has always been angry and we agree that he remembers himself that way. His is a third-degree impasse, because he experiences his anger as somehow genetically acquired and as an integral part of himself. We say, *"Where did you live when you were little?" "Brooklyn." "OK, walk in the front door and see what is going on. What are you angry at?"* He discovers that he wasn't as angry then as now. He was frightened at the anger displayed by his parents and relatives. *"They are impossible ... terrible, terrible fucking people. Throwing soup at each other, swearing, always fucking angry. . . ."* Bill worked in an early scene, and separates himself from his family's angers.

On the third morning, Bill reports, *"It's crazy what happened to me on my way here. I was driving down the same road I always take and traffic was as bad as ever. And I say to myself, I don't have to be mad at this fucking traffic. And then I see this cop and I say to myself, I don't have to be mad at the fucking cop. And all of a sudden this crazy thing happens. I see this beautiful white horse on this green hill. I must have seen him a thousand times before ... and I never once saw him until this morning. All of a sudden I'm enjoying myself, seeing all sorts of things I never saw before."* He did more work that week to firm up his redecision to have a happy life and to enjoy himself. He is a thoroughly gutsy, gusty man and our wish for him is lots of years enjoying white horses and green hills and himself.

When dealing with an angry client, the first step is to assist him in separating feeling from behavior, so that no matter how angry he decides to be, no matter what the provocation, he will not act out his anger in a way that would hurt himself or anyone else. *"I can be as angry as I choose and I still choose my behavior."* An angry, acting-out person may enjoy finding non-hurtful angry behaviors, such as smashing kindling wood or throwing eggs at trees.

The next step is to recognize that he can think and feel at the same time and can continue to think even while feeling strongly.

Mary: OK, I hear that you are furious at your department head . . . and that you believe all you can do is rant and rage. . . .
George: I'm so mad I can't think.
Mary: No, you are not. You are very bright and you can always think. Experiment. Stay as angry as you are, put the stool in front of you . . . that's it . . . and now, while pounding, screaming, give two quick, creative ideas on how to handle the situation.

After recognizing that he thinks well even though angry and that he is not going to hurt anyone, the client may need permission to enjoy his anger rather than to use it to bedevil himself,

Bob: So, you are mad at him. Fantasize what you'd like to do to him.

We want clients to learn that fantasies are fine, so long as they are not acted out. Bob has told clients of the time he was angry at Eric Berne. He went to see his very close friend, Fritz Perls, and this is the conversation as he remembers it.

Bob: Fritz, I am angry as hell at Eric and I'm getting in my way with it.
Fritz: Ya. What would you like to do to him?
Bob: I'd like to kill him!
Fritz: How would you like to kill him? Tell your fantasies.

Bob: Oh . . . I'd like to hang him by his toes and drop him slowly into a vat of boiling water.

Fritz: (*Laughs*) Ya. Say more.

Clients may think they need anger in order to be powerful. *"If I weren't angry, I'd never get what I want."* That may be true in families that do not respond until someone has reached a certain pitch of anger. This belief can be disposed of in group or family therapy, as individuals learn and practice the difference between assertion and aggression.

Will is angry at his daughter and believes that if he learns to be even angrier, he will be more effective in dealing with her:

Will: (*Talks to Vicky in fantasy*) What I am angry at you about, Vicky, is you act like you have a silver spoon in your mouth. You've been out of college two years and you play around skiing and doing a bit of work here and a bit of work there, and now you are back home looking for a job. And I'm supporting you. . . .

Mary: So, on the one hand you tell her not to grow up . . . you support her . . . and on the other hand you get mad that she doesn't.

Will: That's right. When I get tough with you I feel really mean. . . .

Bob: Be mean and tell her where you are at. Be vigorous.

Will: Damn it, Vicky, I want you to be on your own.

Bob: Don't tell her about her. Tell her where you are.

Will: Here's where I am. . . . I'm tired of being the softie, I'm tired of being set up so I have to give more than I intended. And. . . .

Bob: You aren't being set up, you set yourself up.

Will: That's true. I set myself up by giving more than I want to give and then I get angry at myself and at you.

Mary: That's the trouble with anger contracts. So what's the difference whether you are angry or not angry . . . you're still going to be slipping her money, I hear. And, as long as you decide to support her, seems like it would be more enjoyable to be happy about it. I'll be glad to work with you so you'll enjoy giving her your money for the rest of your life, if that's what you choose, or enjoy not giving her money. I hear your "stuck" is that you are supposed to feel bad either way . . . angry if you do, guilty if you don't.

Will: Hmmm. Yes, I want to stop feeling guilty about refusing . . . or angry. . . .

Mary: So you are ambivalent. OK. Experiment. What I want you to do is remember yourself at Vicky's age. OK?

Will: Yeah. I was putting myself through medical school.

Mary: Fine. Was your father alive?

Will: Yes.

Mary: In fantasy, tell your father, *"I've decided to fool around for a couple of years, ski and stuff like that. I know you'll support me."*

Will: (*Laughs*)

Mary: What's your laughter?

Will: Dad wouldn't cotton to that at all. He didn't give me anything after I was 16 years old. (*Pause*) If I were like my father, I suppose my daughter would be self-supporting. Or married. I'm not angry now. And there's no point in being guilty.

Mary: Well, Will, you aren't alone. Most of us therapists got where we did by buying *"Don't be a child"* messages. Fine messages, really. We should thank our folks. What happened, then, is we'd all secretly have liked to stay children so we live vicariously through ours. We say to our offspring, don't worry, I'll take care of everything, you can do the skiing I never got to do, get all the things I didn't get . . . and they end up babies and we end up resenting them.

Will: Absolutely. That is right on. My kids are very bright and creative.

Mary: My guess, then, is that as soon as you see your daughter as a woman rather than as a kid, she will find a way to support herself.

Bob began by following the direction Will desired, to set up the groundwork so that he will experience and voice his anger. Of course, this rarely brings resolution. Will will be happier resolving his ambivalence rather than practicing his anger. Like the client who doesn't have to write an article as long as he feels unhappy about not writing it, Will doesn't have to toss his daughter out of the nest as long as he remains angry at her for not leaving on her own.

Some clients use anger to justify behavior that they would not otherwise permit themselves. In TA, this is called collecting anger stamps in order to buy a guilt-free resignation from a job, a guilt-free divorce, or a guilt-free drinking spree. When working with such clients, we'll first ask them to recognize that they can divorce, resign, or drink, if they choose, without collecting stamps to trade in.

Mary: Hey, what's wrong with simply deciding you don't want to live with him anymore. How come you have to be angry to split?

Gwen: It wouldn't make sense . . . you can't just leave someone without a good reason. . . .

Mary: (*Plays back her words on tape recorder*) Listen to the *"you."* "You *can't leave someone."* That's the programming. "You *can't leave,"* says one part of you. The other part says, *"Oh, but, Mama, I've got good reasons, he is so bad! Listen to all the reasons I have for being mad at him!"*

Gwen: Hmmm. Well that fits. Nobody in my family gets a divorce. In fact, I've already written my mother letters telling her about him, hoping she'll say, *"Get a divorce."* Instead she says, *"Try harder."* (*Smiles*) I just thought of something kookie. When she says, *"Try harder,"* I try harder to find more things wrong with him.

Although each of us has many other ways of stimulating ourselves to do certain tasks in this world, the angry client believes she needs anger as a trigger for action. We give such clients these questions to ask themselves whenever they are angry:

1. *Is the situation I'm angry* (or sad, guilty, etc.) *about real or fantasied?* If she is angry about what may happen in the future, the situation is fantasy. If she is angry in response to an interpretation or guess she makes about someone else's behavior, it is fantasy until she checks out the facts.

Sara: My husband doesn't care what I think and it makes me so damned mad.

Mary: Tell him what you think and find out from him whether or not he cares about that thought. Maybe he does, maybe he doesn't. So long as you don't ask, you can only guess.

2. *Is there something I can do?* If Sara discovers that, in fact, husband is not interested in her thoughts, she can divorce him, stop telling him those thoughts, find out what he is interested in, or go right on telling him—but without being angry when he doesn't care.

3. *Do I choose to do it?* After listing possible options, Sara may choose to follow through on one of them or may choose to do nothing. Whatever her choice, her anger is no longer in any way valuable to her.

When a client thinks her anger is inevitable because it is the only possible or logical response to a situation, she is believing that people and situations make her feel. We often use fantasy to point out that each person chooses her own feelings:

"Shut your eyes. Pretend you are driving your car. You are driving a few miles over the speed limit. The car ahead of you stops suddenly without signaling and you apply your brakes immediately. Your car hits the car ahead and you are not hurt. Sit in your car a moment. What do you feel? Get out and inspect the two cars. You see that your bumper and radiator grill are bent. What do you feel? What do you say inside your head?"

When a group of clients do this experiment together, they immediately learn that each of them had different feelings and that each person's feeling is dictated not by the event but by what she tells herself about the event. The fearful make up *"I could have been killed"* stories. The guilty scold themselves or fantasy that the insurance will be cancelled because they were speeding. The sad may decide that they'll have to spend their vacation money on having the car repaired. The angry focus their attention on the slob who braked without signalling.

If a client continues to believe that people or situations make her angry, the therapist may be tempted to capitulate, particularly if the therapist also responds with anger to similar situations and so secretly believes that anger is justified. Therapist and client may, then, involve themselves in a "counseling" rather than therapy contract, as they ignore the client's pathology while proceeding with problem-solving. This approach may result in the client's solving external problems, but if she solves problems and remains angry, she'll create new problems in order to justify her angry life position.

Long ago, when we were first co-leading groups, we listened to Ruth and Si quarrel. Si's favorite subject was his wife's refusal to clean two rental units. For three months, after the tenants left, the couple couldn't rent the apartments because they were not clean. Ruth alternated between pleading guilty and attacking Si for only wanting her as a cleaning woman. As Si continued the tirade, Bob interrupted only to ask facts, which he wrote on the blackboard:

$$
\begin{aligned}
\text{Loss of rental: } \$150 \times 3 \text{ months} \quad &\$450 \\
\$200 \times 3 \text{ months} \quad &600 \\
\text{Cost of therapy: } \$15 \times 6 \text{ sessions} \quad & \\
\times \text{ two people} \quad &\underline{180} \\
&\$1{,}230
\end{aligned}
$$

Bob asked how many hours it would take to clean the apartments and wrote:

$$
\begin{aligned}
\text{One cleaning person } \$3.00 \times 40 \text{ hours} \quad &\$120 \\
\$1{,}230& \\
-120& \\
\hline
\$1{,}110&
\end{aligned}
$$

Bob said, "*Your anger is very important to you. You are willing to lose $1,110 just to stay mad at your wife.*"

There are several ways to work with such a couple. The anti-therapeutic method would be for the therapist and the group to decide which of them is more to blame and then pressure that one to change. The non-therapeutic method would be to help them problem-solve. Each member of the group may have a solution or the couple will be asked to find and report solutions. If that is the entire focus, two angry people will solve one problem, only to come in the next week with another. They would continue to set up situations in which they hurt themselves and would remain estranged in the service of maintaining old life positions.

To bypass problem-solving, Bob sneaked in an obvious solution and then rapidly focused on the man's pathology, his non-functional anger. Before the session was over, we pointed out the wife's *"Kick Me"* game, in which she asks for kicks by promising to clean the apartments and then not cleaning them. With both, we focused on their difficulties in being emotionally close.

During a following session, we showed them their Wall of Trivia:

Bob: You, Si, say you are angry because she won't have sex in the morning.

Ruth: Of course I won't have sex in the morning. The children are awake. You don't care about the children. In fact, sometimes I think the only thing you care about is the damned TV and your apartments.

Si: It's hopeless! (*Said in very angry, loud tone*)

Bob: (*Draws the three circles for each, then two bricks, labeling each brick "Sex." See Figure 22.*) You are both angry about sex. Ruth, you're angry about Si's something or other with the children and about Si and TV. (*Bob draws two more bricks, labeling them "children" and "TV"*) What else are you angry about, Si?

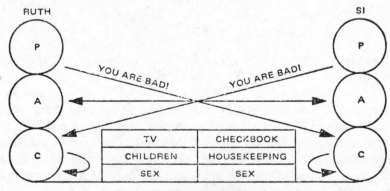

WALL OF TRIVIA
Fig. 22

Si: I don't get what you are getting at. Angry about? Lots. The way she keeps house . . . doesn't keep house, I should say. The mess the checkbook is in. . . .

Bob: OK, that's enough. (*He draws in two more bricks; then he draws transactional lines between the ego states.*) This is what we call the Wall of Trivia. Trivia that you've made more important than intimacy. See what it does for you? It's low enough for you to keep on haranguing each other from your Parents. Low enough so that you can sometimes talk Adult to Adult. But look what happens when you want to play. The wall prevents you. And you two put up the wall and maintain the wall.

Ruth: That means that we have to solve all those problems. . . .

Bob: Not at all. That wouldn't work. For every brick you removed, you'd put up six more bricks. The question is, do you want to be close, intimate? If you don't, that's OK. The focus will be on how you two can maintain your distance without using the wall to distance you.

At the next session they were ready to look at how their early decisions are affecting their current lives.

Ruth: I don't understand our Wall of Trivia. I don't think it's trivia but I get the idea. If we were madly (!) in love, we'd find time to have sex and not. . . . I am too angry at him to want sex.

Mary: Yeah, you find him difficult. Who were you angry at before Si?

Ruth: No one the way I'm angry at him.

Mary: Test out. Shut your eyes and go back into your childhood. . . .

Ruth: (*Doesn't take time even to shut her eyes*) Oh, you mean childhood? My damned brother is exactly like Si.

We use a scene between Ruth and her brother for her to recognize her early decisions about boys and girls, men and women, anger and intimacy. She laughs freely as she realizes, in redoing an early scene, that her brother's antagonism was his way of creating distance in order to squelch his possible sexual desires toward a truly attractive little sister. As she takes her brother's face off her husband, she is freer to look for ways of achieving intimacy with him.

In working with early scenes, Si recognizes that his original anger was directed at his father, who deserted him, and at his mother, who persecuted him.

Si: I have every right to be angry at you. You left us and I was only six years old. You expected me to cope with mother . . . you bastard!

Bob: You have every right, if that is your choice. Tell him, "I choose to stay angry at you until you change."

Si: Damned right. I'll be angry until you change and you'll never change.

Bob: I'll be angry at you until you change when I was six years old.

At this point, most clients recognize the craziness of their position and give up their anger spontaneously. Si is more stubborn than that!

Si: I am going to stay angry at you forever.

Mary: That is exactly where you are stuck.

Si: Well, you know, he is still alive. . . . I still see him. He's still the same . . . still all for himself. Not for anybody else. (*Very angrily*)

At this point, we might stop work, letting Si experience remaining in the impasse, or we might suggest *"Dream on it tonight and see what your dream tells you,"* or we might do a number of other things. Mary decides to take him on a fantasy trip which is a favorite of hers:

Shut your eyes and pretend that you are sending your father to our next four-week workshop. You want him to change so much that you saved up and blew the $1,200 for him to come here. Now, fantasy that the workshop is over and that your father has changed more than you could ever imagine in your wildest dreams. He is a totally new man. He is loving, kind, considerate, and adores whatever you do. Whatever you are and do, you are exactly what he has always wanted. Keep imagining. He is walking down the street to your house. He rings your doorbell. You let him in and he hugs you. He says, "Forgive me for the past. I didn't do right when you were young or even when you were grown up, and now I am going to make it all up to you. I am moving in with you and am going to stay with you the rest of my life."

As Mary finishes the last sentence, Si screeches, *"No way!"* and begins to laugh. The whole group is laughing. With this fantasy, Si abruptly cuts the symbiotic umbilical cord to the past and gives up waiting for his father to change.

Anger is often used by children to defend against the giver of injunctions. Children from seemingly fine environments may use anger in order not to capitulate to saccharin parenting. Nice, smothering parents say, "I'm cold, put on your sweater," "You aren't really angry at your little brother, you're just tired," or "My brave little man isn't really scared." The injunction is "Don't feel what you feel, feel what I feel." Parents also give injunctions against thinking: "Little girls don't know anything about motors, darling," "The dogs are just playing . . . don't worry your little head about it," or, "Of course, Santa can get down the chimney." People who believe such messages become as banal and pseudo-stupid as their parents. Angry children may preserve their rights to think and feel, and thereby may become more interesting adults than their docile brothers and sisters.

Some clients used their early anger to defend themselves against lethal injunctions. Instead of agreeing that they are worthless, crazy, or the wrecker of their parents' lives, they fight back in anger. Listening to the early histories of delinquents and criminals, we often recognize their angry actions as an alternative to a capitulation that would mean profound depression or psychosis. Such clients need to know and appreciate the life-saving aspects of their early angers, while at the same time recognizing that they now have other options for solving today's problems.

SUPPRESSED ANGER

Sometimes angry children frighten themselves as they realize what they have done or could have done, and suppress their anger from then on. Hank, growing up in a series of bad foster homes, acted out his angers and then, suddenly, without therapy, redecided. He finished college, became a fine therapist . . . and in the process kept attempting to bury his anger.

Hank: Yesterday one of the men here gave me an elbow shove in the ribs. What concerns me most. . . . I felt comfortable saying, *"Hey, knock that off, I don't like it."* And shortly after that I was back to picking stupid verbal fights with people. I want to stop my nitpicking fights.

Mary: But you didn't and don't want to fight with the man who gave you the elbow shove.

Hank: Not him. I didn't fight with him. I really would have liked to bounce him off the floor. And chose not to, and won't do that. But I don't know what to do with my feelings. (*Speaks in a very matter-of-fact tone*)

Bob: What would you like to do to him?

Hank: What I'd like to do is just say. . . .

Bob: Say it to him.

Hank: My fantasy is, *"Knock that shit off. I am not going to be the object of your rage. Don't do that again to me."*

Bob: You had fantasies about hitting him.

Hank: Not really.

Bob: Bounce him off the floor?

Hank: Not really. No. I just want him not to elbow me.

Bob: Fantasy hitting him . . . out loud.

Hank: I am really afraid to hit him.

Bob: In fantasy.

Hank: I am really afraid.

Mary: What's your fear?

Hank: (*Very constricted voice*) I am afraid that if I start hitting you I won't stop hitting you. (*Starts sobbing, stops*) I am afraid there is something wrong with me. . . . I see people like you, people as angry as I am, I want to . . . learn not to be angry. I want no part of this anymore.

Bob: I am aware that you are refusing even to fantasy rage.

Hank: That's right. I am.

Bob: You said, *"I don't know what to do with my rage,"* and refuse to fantasy what to do with your rage. Will you go ahead and fantasy?

(Mary brings heavy pillows.)

Hank: I don't want to. . . . I'm scared (*Long pause*) I want you to get your elbow out of my ribs. . . . Fuck you. . . . (He hits pillows twice, very lightly, and stops.)

Mary: What happens is, you're angry and manage to repress very quickly by being scared, fearful. You scare yourself with what you might do in actuality. Will you let yourself be physically angry in fantasy. . . .

Bob: Clobber the pillows.

Hank: (*Shakes head*)

Mary: Start with, "*I don't dare hit the pillow.*"

Hank: I don't dare hit the pillow.

Mary: How come?

Hank: I don't feel like it. It's stupid.

Bob: So it's stupid. Do it anyway.

Hank: (*Explodes . . . hits pillows, kicks them, beats them with his fists and other pillows.*)

Mary: How do you feel?

Hank: Tired. My hands tingle, my muscles are still tight.

Mary: Then do some more.

Hank: (*Pounds and beats and yells "AH" and "FUCK YOU." He stops and sits down.*)

Mary: What are you feeling?

Hank: I feel at peace. My stomach is relaxed. I am aware of my breathing. I think I needed to do that.

Bob: Yeah.

Hank: Yeah. When I am angry, I am not sure what to do. I hold it in. And the more I hold it in, the more I go around looking for verbal scraps to let it dribble out.

Bob: That's why I wanted you to do something physical . . . within a fantasy.

Hank: This is becoming very clear to me right now.

Mary: Would you thank the part of you that is angry? Up to now you've repressed . . . see what kind of appreciations you have.

Hank: Yeah. Ah. You are the part of me that keeps me from feeling scared. I appreciate how handy you were for me when I was little. And I appreciate how you energized me when people were doing things to me that they shouldn't be doing. You helped me stick up for myself. And you are damned good to have around if the going ever got tough and I needed you.

Mary: Are you willing to recognize, too, that you are in charge, not your angry. . . .

Hank: That's not true. (*Long pause*) I have been very afraid of my angry part that used to be out of control. Yes, used to be. I am in charge of you. And I will tell you when I am going to use you. . . .

Mary: And how.

Hank: And how. I won't be letting you do anything that is going to get me into a bad place . . . of hurting people. Of hurting my life.

Mary: True?

Hank: Oh, yes.

Mary: Then it is OK to experience your anger.

Hank: Not comfortable. It is OK to be angry. It is not OK to be as angry as I feel sometimes.

Mary: Not true. Test out, I can feel as angry as I want to feel. . . .

Hank: OK. I get you. I can be as angry as I want to be because I am in charge. That makes better sense. It is OK to be as angry as I feel . . . ah, even though you, my angry feelings, are very intense, I am not going to act on you.

Bob: Any fantasies about what your original anger is about?

Hank: I am. . . . I still feel very responsible for the violent things I did in the past.

Mary: A long time ago?

Hank: Yeah. Well, up through my adolescence I was extremely destructive.

Bob: My question is, do you have any idea of what your original anger was about?

Hank: Yeah. I . . . have done good work here with Ruth and with Jim (our partners). I learned to be angry and enraged because all the people around me . . . in my foster homes . . . on the streets . . . were angry and enraged. I am through with that. I live happily, I would never kill myself or anyone, I have a good life. I think this was a last piece . . . finding out I could be physically angry again and be in control . . . so that I'd hit pillows, not people. As a child, I used anger . . . all the times I was sent off to different places, I never gave in.

Mary: So you used your anger to keep you from being psychotic?

Hank: I really think so, Mary. I knew, when I worked at the state hospital, how close I came to landing there. . . . I was really a fucked-up kid.

Mary: Fucked over.

Hank: Yeah. I think some part of me may still want to get even for the past, but I am satisfied for now. I feel very good.

Hank learned that he could appreciate his angry self, that he had needed his anger when he was a child and, most important, that he can experience anger without becoming violent. The next morning, he finished this work:

Bob: Hank, when you worked last, you decided you are in charge of when you are angry and how you show your anger.

Hank: Yes, that's correct. I feel relieved. I feel very free.

Bob: One more piece. I'd like you to experiment. . . . I'd like you to get to know that angry boy back then. Willing?

Hank: Whew. I'm willing.

Bob: Shut your eyes and see yourself back when you were violent.

Hank: I'm ashamed. . . .

Bob: No. See him as a kind therapist would see him. How old is he when he first starts to be violent?

Hank: Would you believe seven?

Bob: I believe seven. See the seven-year-old. Now be you as you are today. What would you do for that child?

Hank: (*Crying*) I should be saying I'd love him. He's so unlovable back then. . . . I would not find other children so unlovable. This is very difficult.

Bob: Hold him in your arms.

Hank: He'd fight like a tiger. (*Pauses. He is sobbing and laughing alternately*) You are lovable, and I'll stick with you. I did, in fact, stick with you. I love you. I love that you fought back, I'm sorry that you committed crimes when you were so little, and that you hurt people physically when you grew stronger. I see you, lovable and unloved. Yes. Thank you, Bob.

Joe also suppressed anger. His contract is to enjoy competition rather than "act as if every silly ping-pong game is a life and death matter."

Joe: I'm too old to make such a big thing out of competition. I feel as if I were in high school.
Mary: Be in high school. What's going on?

Joe says that he is the best football player on the team and also plays basketball well.

Joe: I don't enjoy it, though.
Mary: How come?
Joe: Same reason. . . . I don't know. I have to prove . . . (*Long pause*)
Bob: What do you have to prove?
Joe: It starts even younger, when I am eight or nine. People don't like me.
Mary: How come?
Joe: (*Long pause*) Because . . . of my background. My origin is Spanish. . . .
Mary: Be there.
Joe: My mother is Spanish. All the Spanish kids are supposed to go to the other school . . . the poor school. They can't kick me out because my name's O'Brien. But nobody likes me. Nobody ever invites me to his house . . . ever. And I don't know any Mexican kids. (*He speaks sadly*)

We ask him to create a specific scene when he is competing and not being liked. He remembers being the star athlete and not being invited to a private party celebrating the victorious football season.

Bob: What do you want to tell them?
Joe: Nothing.
Bob: See what you are doing with your right foot.
Joe: Tapping.
Bob: Do it harder. (*Exaggerating body movement is an excellent way to break through suppressed affect.*)

Joe: Yeah. (*He stamps*) Goddamn!
Bob: Wait a moment. The floor is too hard. (He and group members bring a pile of cushions. *It is important to protect clients from hurting themselves physically during "anger" scenes.*)
Joe: (*Explodes, kicking, pounding, screaming*) Goddamn you all! I HATE YOU! I HATE YOU ALL! (*He continues screaming and pounding, then rests on the cushions.*)
Bob: Where are you now ... with those kids?
Joe: I am as good as they are.
Bob: Maybe better. You were treated outrageously.
Joe: Yeah. And that was a long time ago. I didn't know how much I cared. I don't have to prove anything to anyone. I guess that's been a long time coming. I'd like to hug you both.

Joe and Hank no longer have to be estranged from their own feelings. Both report relief and an ability to relax which they had not previously experienced. They are in no danger of becoming "angry men"; in fact, when clients stop suppressing, they almost always find little current reason for the feelings they had held back. The primary experience is enrichment and greater self-intimacy.

BLAME

Blamers may be angry or sad. Although they believe that they want to change someone else, their primary goal is to have the other person plead guilty. Si, complaining that his wife didn't clean the rental units, wanted the world to know that she was to blame. Because blamers have low self-esteem, we choose at first to find a way to sympathize with the blamer's Child.

Sue is in a tirade against her husband.

Bob: I get the picture and I am feeling sorry for you.
Sue: You are? Why? (*She is amazed. Although she wants sympathy, she expects counterattacks.*)
Bob: Because it must have been hell at your house when you were little.
Sue: Maybe. Why do you say that?
Bob: Because I imagine you wanted desperately to get recognition

and didn't know how. So I guess that you were a nice little kid who didn't get recognition.

Bob: I feel sorry for you.
Yates: You do? Why?
Bob: I guess that when you were growing up they made one hell of a fuss about milk that is already spilled, instead of just wiping it up. Because that's what you are doing now.

Bob: I feel sorry for you.
Will: Why?
Bob: Because your father must have been a horror.
Will: How did you know that?
Bob: Because kids copy their parents. I've been listening to the father part of you, blaming your son.

Will Cupchik[1] taught us a technique to use with a blaming client. We ask the client to collect as many empty chairs as there are members of her original, extended family. In each chair she will identify who she is and whom she blames for what.

Verna: (*Sitting*) I'm mother. I blame my husband for ruining my life.
Mary: Good. Mother, tell what he did to ruin your life.
Verna: The second year we were married, he ran away with another woman. He came back, but I never forgot. . . .
Mary: Switch chairs.
Verna: I'm father. I blame my wife for ruining my life. With her nagging.
Mary: Switch.
Verna: I'm grandmother. I blame my husband for ruining my life. He took me away from my mother and he never earned enough money in America. (*She begins to laugh as she switches chairs*) I'm grandfather. A fairly nice guy. I blame the capitalistic international conspiracy. (*Switches, still giggling*) I'm Aunt Maude. Great old Aunt Maude. Her . . . the man she was supposed to marry got kicked by a mule . . . she died an old maid. I am Aunt Maude. I blame my lifetime of virginity on a mule!

At this point, the entire group is laughing with her and she says, *"Now what will I do? Everytime I want to blame, I'll have to think of Aunt Maude and the mule."*

Another technique is to ask the person to pretend she has won. She has convinced everyone that she is blameless and the others are to blame. We ask her to be there, look around, see who is finally impressed. Whom is she running up to, saying, *"I've won! I've finally proved I'm right!"* We ask her to visualize what is the prize for winning. Very often, the blamer is operating out of a desperate Child position, trying to find some way to persuade the world she is just as good as her big sister or baby brother. The longed-for prize is love. Recognizing this, the blamer is ready to redecide that she is lovable even if the important people didn't love; then she is ready to drop blaming and find effective ways to get love.

In order to work successfully with blamers, it is essential that the therapist, no matter what the provocation, keep from taking sides, passing judgment, comparing, or giving prizes, negative or positive, for blaming.

SADNESS

Come to me my melancholy baby,
Cuddle up and don't be blue....

Smile, my honey dear,
While I kiss away each tear,
Or else I will be melancholy, too.[2]

Girls and boys may sidestep growing up by being melancholy babies. If a girl finds and marries a daddy who loves melancholy babies, she will be stroked for sadness just as long as he agrees to stay stuck with her in this damp symbiosis. Sad "little boys" marry mommies who are supposed to kiss their scratches and make everything right. Herman married a melancholy baby and then cheated her. Instead of spending his energy trying to make her "not blue," he chose to compete in a mostly unsuccessful attempt to be even more sad than she. Each of them wants to be the comforted one, rather than the comforter.

Herman: I want to be happy at home.

Mary: OK. Shut your eyes. You are walking into your house. OK? Walk in happy.

Herman: OK.

Mary: Where are you in your house?

Herman: In the kitchen.

Mary: Still happy?

Herman: Yes.

Mary: Look around. Tell me what you are happy or unhappy about.

Herman: I'm in the kitchen. My wife is there working on something. I say, *"Hi,"* I take off my coat, hang it on a chair.

Mary: Still happy?

Herman: Yes. Pretty good mood. I . . . ah . . . Now I'm in a bind. I want to talk about me, just talk . . . and I get into a fight with myself and the fight is . . . shall I share some of the things I am thinking or shall I talk about what she wants to talk about?

Bob: So you rehearse?

Herman: Not the talking, the issues. Do you, don't you?

Mary: Then?

Herman: I begin to talk. The conversation sort of . . . I say something. . . .

Bob: Be there. Say it to her.

Herman: So I walk in and tell her, *"I have had some sad feelings about Annie."*

Mary: Who is Annie?

Herman: Our daughter who died three years ago.

Mary: So you walk in and tell her something sad. And then. . . .

Herman: We are both sad. After about one or two sentences, she talks about her sad feelings about Annie, and then it goes into a long conversation about her feelings about Annie and then I clam up and listen. I'm tense, I didn't get to do my talking about my feelings. . . .

Mary: OK, one contract is to say goodbye to Annie. Also, I hear you two compete with your sadnesses.

Herman: I don't get mad that she is sadder, but she doesn't listen to my bleeding.

Mary: You know, it is too bad you had a child who died. I suggest that you found things to be sad about before that.

Herman: That is true. I am not used to . . . to happiness.

Although we do not consider Herman suicidal, we always check this out with sad clients. He says he is not, has fantasied suicide only in quite romantic terms that include last-minute rescue, and says that he will not ever make a suicide attempt. He states easily that he will never kill himself accidentally or on purpose.

We then ask Herman to experiment with telling only happy stories to other workshop participants and to report back during tomorrow's session. We do no further work with him in this session. When treating a client who is perpetually sad, we immediately set about changing the stroking patterns. If we simply deny strokes for sadness, he may become depressed due to stroke deprivation. We want to be certain that he asks for happy strokes, gets them, and takes them in.

In later sessions we learn the genesis of his unhappiness and do redecision work with him, during which he finds a way to be happy in spite of what is going on around him during his childhood. He says goodbye to an absent father and then to his dead daughter. His last step is to stroke himself for his own creative, bubbling happiness. In preparation for his return home, he reenacts several times the "kitchen scene" until he recognizes that his wife has a right to feel whatever she feels and that his feelings need not be dependent on hers. He plans to invite her to go to a marathon with him and asks us for a referral near his home. He says he'll enjoy his life whether or not she attends a marathon or makes personal changes.

Julien, a 50-year-old architect from France, is referred by a friend because he "has no reality reason to be sad" but remains perpetually sad. For the first few days of the workshop, he defends against working on his own problem, although outside of the therapy sessions he has let us know that he is very sad about his decreased sexual abilities. On the fourth day, he begins to work:

Julien: I am so tired. I am so tired. I am exhausted. I am too tired for making love, too tired for living.

Bob: It is hard to keep your energy up, when you have stuff you are not dealing with. I think you use a lot of energy not working through where you are stuck. (*Said very sympathetically*) What is it like when you are a little boy and feel sad?

Julien does not remember being sad as a child. He was a child genius, stimulated by his father to be precocious. Every afternoon father would come home to teach young Julien advanced mathematics and then would take Julien to the university to show off to professors and graduate students. Julien says he loved doing this, loved his father, and adored his mother. He finds nothing sad in his entire childhood. We then ask when he began to be unhappy.

Julien: When I am 13 years old and am sent away to a university. I love my mother so much and I miss my mother. I knew to be a man I must live away from her. That is life. That is how it is when you grow up.

Mary: Were you suicidal then?

Julien: Never. And I am not now. I would not kill myself.

Mary: Good. Are you willing to consider giving up suffering?

Julien: Oh, yes! That is why I am here.

Mary: Your program is to suffer . . . the way to be a man is to suffer . . . even the way to prove your manhood is to suffer. That's what you said about going off to the university.

Julien: Yes?

Bob: You don't sound sure.

Julien: I . . . You are suggesting that I make myself suffer?

Mary: More or less. I imagine you had the church and the church schools showing you how. Everyone knows that the important saints are the ones who suffered most exquisitely rather than the one who did something worthwhile.

Julien: (*Laughing*) That is true. And I used to imagine being a priest . . . a very melancholy priest. I made myself sad? I am amazed. I can't explain. I thought my sadness was very complicated and it is very simple? I make things sad?

Mary: Yes. Hey, who taught you how to suffer? Who's the sufferer, mother or father?

Julien: Both. Especially my mother. Yes. She did that.

Mary: How did she do that?

Julien: How? She had what I call the galloping cancer for the past forty years, since I was a little boy.

Mary: She had cancer?

Julien: No, she never had cancer. She always has pain that she believes is cancer. She is always suffering terrible pain when there is no cancer. Or else she is believing she will have cancer when there is no pain. I go to visit her now. I love her, yes? She is 80 years old. I walk to the doorway and before I close the door, I learn a cousin has pneumonia. (*Julien begins to gesture, speaks expansively, and laughs as he talks.*) A neighbor is dying, my mother has a pain in her shoulder so terrible she cannot do anything, she almost could not make a dessert for me but she made it anyway. (*He is laughing heartily.*)

Group members are also laughing.

As he tells this story, Julien begins the process of separating himself from his mother's creed of sadness. For the first time since he arrived for the workshop, he is breathing deeply and his voice is lively.

Mary: OK, Julien. See your mother there . . . lamenting, suffering, showing her sadness. Be there in fantasy with her. OK? Now say to her something different. Say, "*Mother, I feel really great. I have never in my life been happier.*"

Julien: Oh, no. That would be very bad. That would be cruel. You are not supposed to be happy when your mother is suffering. (*Laughs*) I am understanding a great deal.

Julien has given the Parent command: "*You are not supposed to be happy when your mother is suffering.*" If Julien were a therapist, we would play his words back on the tape recorder so that he would hear and understand the "I-You" switch. We want therapists to hear themselves so that they will learn to hear their clients. We don't stop Julien because he is working well.

Mary: And what if you say to your mother, "*I've got such terrible pains in my stomach. . . .*"

Julien: Oh, Christ! She would have all the medication, she would want me to move back to the house, she would have my room ready, she would keep the conversation going for hours.

Julien was stroked for achievement and unhappiness, even though he doesn't remember being unhappy. Perhaps mother's way of loving made unhappiness seem like happiness. He's probably correct that he needed to get away from her when he was 13 and yet his lifelong racket may be a Child attempt to return. *"She would have all the medication, she would have my room ready!"* There is in this one session ample work for many hours of therapy . . . and Julien does not need many hours. Already he is changing.

Julien: I love my mother, but I do not want her attention for this any longer. She was always good to me when I was sick. (*Laughs again*) I never understood before. All this time I have been sad and didn't understand. I was aware she was a bit crazy about these things, all her illnesses, but I was not aware that I, too, have been perhaps a bit crazy about my sadness.

Mary: Great understanding! Now . . . from your new, cheerful, non-suffering position, dismiss your mother and bring in your wife. Now, without tragedy, say, *"I don't want sex tonight."*

Julien: It is true. We have made this a suffering, like cancer. *"Darling, tonight I do not want sex."*

Mary: Still happy?

Julien: Yes.

Mary: I'd like you to know this absolutely. Really understand that it is OK to be happy any night, whether or not you have sex. Are you going to take that knowledge home with you?

Julien: (*After only a short pause*) I will remember that just because I don't have sex one night does not mean that I am sick or a failure. (*Begins to giggle*) I know what I will do. I will bring my wife home a present. A vibrator.

(*Whole group whoops, cheers, applauds.*)

Julien: And from my non-suffering position, I will like the vibrator, too!

We are delighted with his idea of the vibrator; he will not be giving his wife the injunction that his mother gave, *"Do not be happy when I am not happy."* We dealt with his sad racket before his sexual problem in order that he not continue to believe that his happiness depends on his solving that problem.

We will reverse the order of treatment if the behavioral problem is more important than the affective response. If Julien, for example, was sexually impotent because of prolonged use of alcohol, we'd want him to quit drinking rather than figure out a way to be a happy, non-sexual alcoholic.

Some clients won't consider a contract to be happy, because they believe they have never been happy:

Jim: I was always sad. I don't know. I have always been this way.
Mary: What's the myth of your birth? (*We ask this question when a client says he has always been a certain way, to find out what the earliest injunctions are.*)
Jim: I don't know what you mean.
Mary: What's the story about your birth? What do they say?
Jim: I have no details . . . about me. I was told . . . It was a family joke that I was born the day after they dropped the bomb.
Mary: What's so funny about that?
Jim: Nothing.
Mary: You said it was a family joke. That means it's supposed to be funny.
Jim: Well, what they meant was . . . two disasters in as many days.

Jim did many pieces of work . . . to decide to live, like himself, accept his own importance, and, finally, to be happy. Because he had no concept of himself as a happy child, we asked him to go back through time, searching for one instant in which he was happy. (So far, we have never found a client who fails to find a happy scene, even though many at first swear they were never happy.) Like many chronically sad people, Jim finds a scene when he is alone and outside of his own home.

Jim: (*After a very long pause*) OK. I used to have fun playing by the creek.

We ask him to describe the creek, describe little Jim, and describe what Jim is doing. Then we ask him to see sad Jim and set up a dialogue between the two: "*Be each of the young Jims in turn.*" Each is to begin with "I am important to grown-up Jim because. . . ." The work is finished when Jim decides to quit dragging sad Jim around with him and to use this sad Jim only when he has suffered an actual loss. "You'll be around only when I need you. You are no longer my albatross."

Other clients, seeing their sad and their happy aspects in this manner, may recognize that the sad sack has been valuable for stroke-getting. Their assignment, then, is to look for other ways to be stroked.

Don keeps himself sad by labeling his environment sad and refusing to change it:

Don: I want to stop feeling so burdened.
Bob: Put your wife in front of you and tell her she's a burden.
Don: She is. You are. You are a burden. You've been drinking too much for the past 15 years. I can't trust you when you drink. I worry about you constantly when I am away.
Bob: Tell your wife how your worrying changes her behavior?
Don: It doesn't, of course. But I can't help worrying.

We work with him on his "can't" position and ask for more details about his current life. His wife does not harm herself or others, except for the possible harm she is doing to her body by overuse of alcohol. Don doesn't really like her or have fun with her. His children are away from home, in college. We ask what he was "sad and worried" about before he married his wife. He talks of a variety of worries, then:

Don: . . . my mother. I worried a lot about her. She wasn't happy. My parents were never happy. I wouldn't call it a marriage. They stayed together because of me.
Mary: Lucky you. (*Sarcastically*)
Don: I know, it was bullshit. I didn't know it then. I . . . it was a burden. Trying to keep her happy.
Mary: So that's the original burden. That's how you learned to label women burdens, and how come you married one and declared her a burden, and how come you haven't divorced. And you teach your kids that marriages are lifetime burdens so that someday they can be burdens or burdened.

Mary is being tough with him because, like many sufferers, he does not act in his own behalf and he expects positive strokes for enduring rather than changing.

Other clients, who pride themselves on being sensitive to the world around them, explain their sadness by suggesting that it would somehow be indecent to be happy in an unhappy world. One way to tell what racket is favored by each client is to say, "*Shut your eyes. Give yourself time to see the world as it is. Go to different places in the world and look at what is going on. What do you feel?*" (We do not suggest "happy" or "unhappy" places.) Most report feeling their rackets, which they consider natural and appropriate responses to the circumstances of the world. We suggest they may make the same commitments to work to change the world from a happy position that they now make from a sad position.

More sophisticated clients believe that the unconscious controls emotions and that, therefore, it is not possible to substitute happiness for sadness without a prolonged examination of the unconscious. As in the case of Julien, this is not true.

Sad clients use sadness as angry clients use anger . . . to manipulate or pressure others into changing.

Jo: I told him I want monogamy. I . . . (*weeping*) last night he called me and I told him and while he was talking to me . . . (*sobbing*) he had someone else in our apartment. What I want to do is decide . . . to tell him . . . marry me and don't have sex with anyone else . . . or I am leaving.

Mary: OK. Feel good about that?

Jo: No. I feel very sad.

Mary: So you want him to change? Is there a piece of you that says, If I'm sad enough I can convert him?

Jo: I go over and over how I feel . . . plead with him . . . to show how hurt I am. And that doesn't do a bit of good. That is what I am beginning to understand. Your lecture on rackets and the attempt to change others . . . that is where I am bogged down. I want him to see how mad and hurt I am, so that he'll be faithful to me.

Bob: So he'll change.

Jo: And that doesn't work. That's how I keep myself from finding a way. By showing him over and over how hurt I am. (*Sobbing*) I hate his sloppy, lousy . . . self! I WANT HIM TO CHANGE.

Mary: And if he were here, what would he say now?

Jo: He is not going to change. He sees nothing wrong with . . . lots of lovers. And he says I can have lovers, but I don't want them.

Mary: So what are you going to do?

Jo: Just what I always do . . . try to make everything so good for him that he'll want me. And beg him to change. (*Weeps again*)

Mary: I predict the following sequence. First, you stay sad to get him to change. Second, he refuses to change. Third, you get sadder. Fourth, he says, "*I don't want to live with such a sad person*," and he kicks you out. And then he sets up housekeeping with the next great love of his life, who is whomever he is screwing at the moment he tires of you.

Jo: I see that is the sequence.

Bob: And consider that you must have known this sequence when you set yourself up by being the newest great love of his life. A part of you must have known his pattern.

Jo: I see very clearly. Yes, I knew about his other loves. The challenge was to be so much better . . . oh, hell, I want to quit being a loser. I am a loser with men.

Mary: How will you do this?

Jo: First, I am going to be happy whatever he does. I may not stay with him. I may not even go back to him when this workshop is over. I have three weeks to work on this. I am starting by being happy here. And then I'd like to clear up the stuff in my past . . . whatever it is . . . that I . . . that has to do with being second fiddle to any man.

Bob: I like what you are saying and I like you!

Later in the workshop she traces her sadness back to many childhood scenes in which she decided, "*I'll never get what I want*," and was sad.

June secretly hoped that her unhappiness could change her mother-in-law or her husband. Her work is an example of two different approaches to the same sad material . . . with dramatically different results.

June: I want to cope with my mother-in-law. She doesn't speak English and I don't speak Mandarin. I speak Cantonese. So I can't talk to her.

Therapist/Trainee: See your mother-in-law, pretend she speaks English, and tell her.

June says that her mother-in-law invites people to June's house without her permission, interferes with the raising of the children, and acts as if she is the "boss of my home." June then explains that the whole situation is hopeless because of the customs in Chinese homes.

Therapist: Give your mother-in-law a specific example of what you want to change and what you want her to change. (*This therapist is skillful and is doing a good job.*)

June: I want to be the woman-boss in my own home. When I come home from work I want to be in charge. Specific example? (*Sighs several times*) Saturday, just before leaving for this workshop, I had to cook for all her guests from Hong Kong.

This information is too much for the female therapists in the group, including Mary. (The male therapists maintain a discrete noninvolvement. Bob is not present.) The group suggests that June force her husband to talk to his mother, that June simply leave the house and do nothing to serve mother-in-law, that she have mother-in-law do the cooking. June successfully says "Yes, but . . ." to all suggestions:

June: I don't want her to cook in my house. If any cooking is done, I want to do it. I don't want her in my kitchen. I don't want her even touching my pots and pans. (*Long pause*) I've worked on this problem a lot in my therapy group in San Francisco. And I have clients with the same problem. I don't know if there is an answer. (*June begins to weep*)

The following day she brought up the same problem in a therapy session led by Bob and Mary.

June: I worked on this yesterday in the training group. I feel so victimized. I don't have any rights in my own home. I'm afraid my husband will reject me. . . .

Bob: Example.

Mary: If she doesn't cook for her silly old mother-in-law and all the tourists from Hong Kong! Yuck! (Mary leaves the therapist's chair and sits behind the group. She shakes her head in exaggerated horror and defeat, then holds her head in her hands.)

Bob: What's the matter? Isn't your mother-in-law a good cook? I thought all Chinese mothers-in-law were good cooks. How did you pick such a bummer?

June: (*Begins to giggle*) She's a marvelous cook.

Bob: So how come you are cooking?

Mary: (*From back of the room*) It'll blow your mind, Bob. You'll never believe it!

June: (*Still giggling*) Well, I don't know why I am cooking, I really don't. I remember why I said I was cooking . . . in the group yesterday. But I don't know.

Mary: I know why you do it. You do the cooking to punish them!

June: My God! You're right!

This was obvious to Mary the previous day, when she heard June's refusal to find a solution. Mary was not sure June would accept this conclusion, so played the whole scene humorously to get June into her very bright, perky, creative Child instead of her sad, sulky adaptive Child of yesterday. And, Bob, although not knowing what was going on, did the same.

June: Oh, boy. I can just see the scene. (*She is speaking between explosions of laughter*) It's so funny. This is the day . . . that day . . . before I came here. All these terribly proper, prim Hong Kong people in their black suits and white shirts. (*She is laughing so hard she can't talk for a time*) No one on earth is so stiff and proper as the ones from Hong Kong. (*She is weeping from laughing*) Oh . . . oh . . . I decided to have a barbeque. It was awful. My husband had to go out to get briquettes and the fire wouldn't start and they don't like steaks anyway. Oh . . . oh . . . my husband does the barbequing while I make the salad and rice. Oh . . . oh . . . I never thought . . . the only thing they would like on the whole menu . . . the boiled rice . . . oh . . . I cooked it and forgot to serve it. I never knew . . . I do all this to punish them!

We stopped at this point. People who expect clearly stated redecisions will not find one in this work and yet June stopped being the sad sulk, stopped blaming mother-in-law or waiting for her to change, and no longer considered her case to be hopeless. She figured out how to use mother-in-law's domesticity to her own advantage. Most important, by giving up sadness and the role of the martyr, she freed herself to have fun in her life.

SUPPRESSED SADNESS

Roy: I never cried when my mother died. . . .

Mary: How come?

Roy: We don't. In our family we don't . . . cry. I was only nine. I have not cried since.

Mary: Willing to be there and let yourself feel what you feel?

Roy: I am not sure. I am not sure I want to be there. I want to stop for now.

Mary: OK. Someday you may want to let yourself feel what you feel . . . feel what you would have felt back then if there had only been someone around to understand.

Roy suddenly begins to weep. He cries for about five minutes, while another client holds him.

Bob: Where are you now?

Roy: A little embarrassed. Mostly OK. Softer. I encourage my own patients to feel. I hadn't encouraged me . . . up to now.

Mary: I am glad you let yourself know your sadness. My theory is that people who repress anger are in danger of being victims, because they don't say, *"Goddamn, get off my foot!"* People who repress fear may do so in the service of getting themselves killed. And people who repress sadness seem to mute their joy.

Roy: Thanks, I like your theory and I think you are right.

Clients who are phobic of their own anger can still do meaningful work for themselves. They give up guilt, sadness, anxiety, decide to live, to enjoy their sexuality, to become more productive. Later, after making other important decisions in their lives, they are ready to deal with their fear of anger and to desensitize themselves. Clients who are phobic of their own tears are far more difficult to treat, because they rarely do important work until they have desensitized themselves. We were delighted that Roy allowed himself to weep. Crying once is usually sufficient for desensitization if handled properly by the therapist and the group. After this session, Roy let himself move ahead to other areas, instead of remaining the intellectual, non-feeling, mildly depressed psychiatrist he had been for 20 years.

Roy is one type of client who is afraid of showing sadness. Another type we call "Superman." During the contract-setting period of a workshop, Superman enters the room late and either slouches into an exaggeratedly relaxed position or sits very tall with his arms crossed on his chest. He stares away from the therapists, as he declares, *"I have thought a great deal about what I might want to work on here and I don't seem to have any problems. If I come up with something, I'll let you know."* During the rest of the workshop, he'll play "strong daddy" to some "helpless" woman or find some equally tear-phobic buddies with whom he can play a minor game of "juvenile delinquent." They'll miss sessions, crack jokes about treatment, and find inconsequential rules to break. In either role, this therapist defends successfully against doing personal work. He typically is employed to work with delinquents or criminals and resembles his own caseload except for one all-important difference: he is not a psychopath. He is a law-abiding and deeply caring human being who decided early in childhood that *"nobody can make me cry"* and grew up terrified of showing either sadness or fear. That is why he comes on as "Superman."

When such a person finally permits himself to work, the results are magnificent.

Zip does no work during a one-week workshop until the final morning. He then says he wants to *"understand"* a dream that *"bothers me somewhat."* As he begins to tell the dream, he becomes increasingly panicky, twisting his hands and tightening his voice in his struggle against his emotions. His dream, summarized, is: *"I am sitting at my desk in my study and suddenly realize that my son is not with me. I run outside to the back yard and see him floating dead, in our swimming pool."* He is very agitated by this dream and confesses that he has tortured himself with interpretations based on what he knows of "unconscious hostility" and "death wishes." He adores his son.

Bob works very slowly, having him be each part of the dream and claim each part as an aspect of his own personality. Zip becomes the desk: sturdy, solid, dependable; the study: closed-in, never disorderly, full of information; the brick walk leading to the pool: solid and not too interesting; the pool: cool, contained. So far he has claimed all of these attributes as part of himself. Throughout his work, he fight tears and when he becomes the pool, he begins to sob. He continues sobbing for several minutes before he is again ready to work with the dream.

Bob: Be the child in your dream.
Zip: I am beautiful, lovely, the most important thing in Zip's life. (*Again he is sobbing*)
Bob: Say more.
Zip: I'm bright. I love life. I . . . am dead.
Bob: See if it fits. . . . I am the part of Zip that is beautiful, lovely, bright, loves life, Zip's most important part. And that part of Zip is dead.
Zip: Thank you! Yes, it fits! I have drowned in work . . . in . . . yeah, it fits! I've drowned the alive part of me. Thank you, Bob. I'm finished! I'm not drowning me anymore!

When a client like Zip allows himself to express feelings, it is vital that the experience be a positive one. To urge a client to feel and then to leave him without a redecision can be a therapeutic rape. We ask therapists not to promote intense feelings unless they know exactly how to promote a successful conclusion. Zip would have been treated anti-therapeutically if he had been allowed to continue his assumption that the dream was an expression of "buried hostility," or if he'd been left sobbing, without resolution. Instead, he accomplishes a beautiful redecision, *"I'm not drowning me anymore,"* while also learning that it is safe to feel.

FEAR AND ANXIETY

We define fear as an emotional response to a real or imagined *present* danger and anxiety as a response to a real or imagined possible *future* danger. A person is as afraid of a toy gun as a real gun, if she believes it to be real. A phobic knows her fears are imaginary, but is as frightened as if the danger were real. The anxious person tells herself scary stories about what she may some day encounter.

In all the years that we have practiced therapy, there has never been a real danger in our therapy groups; therefore, the fears we hear about in the room are imaginary. However, the fears and anxieties clients report in their everyday lives may at times be real. The first job of the therapist is to determine the facts as to the reality of the danger. A person afraid of a dangerous spouse needs help in deciding how to protect self. Clients who expose themselves to real danger and do nothing to protect themselves may be living out the despairing decision, *"I'll get you to kill me"* or *"I'll let you kill me."* The crucial aspect of treatment is a self-protection contract and then a redecision to value and protect self.

When a person is afraid of a non-dangerous current or future situation, we look for an earlier scene that is the prototype of today's fear.

Jay: Oh, shit, I'm scared to work in a group, did you know that?
Bob: I know you haven't worked yet. You wait until last in order to maintain your scare.
Jay: No, I didn't. I waited because I was scared.
Bob: If you'd wanted to stop being scared, you'd have worked first and then relaxed for the rest of the day.
Jay: I . . . when I am scared . . . I postpone and postpone and keep getting myself more scared. You're right.
Mary: I call it the "high dive" syndrome. Remember when you were a kid? At the beginning of each summer, the brave ones simply walk to the end of the high board and dive off. The non-brave don't even consider going off the high board and have their fun

swimming. The self-torturers walk to the end of the board, look down, tell themselves terror stories, and walk back. They do this time after time before they finally dive off the high board.

Jay: Yeah. I've been doing that here. All set to work, then don't. I always wait until last.

Bob: What terrible thing happened to you in the first or second grade? (*Bob is "diving right in," going to Jay's past.*)

Jay: I remember second grade. I lost my place. Everyone was taking turns reading out loud and I got interested in the story. I lost my place and the teacher put me in the corner. Fuck her, no one is going to put me in the corner again. Hey, that must be why I won't go to X's (name of therapist) marathons . . . because I heard she treats people by putting them in the corner. No one is ever putting me in the corner again. (*Laughs*) I am through . . . I'm ready to work.

Bob picked "first or second grade" because he was disproving Jay's belief that he "always" was afraid in a group. We have found that fear of speaking out in groups often starts in the first two grades of school and is the result of teacher's and students' teasing or shaming. Reading aloud is a traumatic event in the lives of many children.

There are several other approaches we might have used with Jay. We might ask him to look carefully at each person in the group. Often a person drops anxiety by seeing individuals rather than an unfocused blur. If he is still anxious, he might say to each person, "*I am afraid of you because . . .*" or "*I am not afraid of you because . . .*" We'll then work with him to claim his own projections and to be aware of his ability to write scary stories about other people. While he is making rounds in this way, we ask group members not to respond. If they reassure him, they are rescuing, which means that he is seen as helpless to change himself.

We may want a client to recognize that his anxiety is enthusiasm held in check.

Alf: I'm anxious. Very anxious.

Mary: Go inside your body and report what you are experiencing.

Alf: I'm anxious . . . my heart is beating quickly. My heart is pounding and I am sweating.

Mary: Same sensations you have when making love, right?

Alf: (*Snorts . . . a half-laugh*) It doesn't feel the same.

Mary: What can you do to make your sweating and your rapid heart beat pleasurable? Your brain translates anxiety. See what you can do to get your brain to translate excitement.

Alf: Crazy thought! Turn a somersault . . . jump around. I'd like the rest to jump with me.

Mary: Ask them.

or

Liz: My hands are trembling.

Bob: Exaggerate your tremble. That's it. Exaggerate more. Stand up and let your whole body be involved. Yeah. What do you experience?

Liz: Excitement.

Bob: Good. Your trembling was you wanting to be excited and holding you back. Fritz (Perls) said the difference between anxiety and excitement is one deep breath.

Another technique is to follow "catastrophic expectations" to a fantasied conclusion. We ask Hubert what is the worst thing that can happen. He says that he is afraid the group won't like him. He believes he won't have anything interesting to say. "*And then, what is the worst thing that can happen?*" He believes they won't talk to him or socialize with him. "*And then, what's the worst thing?*" He'll feel lonely and withdraw. "*And then?*" "*Well, I won't die or dry up.*" Hubert smiles. "*I will find something interesting to do on my own.*" He recognizes that he has never had to stay alone forever, so he says that he will seek someone out. Even if his catastrophic expectation does take place, he will cope. He then says that his expectation was grossly exaggerated and that he is no longer anxious.

Another technique is to divorce beliefs from affect. This technique is especially good with clients who do not know that they can think and feel simultaneously.

Flo: What I'm afraid of is I'll forget what to say.

Bob: OK. Pretend you have forgotten what to say. Why should you be anxious about that?

Flo: I'd just naturally be anxious.

Bob: No. My grandson, Robert, only remembers how to say about 10 words. He's not anxious. Why do you connect being anxious to forgetting words?

Flo: Well, naturally, I don't want to be anxious. . . .

Mary: That is true. There you are and you have forgotten what to say next and you want to remember what to say next. Why are you anxious?

Flo: Well, that's interesting. I always connected . . . I am anxious because I think I'm supposed to be. Because I tell myself what will people say. . . . I am ready to stop. I'll come in later. I want to think about the way I connect automatically to anxiety. I am going to start deconnecting.

The anxious forgo the present in order to spend their psychic energy peering fearfully at an imagined future.

Gem is extremely anxious about the future. She has had a father, brother, and husband die of heart attacks while living with her. She is planning to remarry and terrifies herself that her new love will die.

Gem: It is getting so bad . . . every time I am with him I am afraid tonight is the night he'll have a heart attack.

Bob: How come you fill yourself full of bad stories of the future instead of enjoying yourself in the here and now?

Gem: I don't know.

Mary: I gather that your husband wasn't like you in this respect. You said he knew for two years that he might die any day of a coronary, and yet you said you and he had a beautiful time. He wasn't obsessed with scaring himself about death?

Gem: Not at all. He lived richly.

Mary: Is that your goal for you?

Gem: Yes.

Mary: I'm glad.

Gem: How do I stop myself?

Bob: I don't understand your question. You are the one who is thinking these things.

Gem: How do I stop myself thinking these things?

Bob: Have a sexual fantasy instead.

Gem: What will happen with a sexual fantasy is I'll end it up with death.

Mary: The trouble is, you really don't believe you are in charge of your head.

Bob: That's right.

Gem: I'm in charge of my head but I'm not in charge of the facts that happened.

Mary: I am sure that long before anyone died your mother taught you to move ahead into the future in order to feel bad. My guess is that she predicted future trouble and you would hear this from her and be scared. Her or father, or grandmother, or someone.

Gem: Yes, she was always afraid of what might happen.

Mary: So your mother carefully taught you how to run your brain . . . how to go to the future and be miserable. And you were smart enough to marry a man who ran his brain differently.

Gem: Yes. He was never afraid of the future.

Mary: And your new man? Does he go around being afraid of the future?

Gem: (*Laughs*) No way.

Mary: That's nice. You are smart to pick men who do not tell themselves scary stories.

Gem: I do understand that I go into the future. Yes, and scare myself.

Mary: Good. And are you now ready to start running your brain a different way?

Gem: Yes. These are new ideas. I am chewing up what you say.

Mary: And then you can either swallow or spit out the new ideas.

Gem: (*Laughs*)

Mary: I'll give you a technique which is fun if you like to play with it. Go on doing what you are now doing and brag about you. An example. I used to be very phobic about airplanes. There's all kinds of magic involved. If I keep watch very carefully, the wing won't drop off. I don't know if you understand this?

Gem: I certainly do. (*Laughs*)

Mary: And I keep a close watch over what may be going on behind that important closed door . . . up front in the pilot's cabin. . . . I make sure they are all *there*. And listen to all noises. That's so I can rush up front and tell the pilot if the motor drops off. (*Gem is laughing*) And watch to see what food is taken in to the pilots, because if they eat fish they might be poisoned and I'll have to find someone who looks capable among the passengers and tell him, *"They are all poisoned up front and you look like just the kind of man who can take over and land this 747."* Now, Gem, the important step is the next one. I congratulate myself. Look how creative I am! Any old banal phobic can come up with scare stories about engine noises, but look at me. I can even scare myself about botulism. Understand?

Gem: (*Laughing*) Yes, I do. I really do.

Mary: Will you spend the rest of today spoofing yourself every time you start to spook yourself?

Gem: I . . . OK. I think I am going to have fun.

With this experiment, Gem begins to take charge of her own fantasies. She has other important work to do later. She says goodbye to her dead brother, her father, and her husband, and she gives herself permission to have fun even though they are dead. She drops her magic: *"Don't feel too good or something bad will happen."* Bob suggests an anti-disaster amulet to wear in place of her fear.

Gem: I don't understand about the amulet.

Bob: Well, this is my amulet (showing a pendant) and it keeps tigers off our property.

Gem: There are no tigers in California.

Bob strokes his pendant and nods wisely: *"Of course. There are no tigers because my amulet keeps them away."*

For additional material on working with fearful or anxious clients, see Chapter 11, *Phobias: One Wednesday Afternoon.*

SUPPRESSED FEAR

Suppressed fear may be in the service of self-destruction, as when men and women volunteer for dangerous service during wartime or find dangerous hobbies or careers. We don't believe counter-phobic behavior is behavior used by the client to repress phobias. We believe counter-phobia is a Child method of suppressing Adult facts and normal care for self in order to live out *"I'll get myself killed and then they'll admire me"* decisions. Counter-phobics are not afraid when they should be; phobics are afraid when there is no danger.

The switch from counter-phobia to phobia occurs when the client lets the dangerous facts into his awareness and says internally, *"I don't want to get killed!"* The ex-counter-phobic, justly fearful of his own past lack of care for self, may then develop a phobia as a magical means of self-protection.

Drake is a "Superman," who makes no treatment contract with us and explains that he is attending the workshop because his agency sent him. During mealtimes, he entertains the group with wild tales about his mountain climbing and his dangerous motorcycle racing. We begin confronting him by saying, "I'm not laughing at you hurting you. I won't give you strokes for risking your life." He argues with us, saying that he knows how to take care of himself and that a risk-free life would be boring.

Finally, we bring his material to a therapy session, even though he still refuses to make a contract. We ask him to test out experimentally what happens when he tells his stories to the family of his childhood. He tries to shrug us off, saying, *"I don't know what they'd say. Father'd be interested maybe, if he wasn't drunk. The others. . . ."* He shrugs.

We ask if he's willing to do this, even though he doesn't know their reactions. He agrees and tells them about his most recent hair-raising escapade on his motorcycle. What he is in touch with and defends against is that his family does not give a damn whether he lives or dies. So he picks buddies like himself and they stroke each other for risking death.

Drake is now listening to himself as he recognizes that a part of him is trying to die. We ask him as an experiment without yet committing himself to tell his family and his buddies that he is going to care for himself. He tells them he is not going to risk his life ever again. He sees that his mother is pleased to the extent that this depressed, beaten-down woman can be pleased. His big brother and his friends call him "chicken." His father is so busy killing himself with alcohol that he doesn't listen. Drake is profoundly impressed and decides to enter our weekly training program. We believe there are thousands of men and women like Drake, risking their lives blindly and not recognizing their need for changing their early decisions. Physicians and attorneys, when they see them after accidents and injuries, would do well to refer them . . . even though such clients might not immediately accept the referral.

SHAME

Mary's daughter Claudia and grandson Brian were playing peek-a-boo when, in a burst of joyous excitement, Brian suddenly bit Claudia hard. Claudia screamed instinctively and pushed him away. He slid to the floor, covered his eyes with his hands, and began to sob, a deep, despairing sob we hadn't heard before. Eleven-month-old Brian seemed to be experiencing shame. Claudia picked him up, kissed and cuddled him, as she said, *"My goodness, I'm the one who's bit and you're the one who needs comforting."* Soon he was happy again and they continued playing peek-a-boo.

All "shameful" scenes do not end that well. Clients remember what happened when they wet their pants, were discovered in sexual play, forgot the ending during a musical recital, and were laughed at or punished publicly. These minor incidents are of major importance in childhood and constitute the reasons people believe, *"If they really knew me, they'd find out how bad I am."* Remembrance of past shames and fear of future shame become a straitjacket against spontaneity and knowledge of self-worth.

Ara, a very competent psychiatrist, keeps herself constricted whenever she imagines that people are evaluating her. We look for an early scene:

Ara: I remember. . . . I'm three years old. My brother is a baby. And I wet my pants. Even saying this, I am so ashamed. I don't want to talk about it.

Mary: You sound very sad and ashamed.

Ara: I'm wiped out. (*Sobs for some time*) I'm so humiliated. They put this big dishtowel on me. They say I have to be . . . like that . . . until I change. Until I stop wetting. They both laugh . . . they laugh at me. I'm . . . wiped out.

Bob: Wiped out. Instead of being wiped out, would you this time holler back at them?

Ara: It's no use. I . . . it's a kind of despair I can't even explain.

Bob: Holler back at them.

Ara: Both of you, get off my case. (*Sighs several times, wipes her eyes.*) I don't feel as if I have the strength to yell.

Bob: You do, though.

Mary: Will you tell them it is perfectly OK for a three-year-old to wet her pants?

Ara: Yes, it is OK. Three-year-olds can wet their pants. I can wet my pants. I don't have to be laughed at or put down.

Mary: Feel that?

Ara: No. I feel so hurt.

Mary: Look at your parents. See how you can put them down. After all, they didn't get an A in parenting that day.

Ara: I'll tell them what they did wrong. You are lousy parents, did you know that? You think you are so big, you think you are always right, you mean well, sure . . . hmmm. . . .

Bob: What's the hmmm?

Ara: Hmmm is all that I could do in that situation was stand and take it.

Bob: And now?

Ara: And now that is exactly what I have been doing, standing and taking it. Taking it from other people. In some situations, not all.

Bob: So do something different.

Ara: OK. I sneer and walk off. Yes! (*Laughs*) See, it's them, not me. I'm acting normally for a three-year-old. It is not me, it's you. You are acting crazy, all upset about a little piss. I am not listening to your tirade, your craziness. (*Pause*) I just thought of something. They are 20 and 21 years old when I am three . . . they are ignorant babies coping with two kids. My God, I'm twice as old as they were. And I'm educated. They weren't. I am not allowing my importance to depend on you two ignorant kids. Actually, you did pretty well, considering that you didn't know anything about babies. I'm done. I feel free, really free . . . for the first time I can remember.

Our technique for resolving early shame is to get the shamed client out of the victim role so that she can fight back against the early persecutors, as Ara did when she told her parents they were wrong. Usually, a client fights back in anger, although sometimes she will create a humorous fantasy instead. One woman, who had been made to stand in the corner for being "a smarty" in the third grade, wove a fantasy of putting her teacher in the corner, writing "dummy" across her forehead in red paint, and then forcing her to confess her various stupidities in her dealings with her pupils.

When a client imagines therapy to be a painful process, he may be concerned with having to tell his own shameful behaviors or fantasies from the past. Marv, a quiet, lovely man who has been monogamously married for 25 years, confessed with great shame that he occasionally has homosexual fantasies.

Bob: Congratulations.
Marv: What?
Bob: Congratulations.
Marv: I don't understand.
Bob: I am congratulating you for being free enough to have a full, rich sexual fantasy life. Good for you!
Marv: (*Long pause*) Well. Well. Well. I don't think my colleagues would agree with you.
Bob: Fine. Then don't tell them.
  (*Entire group laughs*)

One of the advantages of group treatment is that all members benefit from each individual's work. This time, after Marv finished, several people brought up secret shames about their sexual fantasies and decided for themselves that their fantasies were all right.

Ben used the group setting to permit himself to dance. He'd danced in high school, been laughed at, and had never danced again.

Ben: I wish I could dance. I'd like to, but I feel ashamed.
Mary: What is your catastrophic expectation . . . the worst thing that could happen?
Ben: People would laugh. (*He tells high school scene*)

Mary: Being laughed at in high school is awful. How about right now?

Ben: I don't know.

Mary: Here is my idea. . . . I learned it from Irma Shepherd and Joen Fagan,[3] the gestalt therapists. The idea is . . . we'll have an awkward dance right now. That means everybody dances as awkwardly as possible. You game for that?

Ben said he was, so we turn on the radio and the group has a wild, hilarious time dancing awkwardly. They continue dancing, this time not awkwardly, and Ben joins in. He is not a good dancer, but he enjoys himself dancing.

GUILT

Guilt, technically, is a judgment rather than an emotion. A person judges self guilty and then experiences sadness, anger, anxiety, or shame. There are three categories of guilty people. Most guilty neurotics rarely do anything hurtful or wrong. In fact, their worst fault is that they use guilt in their child-rearing with the result that their children also grow up guilty. The pseudo-guilty wear their guilt proudly in order to feel honorable and sensitive. They believe that their pseudo-guilt about the starving of the world excuses them from having to send food or money. The third group does harm others, feels guilty, and continues harmful behavior. They may be guilty child abusers.

Whether or not the person who is neurotically guilty is overtly depressed, the first step in treatment is a no-suicide contract. The client is asked to contract that she will not kill herself no matter what she does that she thinks is wrong and no matter how guilty she decides to be. The next step is a redecision to drop her guilt and substitute self-esteem.

1.

May: I feel so guilty. I'm spending $300 a month on tuition alone, $3,600 a year, and I'm not getting my dissertation written.

Mary: I hear you are not writing your dissertation and this is very important for you. I'm willing to work with you so that you'll solve this problem. First, though, 1 think it is important for you to give up your guilt.

May: I don't understand.

Mary: OK. If you stay guilty and we work on the dissertation problem, I predict that you will not write the dissertation in order to feel even more guilty . . . like, now you are spending $300 plus the cost of therapy and you can use this fact to increase your guilt. Or you'll write the dissertation and feel guilty because it isn't good enough. Or you'll write it and find something else to be guilty about.

2.

Ned: I never lose weight. I always stay this fat.

Bob: You are, let's see, about 20 pounds overweight?

Ned: About.

Bob: (*Checks out physical problems and learns that Ned has no health reason to lose weight*) And when you think about being 20 pounds overweight, what do you feel?

Ned: Like a pig . . . guilty as hell.

Bob: My contract for you is that you get to like your body exactly as it is, that you stop harassing yourself, and instead enjoy you. Then, when you've done that, lose weight if you want to.

3.

Pete: I don't seem to be able to give her good sex. I feel very guilty. . . .

Bob: For a start, will you let her be responsible for her own sexual response? And stop being guilty? That is the first contract, while you two play at learning to enjoy sex.

4.

Opal: My son essentially has dropped out of high school and I don't know what to do. I know it has to do with my raising him alone. . . . I feel so guilty.

Mary: I doubt if your guilt will get him back to school.

Opal: I know that.

Mary: So. . . . I recommend that you two get into a family therapy group. And the contract I recommend for you is to get rid of your guilt. I imagine you've been guilty a long time.

For the guilty client, we often suggest what we call "hiring a new accountant."

Jana: I feel guilty. (*Speaks very rapidly*) I planned to do so many things this week and I'm not doing what I should be doing. I should. . . .

Mary: Wait, wait, wait! Hold on! That is not what I have heard from you. You set yourself a lot of goals this week, like sitting at the table with us and chatting with us and getting to know other people. In a very few days I think you have done a lot.

Jana: I could assert myself more easily and get to know people more than I have and. . . . (*She goes on with her intense harangue against herself.*)

Bob: The real problem is your accountant.

Jana: (*Suddenly stops talking and laughs her abrupt laugh.*)

Mary: Understand?

Jana: I keep track of my failures and not my successes.

Mary: Exactly.

Jana: I am just beginning to stop criticizing myself. Every time I wasn't actually working, I used to criticize myself and. . . . (*Now she continues her harangue, this time on the subject of how she used to harangue.*)

Mary: (*Shouting to be heard over Jana's barrage of words*) GOOD FOR YOU RECOGNIZING THAT.

Jana: Yes, I feel much better.

Bob: Would you be willing to fire your accountant, who adds up debits and not credits?

Jana: Yes, I'd love to.

Bob: Tell your accountant.

Jana: Damn you; it's you who's ruining my life. I can't enjoy because you keep hassling about the past, about what kind of impression I'm making, you're. . . . (*She does more harassing. This time she is harassing her internal accountant.*)

Bob: Words, words, words! You don't have to justify to your accountant. All you have to do is fire her. Or him.

Jana: You are terrible. You are making me miserable. You are off
   base, you are not fair. . . .
Bob: You are fired.
Jana: You are fired. (*She said this clearly and slowly.*)
Bob: I like the way you said that.
Jana: I do too.
Bob: Would you like a new accountant?
Jana: Sure.
Bob: Go ahead. Stand up and apply for the job. Tell you how you
   are going to keep the books from now on.
Jana: (*Standing*) I am fair. I am going to look at all the little things
   and all the big things and keep score. Your last accountant had
   no sense of proportion. That is true. She put down all the little
   things she could find to add up against you. And she kept adding
   the same item every month instead of just once. Yeah. I am
   going to give you credit where credit is due. When you do something big. I'm going to give you credit and not just count the
   little things you do wrong. Yes.
Bob: Change chairs. Is that an accountant you'd like to have around?
Jana: Yes. She's fair. Thank you.
Bob: You're welcome.

At a later session, she practices being that accountant and gives
herself specific credit for what she likes about herself.

We ask guilty clients to trace back the history of their guilts.
*"Right now you are being guilty because you somehow consider it
your fault that your grown son is having problems. What were you
guilty about before he was grown?" "Before he was born?" "Before
you were married?" "In high school?" "Grade school?" "When you
were little?"* When a client traces a racket from present to recent
past to past, she stimulates her memory and finds important scenes
in her life. If we jump too quickly to the past, she may not remember. This is also a successful technique with a client who claims to
have no memory of childhood. By going back slowly, the client will
surprise herself at how much she does remember and also may
remember the crucial time in her life when she decided to blot out
her memory of her past.

As the client picks a particular guilty scene for each stage of life, she will recognize both the chronicity and grandiosity of her many guilts. We stop at each important scene and ask her to be there and describe it in the present tense. We may work with any of these scenes in order for the client to give up a particular guilt.

There are many ways of doing this. The client may exaggerate the guilt in order to recognize her grandiosity. She may tell parents that her actions, back then, were normal and then repudiate their guilt messages. She may make fun of the situation. Or, she may merely say, *"Wow, I don't have to be guilty about stealing a silly piece of chalk from that teacher!"*

Ian needed to understand what was going on with his parents, in order to stop taking responsibility and guilt from their divorce.

Ian: My father divorced my mother because of me.
Mary: Be there and imagine the scene.

Ian describes the quarrels, the poverty, and the fact that his father did not want to be tied down to a child. We ask him to be father.

Mary: What is your name, father?
Ian-Father: Michael.
Mary: OK, I want to interview you, Michael. You and your wife have sex, she gets pregnant, and you feel what?
Ian-Michael: Angry. Tied down.
Mary: Interesting. Have you any idea what you felt angry about, tied down about, before Ian was born?
Ian-Michael: No. I don't know.
Mary: Had to be something. You see, if you'd been a happy man, you'd happily have chosen to raise a child or not raise a child. Whatever. Somehow you knew how to feel tied down, angry, and then to split. Make up what happens when you were little. . . .
Ian-Michael: Very strange. I never thought of all that. I . . . am my father. I was always the no-good member of the family. Everyone said so.
Ian: (*Returns to Ian's chair*) Of course, you were the no-good person . . . you never really had a chance. Your family hated you and mother was the martyr. Of all the men she could have

picked, she picks one who'll leave her. Of course. I never thought
of all that. Well, you two, I didn't have anything to do with
your desertion or your martyrdom. And I am not guilty.

A parent-interview is an effective way to resolve a child's sense of
responsibility for a parent's problem. Our goal for Ian is for him
to know in his guts that he was a lovable child (as are all children)
even though his father didn't love him.

As Hannah traces back her history of guilt, she finds countless
guilts at every age, all trivial. Mary asks, *"And when you were very
little?"* and she begins to sob.

Hannah tells of being forced to pray at her father's bedside as he
lay dying. She gets up, runs outside, and he dies while she is playing. She is five years old. We ask her if she is willing to get to know
that little girl better than she now seems to know her. When she
agrees, we set up a scene in which she, the age she is now, interviews
little Hannah. We ask her to see the child, describe her, then find
out what is going on inside Hannah. She discovers, of course, that
the child is frightened and doesn't understand death. Hannah begins to weep and her voice becomes gentle as she talks to little
Hannah. We ask her what she is willing to say and do for little
Hannah right now, so that Hannah won't have to grow up guilty.
She balks, is flustered, then lets herself tell Hannah that she is a lovely,
normal little girl and that it was all right for her to be playing. In
fact, her father probably would have preferred her playing rather
than praying and, anyway, her playing had nothing to do with his
dying.

After asking about guilt *"when you were very little,"* we ask guilty
clients, *"What were you guilty about when you were born?"* Almost
always, we find the original guilt in the birth myth.

An obstetrician, who at this stage in his life certainly is an expert
on childbirth, is asked about the myth of his birth. He is a very
guilty client, who has a strange laugh. He gives a *"Ho, ho, ho"* while
sucking in his breath instead of exhaling.

Jeff: Well, my mother was a hysteric. . . . You know, the old family
    martyr stories. How she was all torn up. . . .
Bob: Be her. Here, sit on this chair in front of Jeff. Sit the way you

sit, Mother. And get your own typical expression on your face, Mother. That's it. Now tell Jeff about *"all torn up."*

Jeff-Mother: You tore me up. You came too fast and tore me up.

Bob: Be Jeff.

Jeff: (*Returns to his own seat and sits sadly, not speaking.*)

Bob: Respond.

Jeff: I don't know what to say.

Bob: Ask her whose uterine muscles did the pushing?

Jeff: I . . . (*Bursts out laughing, a full, exhaling laugh*) I didn't know that I believed. . . . Hey, Ma, your muscles, by damn, did the pushing!

To read this unskeptically would be difficult for a therapist who has not experienced emotionally some of her own irrational Child beliefs. This man, who knows all about babies and uterine muscles, still believed in his Child that he did something wrong in that he tore his mother. Little children do not understand the mystery of birth even in enlightened households. They tend to believe what they are told: *"You came along."* This is more nebulous than the stork or cabbage stories and equally incorrect. Yet almost everyone uses those words:

Jean: Well, the problem was, I came along only 10 months after my brother was born.

Mary: Such strange words. Picture the scene. There is your little brother sitting in his play pen. Somehow he was smart enough to come along at the right time. Now imagine this stubborn baby girl, one day old, crawling up to the front door, holding her tiny suitcase in her teeth, defiantly coming into the house in spite of the "no vacancy" sign.

Jean: That's exactly how I felt.

Mary: Well, it's bullshit, isn't it? Will you ask them who fucked carelessly?

Bob lists three causes of "original guilt": born at all, born intrinsically wrong, and born at the wrong time. Some believe they should never have been born because no child was wanted by their parents. Others believe they'd have been wanted if only there hadn't been something wrong with them. These people were born the wrong sex, too dark or too light for their families, or with a congenital defect such as blindness, Down's syndrome, or cerebral palsy. Others, like Jean, "came along" too early or too late in the lives of their mothers and fathers. The child accepts the blame.

Lea is working to drop her guilt for having been born at all:

Lea: If I hadn't been born, you would have been a lot happier.

Mary: Say, *"It's all my fault for being born."*

Lea: No, it's not all my fault. Even if I hadn't come along, mother would still be miserable and alcoholic and Aunt Ris would still be taking care of people and wearing herself out, but at least it wouldn't be me.

Mary: You're saying it's all my fault I was born.

Lea: It is all my fault.

Mary: That's where you're stuck, isn't it? That little girl really believes it was all her fault she was born.

Lea: (*Nods*)

Bob: Test out: *"It's all my fault I was conceived."*

Lea: (*Laughing*) No.

Bob: Then where are you with it's all your fault you were born?

Lea: It's really not.

Bob: Ready to drop that load of guilt?

Lea: Yeah.

Bob: For the rest of your life?

Lea: Yeah. You know, I can remember when I was only four or five years old, going out and sitting alone in the pasture and wishing I were dead, because I felt like I made everyone sad.

Bob: I hear you. (*Bob is drawing the sperm and egg, with the notation, "I didn't do it!" He autographs it, tears off the sheet and hands it to her.* See Figure 23.) This is my famous $200 painting. You got a bargain. It costs $400 at one-week workshops and $1200 at four-week workshops. Hang it in your bathroom or somewhere and everytime you feel guilty about anything, go look at the picture.

Bob has given this picture to hundreds of guilty clients. On each picture, he writes the client's redecision and then autographs it.

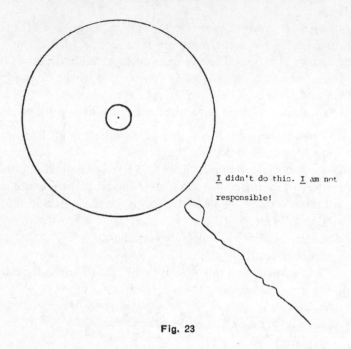

I didn't do this. I am not responsible!

Fig. 23

The pseudo-guilty, who use guilt in place of action, may have exactly the same behavioral problems as the guilty. They may be overweight, procrastinate in writing dissertations, have sons who have dropped out of school, or not have a good sex life. They work at maneuvering therapists into agreeing with their "shoulds" and then will passively or actively rebel against the therapist. These clients are very difficult for Parental therapists, who may begin by working with the client to feel less guilty and then, on realizing that the client is not changing her behavior, will attempt to get the client to be more guilty.

Sue is a Ph.D. candidate who is not writing her dissertation:

Sue: I feel guilty. I really, really do. ("Really" is a Child word, used to convince skeptical parents.) I just don't seem to get started.
Mary: Take both sides. First, *"I don't want to write."*
Sue: (*Gives reasons why it is a lot of work and recognizes she doesn't want to work hard.*)

Mary: OK. Now take, *"I want to write."*

Sue: That's easy. (*She does not take the "I want to write" side but takes the "I want to have a Ph.D." side.*)

Mary: Test out, *"I won't write."*

Sue: I won't write and you can't make me. Wow. Yeah. Nobody can make me.

She becomes aware of the force of her struggle against pleasing parents, in her head and in reality. Her living parents are paying her tuition, while urging her to finish her Ph.D.

The differences between Sue and May (the two women who are not writing their Ph.D. dissertations) are subtle and involve the quality of their guilt. Sue tends to wave hers like a banner and also, in a childlike way, delights in being guilty. May feels very guilty and her energy is bound up in her self-depreciation. The question before Sue at this point is what she, autonomously, chooses to do about getting herself a Ph.D. Her pseudo-guilt is irrelevant. We won't join her parents in urging her to finish nor will we analyze, and thereby stroke, her guilt.

For clients who claim to be guilty about the state of the world, but give neither time nor money toward improving conditions, we agree with labor leader Harry Bridges, *"Put up or shut up."* For those who do work for world improvements, enthusiasm is a more pleasant motivation than guilt.

When a guilty client is destructive to others, we work only with the contract to cease destructive actions.

Bry: I don't mean to spank the kids. I feel guilty.

Bob: I believe you believe you. I don't believe you. Take the side, *"I mean to spank the kids."*

Bry: (*Long pause*) I don't mean to.

Bob: You hit them. You don't hit them during an epileptic seizure. You aim at them and hit them.

Bry: I . . . I get mad at them. I want them to stop making so much noise. I want them to do what I say. They won't go to bed until I explode and spank them.

Bob: So you mean to hit them. I'd like you to find out you don't have to hit kids. Would you for the next week divorce yourself entirely from the discipline of your kids? If you start to mean to hit them, leave the room, leave the house, or whatever. AND NOT HIT THEM FOR ANY REASON?

Bry: I think I could do that.

Bob: I think you could, too. Will you do that?

Bry: Yes. I'm in conflict. . . . I have not controlled myself well in the past. A part of me says I may get too provoked.

Bob: Will you decide you won't hurt your children no matter what they do to attempt to provoke you? Or how provoked you decide to be?

Bry: Yes.

Bob: Fine.

Mary: They have been involved for a long time in your Persecutor-Victim games with them. They won't understand your change and they'll probably behave worse and worse for a while. Like, they now know that they are not supposed to go to bed until you've hit them. They've been trained not to go to bed when they are sleepy, not even to know when they are sleepy, and instead to go to bed after you have been abusive. Do you understand that?

Bry: I'd never thought of it that way . . . yeah.

Mary: So what will you do, while they are retraining themselves?

Bry: I don't know. (*Pause. He seems to be waiting for suggestions.*) What if they don't get enough sleep?

Mary: I don't think that is as harmful as being hit. Whether they get enough sleep or not, you can get enough sleep.

Bry: I see that it will be a hard job. I do feel some relief at the idea of not being the family ogre. OK. I have no good ideas what I'll do. But I won't spank them. I won't hurt them.

Bry was a guilty child abuser,* who considered himself a good father because he earned an adequate living, was monogamous, and wanted what was best for his children. Later, to solidify his contract into a redecision, he went back into childhood scenes and vented his rage at his father, who was also a child abuser. In that scene he said, *"I am never again going to be a brute like you!"*

---

* We consider anyone who physically hurts a child unnecessarily (surgical procedures and inoculations are necessary) to be a child abuser.

We believe clients can control their destructive actions . . . child abuse, shoplifting, spouse-beating, or any other activity that hurts someone else. Further, therapists who "try to treat" while condoning such behavior are giving the secret message to their clients that the clients are victims of themselves or their circumstances. Such therapists are condoning the acting-out of the client by not demanding firm contracts against such behavior.

REGRET

Regret is one of the most solemn and solid of rackets. It is indulged in by people who were taught to walk backwards through life, focusing unhappily on what wasn't to the exclusion of what is or could be. When the regretful person does glance toward the future, she does this to remind herself that she will always remain as she is, backwards. *"I'll always regret that I had no son," "didn't go to college," "was cheated out of my adolescence," "married," "didn't marry."*

Among our many regretful clients, Sally took first prize. She was responding to a life-script questionnaire that contained the following: *"Imagine that you have reached the end of your lifetime. How old are you? Look back over your life and summarize it in a phrase or a sentence."* Sally said, *"I imagine I am 86 and the summary that came to me is, 'I regret that I spent so many years regretting my marriage before I finally got a divorce.'"* This translates that she plans to die regretting and will even be regretting her regretting.

In treating a regretful client, we begin as we do with blamers by asking her to set up a group of empty chairs for all the grown-up relatives she's ever known. She'll be each one in turn, sit in the relative's chair, and begin with, *"I am so and so and I regret. . . ."* or *"I am so and so and I have no regrets."* The client may come from a family in which all members of both sides of the family tree are regretful, or from a family in which just one side regrets or in which just the females or just the males regret. The client may then draw a family "regret tree."

She may enlarge on the subject by being each family member again and adopting the perfect regretful pose, stance, tone of voice, as she describes the regret in detail. She may tell the other members what they are supposed to do for the regretful one: *"I am father and I regret I couldn't go to college because I married young and had to support you children. Therefore, you are to repay me by honoring my regret, by feeling guilty that you caused it, and by doing everything I tell you to do."* She may, as the regretful one, say what she is excused from doing in repayment for regretting: *"I'm grandmother and I regret leaving Armenia and therefore I am excused from learning to speak English. Mostly, I'm excused from ever being happy."*

We use this approach so that the client will realize that regret is a learned rather than natural response. We want the client to know this affectively, by becoming disgusted or amused. We may suggest that she go back into the scene, visualize them all regretting, and tell each that she's no longer a regretful person. Then she may tell them what she is doing and experiencing instead. She may watch and listen to them regret as she fantasies skipping out of the house to play. She may fantasy an object that will be to her the essence of regretfulness. One client imagined a dirty, torn diary full of tearstained pages. We suggest that each time she begins to regret, she instead fantasize giving that diary to one of her regretting forebears.

Sometimes we will work with the magic in regret: *"If I regret long enough and hard enough, what will happen?"* The basic Child magic is that God or Fate will change the past or will take her back to the past so that she can do it over. Regret may also be used magically in place of self-blame or as a defense against blame by others. It is certainly used to keep the person from enjoying the present.

People who have been taught since childhood to regret their actions have great difficulty in making life choices. They have internalized family slogans such as, *"Think carefully or you'll regret it the rest of your life,"* *"If you make your bed, you have to lie in it,"* or *"You're old enough now to be free to make your own mistakes."* One of the most-used words by regretting clients is *"mistake"* rather than *"choice."* The Parental admonition is, *"Be right!"* and the Child warning is, *"Don't do anything . . . so you won't regret your decision."* The injunction, then, is *"Don't."*

Dave has a small farm and also a paraprofessional job in a state hospital. He says he is attending the marathon in order to make one of these decisions: keep on farming and working as he is now, sell the farm to pay for graduate school education in psychology, or resign from the hospital and devote full time to farming. Instead of choosing, he obsesses because, *"I'm afraid that whatever I choose, I'll live to regret it."*

We ask him to pretend it is five, 10 and then 15 years from today and imagine his life, using his three choices, one at a time. As he does this, he recognizes that he plans to regret no matter which choice he makes. Each choice, as he lives it in fantasy, seems less attractive than the choices he rejected. When he understands this, he retells all three choices from a happy position and decides, on an Adult level, that he will be happy in his choices. We refer him to a local therapist for "practicing being happy." Currently he and his wife are enjoying themselves as they combine farming with a new occupation, repairing antique furniture.

When the person, place, job, or opportunity is gone forever, the client may be regretting in place of saying goodbye. In such cases, we use the techniques described in the next chapter, Goodbyes.

CHAPTER 7

Goodbyes

Bob writes, "When I attended my mother's funeral, I first wondered if they had the wrong woman. She was being called by her formal, official first name, which she had never used. Then I wondered if the funeral was in honor of this woman with the formal name or whether it was in honor of Jesus. I decided the latter, because the woman's name was mentioned only twice while Jesus was mentioned repeatedly. I wondered why the essential fact was overlooked: She who lived on this earth is now dead. I wondered why the funeral service concentrated on the possible life after death, while ignoring the fact of death in this life. I wondered why we allowed ourselves to listen to formal words and why none of us was given an opportunity to speak. I decided this was one hell of a way to say goodbye. Later, I said my own goodbye to Mimi Goulding, while burying her ashes on our property beside a new redwood tree I planted in her memory."

Many clients need assistance in saying goodbye. We learned from Fritz Perls[1] the value of creating fantasied ceremonies for this purpose and have since devised a formula for goodbyes: 1) Facts, 2) Unfinished business, 3) Goodbye ceremony, 4) Mourning, and 5) Hello to today.

The fact of death is obvious, except in the very rare cases when the body is not recovered. And yet, in spite of the facts, people have magical ways of denying death. They attend the funeral while busying themselves with details of housing and feeding other mourners; they let the service itself distract them from the fact of death; or they don't attend the funeral in order to pretend the death did not occur. After the funeral, they play "If only": *"If only we'd insisted she see a doctor." "If only I'd had a chance to see her one more time."* They behave like Queen Victoria, who supposedly kept Prince Albert's clothing and toilet water always fresh and ready for him. They talk to the dead and pretend that the dead can hear and even respond.

Clients who do not say goodbye keep a part of their energy locked in yesterdays. They may refuse intimacy in the present and experience extreme difficulties with current "hellos" and "goodbyes." The first task, then, is for the client to accept the facts:

1

Judy: I just can't say goodbye until I know for sure whether he died of a heart attack or committed suicide.
Bob: It's irrelevant.
Judy: No, I . . .
Bob: How he died is irrelevant. It makes no difference. The only thing that is relevant is that your father is dead and has been dead for 20 years.

2

Tom: Sometimes I think I see her . . . in a crowd.
Bob: You lie to yourself to pretend she isn't dead. She's dead.

3

Maris: I think I've said goodbye.

Mary: I don't. You are still wearing your wedding ring. I used to say that wearing a ring is a way of not saying goodbye, but that this is OK for little old ladies. Now that I am edging closer to being a little old lady, I know my words were discounts. A person of any age says goodbye in order to give herself the opportunity to say hello to the living.

Sometimes a client will deny the fact of death even while thinking she is saying goodbye:

Ann: I want to . . . to say goodbye to my uncle. My uncle died the day I graduated from college and I didn't acknowledge his death. He'd always been so far away. . . . I pretended he didn't die. I thought I'd said goodbye until last week, when a friend died. And I became very sad about my uncle too. That was when I realized I was holding on.

Mary: How are you holding on?

Ann: I don't know. . . . I don't know that this has any effect on my life.

Mary: Any unfinished business with him?

Ann: No.

Mary realizes she slid through this part too quickly, so she sets up with her a scene in which Ann can tell her uncle her unfinished business:

Mary: Will you go back to a time when he was still alive and see him and describe the scene?

Ann: I'm playing tennis with him. We're out in the street batting the ball back and forth.

Mary: Is this a child scene or a recent scene?

Ann: Child. 'Cause I didn't see him again until I was 14. And it was only with his family in a restaurant.

Mary: OK. In your scene, will you stop playing tennis for a minute and tell him what he means to you.

Ann: Uncle, you mean a lot to me. I've heard a lot about you from

my mother and I admire you a lot. You played with me. You're
so healthy. . . . I want to take care of you. No, I wasn't thinking
of that then. I want you to be my Daddy. You always seem so
happy, you take time to play. I only get to spend a little bit of
time with you 'cause you live in Canada and I am in England.
I want you to spend more time with me. I know you have two
daughters of your own. They don't play ball with you as much
as I do. You told me that. I spend time with you. I love you.
I'm sorry we don't have lots of time.

Mary: Now will you move up to the last time you saw him.

Ann: You look a lot older. He's had one heart attack. He was still
smoking and working hard and not taking care of himself.

Mary: Where do you see him?

Ann: In a restaurant.

Bob: Tell him what's unfinished.

Ann: I want you to take care of yourself.

Bob: Tell him, "I'm angry you don't take care of yourself."

Ann: I'm angry. You have two daughters who love you and a niece
who loves you. . . . I don't want you to kill yourself!

Mary: Any other angers?

Ann: I'm angry you didn't come see me more. And I know you
couldn't.

Mary: Any other angers?

Ann: No.

Mary: Appreciations?

Ann: I appreciate that you have spent time with me . . . that you
enjoyed being with me. Going to museums with you. . . . I
appreciate that you loved England too, that you . . . that you
were good to my mother. A good brother. I loved you. I wanted
you for a Dad. I miss you.

Mary: Are you saying goodbye?

Ann: Goodbye.

Bob: What are you experiencing? (*She is not showing feeling and is
rushing her goodbye.*)

Ann: Relaxed. My stomach was uptight. When I said goodbye, I
could see him walking away.

Mary: See him dead. He can't walk. He's dead.

Ann: Yeah.

Bob: Did you go to the funeral?
Ann: No. He died in Canada.
Bob: Will you transport yourself to Canada, to the funeral?
Ann: (*Nods*)
Bob: See the casket.
Ann: (*Nods*)
Bob: See him in the casket. Fantasize what he looks like, see him dead.
Ann: I can't see him. All I see is a gray casket.
Bob: Get him in it.
Ann: I'm shaky.
Bob: He's dead. See him.
Ann: (*Screams, then sobs for several minutes*) I'll miss you. You know that.
Mary: He knows nothing. He's dead.
Ann: (*Sobs again, for some time*) I miss you. I miss you. (*Long pause*) And you are dead. Goodbye, dead uncle.
Bob: OK?
Ann: I'd carried a lot of wishes. Thank you. Yes.

In this scene, Ann kept insisting on his being alive. *"I could see him walking away," "I can't see him (dead)"* and *"You know that."* For an effective goodbye, the client accepts the fact that the person is dead in this life and does not walk, talk, or know.

When a client accepts the facts of death, we ask what unfinished business with the dead is used by her to prevent herself from saying goodbye. We suggest she finish, by giving appreciations and resentments. The client chooses a scene when the person was still alive, in order that she not pretend to talk to the dead. Clients usually begin with appreciations. If the client still resents, we will work with her in order that she recognize that she is still magically asking the dead person to change . . . in the past. Part of the unfinished business, then, is the giving up of the magical hope for a better relationship.

If the only resentment is that the person died, we ask the client to move into a "goodbye" scene and to imagine the funeral.

Joe: I resent you died. 1 am angry that you died. . . .

Mary: Wait a moment. Now is the time to see him in his coffin. Will
you do that? See the coffin and open the lid.
Joe: (*Reaches out and pretends he is opening the coffin*)
Mary: Now . . . he's dead and you are talking for you, not for him.
He can't hear you. Tell your anger for your sake.
Joe: I'm angry. It's not your fault . . . you didn't want to die . . .
and I'm angry, angry! And very sad. (*Weeps*)

When unfinished business is completed, we ask the client to fantasize the goodbye ceremony, usually the funeral and burial. Essential to the goodbye is that the client fantasize that the person is dead,
say, "*You are dead*," and say "*Goodbye*."

A mourning process may be unnecessary if the death occurred
long ago. For Ann, a few tears were enough and then she felt relief
that she had said goodbye to an uncle who had been more fantasy
than reality and who had been dead a long time. When death is
recent, the client will mourn for whatever time is right for her. We
want her to know that the purpose of mourning is to solidify the
goodbye and to free her energy for her own present life.

As mourning is finished, the person needs a renewed interest in
today. Unfortunately, our society often gives flowers, comfort, and
company during the time of bereavement and then leaves the be-
reaved alone before the mourning stage is finished. It is during this
period that the client needs support in seeking strokes and finding
activities. Group members can be helpful, as can old-fashioned "social work," in which problem-solving is the focus.

Sometimes a client wants to say goodbye to someone he has never
met, the mother who gave him for adoption or the father who deserted when he was an infant. While asking the facts, we want also
to know his fantasies. "*What did they tell you about your father?*"
and "*What did you make up about him?*" A child may have given
himself important positive strokes and literally saved his own life
by imagining, somewhere out in the world, a father who really loved
him. If so, we ask the client to say goodbye to the father while still
continuing to stroke himself as he imagined his father would stroke
him.

Mort: (*To fantasied father*) My mother would never tell me about you. I sometimes wonder if she really had more than one fuck with you. All I know is that you were in the Army. . . . I don't even know that. She says you were killed in the war. I don't believe her anymore. There are no pictures, no papers.

Mary: Tell him your fantasies about him when you were a kid.

Mort: Oh. That's embarrassing. I thought you were the perfect hero . . . that's how I got my suicidal stuff, wanting to die a hero like you. Well, that's long over. I thought of you as loving . . . loving me.

Mort continues, saying his resentments for never having known this mystery father. He states that he appreciates that his life resulted from this man's sperm.

Mary: Now will you see yourself as a little kid, a kid who has invented a loving hero for a father. And tell that little kid that you'll take over . . . you'll be your own loving father. . . .

Mort holds and loves the little boy who was himself. He also reaffirms his no-suicide position and tells the little kid he'll protect him.

When a child dies, we urge parents to say goodbye and not make a shrine of the child's room or belongings. Failure to say goodbye may give their other children the message that none of them is as valuable as the dead one. If the living children cannot be as good or as loved as the dead child, they may decide that the only way to be loved is to be dead. While saying goodbye to a dead child, parents may choose to say goodbye both to the actual child and to their fantasies of what this child would have become.

Before adoption, we urge parents to say goodbye to the biological children they will not have and mourn rather than repress or deny their feelings. This frees them from past hopes and longings so that they can truly accept the adopted child.

When a client won't say goodbye, one method is to have him take both sides: *"I'll never say goodbye to you"* and *"I'll say goodbye to you"* and find out the advantages and disadvantages of each position.

A client who isn't saying goodbye may have decided in childhood not to say goodbye to someone who died then. One woman was not allowing herself to feel her goodbye to her husband. When we asked if anyone had died when she was little, she recalled going to a neighbor's home to play instead of going to her grandfather's funeral. She went through a goodbye funeral fantasy for grandfather and then said the important goodbye to her dead husband.

Some clients do not say goodbye because they come from families who mourn forever. An American client of Greek heritage, refusing to say goodbye, recognized that her mother and grandmother had been perpetual mourners. She told her mother, in fantasy, that she was going to say goodbye even though none of her ancestors would understand this. She lined up 5,000 years of Greek ancestral women, visualizing them stretching across the plains of Sparta, all dressed in black, and she shouted at them through the centuries, *"Hey, you silly old ladies! I am done with mourning! I am becoming a female Zorba!"* She said her goodbyes and ended with a Greek dance.

Couples who separate may need to say goodbye, especially if they are still "attached" to each other through the custody or property games they play or the injunctions they continue to accept. The client with a "Don't exist" message in childhood may hang onto an ex-spouse in such a way that the ex-spouse wishes he were dead. The "Don't be close" client doesn't finalize a divorce in order to remain lonely and alone. The "Don't grow" client keeps holding onto the ex-spouse to solve his problems, while the "Don't be a child" client tells ex-spouse, *"If anything goes wrong or if you get too depressed, I'll always be available."*

Sue: There's nothing I can do. He keeps phoning me, and. . . .
Bob: You must have a very strange telephone. One that sticks to your hand so you can't hang up.
    (*Group members laugh.*)
Sue: I see the point, but. . .
Bob: *But*. But you are going to keep talking to him and being angry just as long as he dials your number.
Sue: Well, you shouldn't just . . . give up on somebody.
Bob: Shut your eyes and repeat that statement. *"You shouldn't just give up on somebody."* See how that fits your past.

Sue found she was doing for her ex-husband what she had attempted, as a small child, to do for her father. She worked unsuccessfully to make them both happy. When she redecided to skip outside to play, leaving her father to drink if he chose, she decided that she was no longer in charge of her ex-husband's depressions. She gave up "trying to help" and being angry at her failures.

Clients may postpone goodbyes by hiring ineffectual therapists or attorneys. They forget that attorneys and therapists are their employees and instead behave toward them as if they were all-powerful parents. We remind clients of their rights to competent lawyers and therapists who work effectively and quickly for the client.

After the facts are recognized and accepted, the client is ready to say goodbye. An ideal method is to have both partners and all children present. The partners will say their resentments and their appreciations, including how each has grown through knowing the other. They may mourn that the dream of a perpetual, productive, happy marriage is not their reality. They recognize that the end of a relationship is not a failure but a choice. They see divorce as a beginning as well as an ending. They may never meet again, they may meet whenever one partner comes to pick up the children for a weekend, or they may meet for important family occasions such as graduations and marriages. Part of the goodbye will include acceptance that neither has responsibility for the other and that each is giving up any investment in the life of the other.

In this ideal goodbye, the children also give appreciations and resentments. The children are told by both parents that the separation is permanent, that the children did not cause the parents' problems, and that there is no way that the children or anyone else can bring about a reconciliation. Dad and Mom will never reunite. For the future health of the children, it is tremendously important that they are told this as often as necessary until they understand.

As the children take part in their parents' goodbyes, they do not say goodbye to either, but may say goodbye to the family as they previously experienced it. They are encouraged to recognize and state their feelings and they are supported in their mourning.

If the parents are unwilling to arrange such a goodbye, one of them, with the children if possible, may say goodbye in fantasy. After divorced clients say goodbye, we suggest that the "hello to today" include a party as soon as the client is ready. Some clients give themselves a special gift, one that they would not have received during marriage, such as a painting or phonograph record that the ex-spouse wouldn't have liked. They take vacations or join organizations that support a current interest. Each gift says, "I am special to me. I am not a victim."

Such goodbyes are appropriate for all couples, heterosexual and homosexual, married or not, when they terminate their relationship. Other clients cling to the past by refusing to say goodbye to their country of origin. *The San Francisco Chronicle* ran a feature story about an 86-year-old man who fled from Russia in 1919. He stated in the interview, *"I know the monarchy will be reestablished. I just hope it happens while I am still alive."* For almost 50 years, he had refused to say goodbye. All over the world, there are people who cling to such delusions and, in so doing, deny themselves an attachment to their adopted countries. Again, we ask for the facts and, when the client says he is not going to reestablish himself in his childhood country, we ask if he is ready to acknowledge this by saying goodbye. He sets up the goodbye scene that is meaningful to him. He may visualize the family home and the relatives who were living there. Whatever scene he chooses, we ask him to tell this place and these people his unfinished business with them, resentments and appreciations. He tells the old home what is good in his present home and what he will do differently as a result of saying goodbye.

Katie remained depressed for months, refusing to say goodbye to the home in the East which she and her husband had sold when he was drafted during the war in Vietnam. She maintained that she had no choice but to come to California. We pointed out that she could choose to live almost anywhere, although her husband's choices seemed to be restricted to California, Canada, Sweden, or perhaps prison. Before saying goodbye, it was important that she stop defining herself as a victim. Her choices:

1. Stay in the East and be happy.
2. Stay in the East and be sad.
3. Come to California with her husband and be happy.
4. Come to California with her husband and be sad.

She recognized that she had considered that her only choice was No. 4.

Three weeks later she decided to say goodbye to her home in the East. She described her ex-home to the group, walked through it in fantasy, and said goodbye. She was then energized to find a good life in California.

Ex-priests say goodbye to the priesthood, career military officers to the Armed Forces, and retired men and women to the jobs they held. All do this in order to reinvest their energy in the present.

Some say goodbye to dreams they cannot fulfill, such as becoming president of the company. One of our therapist friends spent three years unsuccessfully attempting to gain admittance to a medical school and then decided to accept an appointment to a graduate school in psychology. In his goodbye scene, he pictured the letters "M.D." twelve feet high, in gold, encrusted with diamonds and other beautiful stones. He told these letters how much he wanted them after his name and how resentful he was that he would never have them. He let himself experience anger and grief. Then he said, "Yeah, and I will be doing the same good work as a therapist whether I'm an M.D. or Ph.D. And I won't have to learn all the stupid names of all the parts of the body or deliver babies or stitch up people just to get to be a psychiatrist." He imagined the letters shrinking to a tiny size, then ground them into the carpet.

We suggest goodbyes to loss of parts of body or body functions whenever the person exaggerates or minimizes the loss. One man continued to play football after an amputation and thereby kept re-injuring his stump. Another applied for Aid to the Disabled. Both needed to say goodbye in order to say hello to themselves as men who had lost a leg and nevertheless had potentially rich lives.

A woman, following a mastectomy, refused to undress in front of her husband. We learned that both conspired not to discuss the surgery and no longer physically touched each other. They were both phobic about injury and scarring. Together they said goodbye to her breast and renewed their interest in sexual intimacies.

Goodbyes are important for all who live in the past, in what was or might have been. When the goodbyes are said, the person returns to the present with energy for commitment to today and to the changes he wants to make in the *now*.

CHAPTER 8

Redecisions

THE REDECISION SCENE

In redecision work, the client and therapist set up a scene, much as in a stage drama. The scene may be: 1) the present scene, 2) a recent scene, 3) an early scene, 4) an imaginary scene, or 5) a combination of scenes.

THE PRESENT SCENE is one that is occurring at the moment in the therapy room.

Lee: Joy, I want to work something out with you. My inclination is to be somewhat intimidated and want to please. I . . . ah . . . I was annoyed when you insisted I listen to your tapes when I was planning to go to the beach. So I stayed here with you yesterday . . . and was . . . ah . . . annoyed. (*He is moving to a recent scene.*)

Group Member: Lee, I'm struck by how you are compressing your breathing when you talk.

Lee: OK. Anyway, I . . . I guess there isn't anything further I want now. I . . . ah . . . let you spoil my fun. Yes, there is . . . I want to stop letting people spoil my fun. (*Again, Lee is moving out of the here and now, this time to an unspecified future.*)

Group Member: You are choking yourself even more in your breathing.

Bob: (*Deciding to keep Lee in the present scene*) Lee, stand up. Now breath deep and growl at Joy.

Lee: My feeling is that . . . ah . . . just . . . you don't yell at people.

Bob: (*Hearing "You don't yell," the Parental command*) Disobey that command, that Parental command that says, Lee, don't yell at people.

Lee: (*Stands*) rrrrrr . . . aahhhhh . . . grrrrrrr (*He grins*) RRRRAR-RRRAAARRRR. GRRRRRRRR.

Bob: Now put words to it.

Lee: Joy, WHEN YOU TOLD ME TO MEET WITH YOU, I FELT COMMANDED! (*He is bellowing deeply and the group is laughing in appreciation*) I WILL YELL WHEN I WANT TO AND I WILL GO TO THE BEACH AND I WILL NOT BE NICE TO PRETTY GIRLS LIKE YOU JUST BECAUSE MY MOTHER TOLD ME TO. I WILL DO WHAT I WANT. Thank you. THANK YOU. ARRRRRRR. . . . GRRRRRRR. I AM WONDERFULLY LOUD AND I COULD GO ON ALL DAY! I feel superb.

In this piece of redecision work, Lee could use the present, because his "protagonist" was in the room. Since his injunctions, "*Don't be a child*" and "*Don't want,*" plus his counter-injunctions, "*Be polite*" and "*Don't yell,*" militate against his making a direct confrontation on his own behalf, it was particularly important for him to dare to fight back in the present.

Zoe also used the workshop group in the present to support her redecision. As a child she had accepted the parent-given attribution, "Our little timid one." When she contracts to become exciting and excited rather than timid, the group arranges a fantasy party as a scene in which she can redecide. She's sent from the room and told to return in 60 seconds. When she approaches the workshop room, she hears a loud party inside. The group are pantomiming a children's party, playing games, turning somersaults, and shouting loudly to each other. Zoe knocks timidly and no one answers. She knocks again. The noise increases. Finally, Zoe opens the door. Group members continue to play, ignoring her. Twice Mary reminds her that she wants to behave differently than she behaved in the past. Zoe joins in, pretending to play "Keep-away." Someone passes out imaginary horns and leaves Zoe out. When she demands a horn and toots triumphantly, the group sings "Happy Birthday" to Zoe.

We also use the present in third degree impasse work, when the person, without creating a specific scene, simply expresses the opposing parts of self. Philippe was discouraged about his ability to learn our form of therapy:

Mary: OK. Use two chairs. In one chair be smart Philippe, who is learning. In the other chair be the Philippe who supposedly is not learning TA/gestalt.

Philippe: OK. I am smart. I learn. I like to enjoy. I like to make learning a fun experience. Yes, right. I do learn very quickly. When I am 12, I am sent to live in England one summer only and I make friends and I learn their language very quickly. I learn well. If I can learn English in three months, I can learn TA/gestalt in two months.

Philippe: (*Sits in other chair*) I am harassing myself. I am sure I am not going to be a good therapist. Others are much better than I am. I just can't figure anything out. I feel like I am running and I am far behind and I am choking and I don't have air and I'll never catch up. I am running hard, so hard, to be first . . . at the head of the line.

Mary: If I am not first, at the head of the line, the best in the world, I am no good.

Philippe: If I am not first. . . . (*Bursts into laughter*) Yes! Really! Of course! (*Goes back to own seat*) Case closed!

We treat many clients who believe that if they are not the best, they are nothing. Philippe seemed to redecide very easily. Others say, "Of course, I have to be first!" Like Caesar, who would not be second in Rome, they may put a life and death value on the struggle and be unhappy throughout the struggle. Such clients need considerably more work, including no-suicide decisions if they do not reach their goals. They may work in many scenes, clarifying their positions and making redecisions, before they are willing to enjoy the successes they have, enjoy improving themselves, and stop disparaging themselves for not being the very best in their fields.

When treating clients with somatic complaints we work in the present, while they are experiencing their symptoms.

Troy: I have a headache.

Bob: I'll work with you. During the work, pretend there is no physical basis for your headache. If you don't stop your headache or if you have other symptoms, let me know. OK, be your headache and describe yourself.

Troy: I am large, spreading. I spread over Troy's head . . . over the top of Troy's head. I . . . like, I contain him. . . .

Bob: Be you.

Troy: Go away.

Bob: Be your headache.

Troy: I won't go away.

Bob: Headache, you said you contain Troy. Say more on that.

Troy: I wrap around you, I contain . . . this is . . . I want to say I am almost like a caress.

Bob: I caress Troy. Switch.

Troy: I just thought of something. I used to have lots of headaches. When I was a kid. I'd get to stay home from school and my mother would rub my head. Well, headache . . . my headache's gone! (*Smiles*) I think I was lonely here, coming to this workshop alone. Well, vanished headache, I do not need to stay home and be caressed. So I'm not inviting you back. (*Laughs*)

Troy stopped his headache very quickly. Usually a client requires more time. As a client continues the double-chair dialogue, we ask if the headache is the same, more painful, or less painful. If the pain increases or stays the same, we may switch scenes by asking him to visualize who might be sitting in the headache's chair, saying the words the headache used. Then we suggest he dialogue with that person. If the technique is unsuccessful, we advise he seek medical attention.

RECENT SCENE

Lee might have recreated the scene with Joy, when she asks him to listen to tapes rather than go to the beach. Zoe might have presented a recent scene, at home or at work, where she behaved timidly and that scene could be used for redecision. Philippe might have returned in fantasy to the last time he was leading a therapy group.

Greg, like Philippe, was concerned about his work as a therapist. He describes his client and brings the recent scene into the here and now.

Greg: She's stuck. She's staring at the floor. And I am just as stuck. I don't know what to do for her.

Bob: And what are you thinking?

Greg: I'm thinking . . . I'm trying to figure out what to do.

Bob: Trying, huh? That's the trouble with "trying." So you don't think what to do and then what?

Greg: Well, I keep thinking that everything I do isn't good enough.

Bob: Bring your parents into the therapy room and have them sit beside you. Are they saying that what you do isn't good enough?

Greg: My father is. Yes, it's my father in my head.

Bob: And what is your father's occupation?

Greg: He's a surgeon.

Mary: What does he know about therapy?

Greg: Nothing. (*Laughs*) Not a thing.

Mary: So you are stupid . . . to hire such a know-nothing supervisor.

Greg: (*Laughs*) Yeah . . . yeah. OK, Pop, OUT!
(*Group is laughing*)

Bob: The next time you block your creativity by listening to your Parental scolding, will you see your father sitting beside you . . . and kick him out. He has no more business in your therapy sessions than you have in his operating room.

Usually we use present and recent scenes for clarification and problem-solving rather than redecision. In such scenes the person is being himself at his current age and therefore more easily uses Adult ego state. Lee might have "problem solved" what he wanted to do in the present to give up his annoyance at Joy. He might also have re-enacted the recent scene of tapes vs. beach in order to understand the game he plays when he wants to say "No," instead says "Yes," and ends up irritated.

EARLY SCENES

For most clients redecision is easiest in early scenes, because they *are* children in such scenes. They don't have to struggle to stay in the Child ego state. Also, the redecision is experienced most powerfully when the fantasied protagonists are the people who gave the original injunction. To find an early scene for Lee's redecision, we might have said:

> *"Be a little boy and hear the words, 'You don't yell at people!' "*

or

> *"Who told you not to yell at people? Pick a scene."*

or

> *"Hold your breath in, as you are doing, and hear yourself talking politely. You are intimidated and you let someone else get his or her way. What's the scene when you are little?"*

or

> *"Whom did you give in to, when you were a child?"*

Whatever scene Lee chooses, the purpose of the work would be for him to experience rejecting the injunctions he'd previously accepted.

To find an early scene with Philippe, we would concentrate on his words, "I feel like I am running and I am far behind and I'm choking and I don't have air and I'll never catch up," and see what past scene that evokes. He might repeat the words or might act them out, running in place while he imagines not catching up. He might position his body in a way that expresses what he feels. "Make your body show how you feel when you are unable to catch up." When he has sculpted his body to his own satisfaction, we simply ask, "How old are you and what's going on?"

Zoe's early scene might be exactly the same as the "birthday party." We'd ask if she had ever gone to a birthday party and have her pick one in which she played her timid role. When she was emotionally in the scene, we'd ask her to behave differently than she actually behaved back then. We might have her fantasize the entire scene or have the group play the roles of the other children, as they did in the present scene.

If Troy had not "vanished" his headache, we might have moved to an early scene between Troy and his mother, in which he tells her that he is giving up headaches and caresses because he'd rather play with the kids.

Greg might have selected an early scene with his surgeon father.

Our formula is simple. We and the client find a childhood scene in which the client has the same problem that he is now presenting. For Lee, Philippe, Zoe, Troy, and Greg, we might simply have said, "Shut your eyes and go back in time. How does your problem today fit your problems of childhood? Pick a scene."

We might use the game payoff: the racket feelings plus statement about self and other. Lee feels "annoyed" and "intimidated." In Child words, he is "angry" and "scared." He says about the other person, Joy: "You spoil my fun" and about himself, "I don't get to do what I want to do." Philippe feels "discouraged" and says, "Others are much better than I am," and "I can't figure out anything." We might ask either to shut their eyes, repeat the feeling plus the statements and go back to childhood to find a scene that fits.

There are limitless early scenes available to clients. It is important that the chosen scene fits the client's injunction-decision, so that the scene will be appropriate for the specific redecision.

Don't be. The redecisions will be, "*I will not kill myself*," "*I am loveable,*" and "*I love me and will continue to care for me.*" To make such redecisions, the client finds a scene in which the injunction was given and makes the redecision that is meaningful within that early scene: "*I am loveable even though you didn't know how to love, Dad,*" "*I am loveable even though you say I fought you from the day I was born,*" or "*I am loveable even though the welfare de-*

partment never found parents willing to adopt me." (See Chapter 9.)

Don't feel. The client returns to an early scene in which she redecides by experiencing the forbidden emotions and she tells others that she appreciates her ability to feel and to show feelings, even if they do not recognize or approve of feelings.

Don't be a child. In an early scene, the client affirms her right to wet her pants, go out to play instead of work, or give up responsibility for baby brother.

Don't think. If the injunction is *"Don't think about our family secret,"* the client will return to the early scene to tell the others that she always knew the family secret. If the injunction implies that the client is "stupid," the early scene will be one in which the client repudiates that attribute.

Don't make it. The client returns to a time she was stroked for not succeeding or was negatively stroked for succeeding, in order to redecide, *"I am making it even though you may not want me to."*

Don't grow. Again, the confrontation is between those who wish to keep her a child and the client affirming that she is not staying a child. Often, in this scene, we do a "parent interview" in which we ask the parent why he or she is so afraid of the child becoming a grown person . . . and then the client is free to redecide, *"I am grown, even though you wanted me to remain your baby."*

Don't. The client returns to an early scene in order to demonstrate that she can and does make choices. She may also tell parents that she is returning her fear to them, as they are the ones who were originally afraid when she wanted to swing, climb trees, or cross the street.

Don't be the sex you are. In a world of rules for each sex, those who strive to be the other sex do break the rules. Girls who want to be boys are not as "soft and as sweet as a nursery" and boys who should have been girls allow themselves a softness and sweetness that may be scoffed at by the supermen. In early scenes, the client redecides to like self "as is." If the client feels guilty for being the "wrong sex," we'll ask the client to create a birth scene in which the client will tell parents who is responsible for the client's sex.

Don't be close. This injunction has so many different meanings that it is particularly important to go to a scene in which it is given specifically, so that the client redecides, *"I will be close to others even though you were not close to me," "I am sexy even though you were afraid of sex,"* or *"I now let myself be dependent even though I didn't succeed in depending on you."* Sometimes the injunction was not given, but the decision was made because of trauma. *"Because you died, I decided never to love again. I am now loving . . . even though you died. I dare to love."*

Don't be important. In early scenes, such as at the dinner table, the client gives up his quiet ways to demand that the family listen to him. He recognizes his own importance even if others continue to deny his importance.

Don't be well. This may be the decision of clients with psychosomatic complaints or those who misuse illness to keep themselves from enjoying or succeeding in life. John McNeel and Ellyn Bader,[1] our associates, return a client to an early scene in order for her to stop her pain.

Arda: What terrifies me is the pain . . . even though I know it's not my heart. My chest hurts. . . .

John: Are you willing to be a little girl?

Arda: Ummhm. (*Nods head affirmatively.*)

John: See your Dad and Mom in front of you.
(Arda says she sees them.)

Ellen: And let yourself be little.

Arda: (*Does this and describes herself when little.*)

John: And would you see your parents and describe them? (*She does*) Would you let yourself see the kind of connection of pain that runs between the two of them?

Arda: (*Begins crying hard.*)

John: And as a little girl would you tell them that you are separate from their pain?

Arda: My mother wouldn't let me be separate! (*Sobbing*) I go off in a corner and read and she won't let me. (*She sounds very little.*)

John: Well, you are separate.

Ellyn: As you go off in the corner, Arda, let yourself know how much you wanted to be separate.

Arda: Oh, yes. I couldn't stand the noise and the fighting and the dishes crashing around the walls. I'm so scared, I just want to get away, but . . . no place to go. My mother made me wash my father when he was drunk. I wanted to get away. . . .

Ellyn: Of course you wanted to get away.

Arda: (*Continues to sob*)

Ellyn: And you deserved to have someone there taking care of you.

John: And letting you know that you are a separate human being.

Arda: I am separate. I can look like you. I can feel good things in you, but I am not you. I don't have to take on your pain.

She sees them and tells them that she is separate from them and is not taking on their pain.

IMAGINARY SCENES

An imaginary scene is a scene that did not and could not happen. Arda might have used an imaginary scene, such as pretending to be in a tiny magical canoe that she paddles through her veins and arteries until she finds the place of her pain. There, she describes what she sees that produces pain, such as a place that is knotted, blocked, or stretched tight. She then fantasizes curing that spot.

Philippe might have redecided by treating his fantasy of running and not catching up as if it were a dream. He'd then claim the parts of his dream, the road he runs on, the scenery he creates, the other runners, and himself the dreamer. Lee's roaring could be turned into a fantasy in which he becomes a lion and then owns the lion's imagined power.

Edith, as she starts to work, is asked to go to an imaginary scene when Bob tells her to be her block:

Edith: Many times I am aware I'm blocking. And it rings bells back in my childhood. It rings bells that I am blocking the same way.

Bob: I'm confused. Will you stand up and be the block. "*I am the block.*" (*Said in a loud voice*)

Edith: I'm not that kind of block. I'm fuzzy.

Bob: Great. Be the fuzzy block and tell Edith what you are doing.

Edith: I'm all fuzzy and amorphous and wishy washy. If you try to move me, I'll roll around and come in somewhere else.

Bob: To keep Edith from. . . .

Edith: Thinking.

Bob: An anti-thinking block.

Edith: And I'm a not-remembering block.

Bob: I don't want you, Edith, to remember so that. . . .

Edith: I don't want you to remember so that. . . . I don't know.

Bob: Shut your eyes and keep repeating, "*I don't want you to remember, so that. . . .*"

Edith: Oh. So that you won't get scared.

Bob: Be Edith.

Edith: Yeah, that's all very well, block, but sometimes I'm willing to risk being scared. I wish you would go away, shove off.

Bob: Enough wishes and hope and faith and you'll need charity.

Edith: (*Laughs*) Yeah. I don't need you. I'm going to push you off. (*Big smile*)

Bob: What's happening?

Edith: It evaporated before I had time to push.

Bob: You are so powerful, you didn't need to push it? Instead, you just evaporated it.

Edith: I did?

Bob: Sure . . . who's block was it?

Mary: Nope, you didn't. Bob really did it. I saw him evaporate it with his secret anti-block ray gun. Didn't you see him? And now he's trying to pretend that helpless little you did it.

Edith: (*Giggles*) I'm . . . oh, boy, my head is so clear. I am so clear. I am owning my own anti-block ray gun and you can't take it away from me. I hardly ever feel this clear. I can think . . . I am thinking.

During the next few days, Edith joyously used her ray gun to zap away her anti-thinking block. Later she remembered an early scene in which her mother accused her of stealing money. Edith became more and more confused by her mother's accusations, until finally she confessed to stealing. Mother then cuddled her and told her what a good girl she was to tell the truth. Now, re-entering the scene, Edith affirms that she never stole the money and that she was very smart back then to do what she did. It was better to be confused and loved than to think straight and be called a liar. In her recreation of this early scene, she tells this to mother. She then affirms that she no longer needs confusion for love or any other purpose.

A client who worked with our associate, Gene Kerfoot,[2] dealt with "a wall." She was a lonely, distant woman who was afraid to be involved in more than casual encounters with others. In her therapy she talked of the "wall" she had experienced since childhood. Gradually, she recognized that this wall, which she had considered pathological, was valuable and had served to protect her, in fantasy, from feeling invaded and overwhelmed by her mother. She understood that early decisions are invariably useful at the time they are made and do include positive aspects of self-protection even when the consequences are destructive.

Gene Kerfoot states, "When the early decision contains a metaphor, in this case '*I won't be close. . . . I'll build a wall,*' it is helpful for the therapist to include that metaphor in the redecision. Her redecision occurred as she fantasized building a door in her wall, so that she could go out or stay behind the wall. She was in charge."

Mary's favorite imaginary scene was told her by Graham Barnes,[3] about a client at one of his interracial workshops for Fundamentalist clergy. A minister was keeping himself sad, frustrated, and overworked by concentrating his energy on the ex-parishioners who refused to go to church. He did not believe it was possible for him to be happy until he found a way to make these backsliders change their ways. Graham asked him to make an imaginary trip to Heaven. Face aglow, the minister described the angels, the music, the shimmer of gold. *"Are you happy there?"* Graham asked. *"Perfectly happy, infinitely happy!"* Graham then said, *"Look around you. Are all your parishioners and ex-parishioners in Heaven?"* The man stopped smiling, shook his head, and said, *"No, they're not."* Graham asked, *"And what do you feel?"* He answered, *"Sad. Sad and frustrated."* Then he began to laugh. From a delighted Child position he recognized that he had just programmed himself to be as unhappy in Heaven as he is on earth . . . and redecided.

Dreams, like fantasies, are excellent tools for redecision. The man who dreamed of his son dead in the swimming pool redecided as he recognized the dead son to be the child part of himself. Another man, whose contract was to finish his dissertation, dreamed:

"I take my car to the garage to be fixed. When I return for it, I find that it is repaired but I can't drive it out because someone has dumped a load of bricks in front of it. I complain to the mechanic and he says it's not his responsibility. I find the manager and he says the same. So I just stand there, looking at the car and the bricks. There's nothing I can do."

As he plays each role, he experiences his frustration. No part of him is willing to move the bricks. We ask him to remain in the dream, being the bricks, the car, the mechanic, the manager, and the dreamer—and then experience time passing . . . fall, winter, spring, summer, and fall again. We count the seasons as he accomplishes nothing. Suddenly he says, *"This is intolerable,"* jumps to his feet and pantomimes moving the bricks. As he does this, he enjoys his actions on his own behalf. The next week he sends us the first pages of his dissertation. He is, in reality, moving bricks. George Thomson,[4] an associate, uses this technique. He believes that "the body of the dream represents the past, the emotions on awakening represent the present racket, and the redecision is made most easily in the creating of a new ending to a dream." In this approach, the therapist listens for lack of autonomy in new endings. *"Wow, you have an opportunity to end your dream any way you wanted, and you still write a sad ending!"* or *"When you could write however you please, you still decide to make an ending that depends on other people changing."* The client continues to rewrite the dream until he and therapist are satisfied that the ending contains the redecision.

Future scenes may be as imaginary as the minister's heaven or may be a simple rehearsing of an expected event. Lee, in the next section, begins with an important future scene, his oral examination for licensure, and then uses a combination of scenes, plus Bob's Bullseye for redecision.

COMBINATION OF SCENES

Usually, we advise therapists in training to complete one scene before beginning another. When a client talks to her clienched fist, boss, dead father, and tightness between her shoulders, she's probably going to end in confusion rather than redecision. Lee kept the partial scenes intact as he went from oral committee to being his hands, to an early scene with Maw, and back to oral committee for the finishing touches:

Lee: I am afraid I'm not going to pass.
Mary: Be at the examination and create the scene. First, who are the examiners? Visualize the sort of examiners you'd be afraid of.
Lee: (*He does this, describing his examiners. He then presents himself to them. While giving his credentials, he is polite, stiff, and self-effacing.*)

We ask group members to use Lee's material and deliver it as they would do it. One is scholarly, one enthusiastic, one forceful.

Lee: This is not helping. This is . . . I don't know the *best* way to present myself! And I certainly don't know the *best* way to answer their questions.
Mary: I set this up so that you could see there is no best way. Abe does what is congruent for him, Ann for her, Art for him.
Lee: (*Moves hands in a sharp, downward gesture.*)
Bob: Do that again. That's it. Now be your hands. What are they saying?
Lee: To hell with it! To hell, to hell! To hell with the board, to hell with TA! To hell with everything. (*Lee has learned to be vigorous, since his deep breathing and growling at Joy.*) I am mad at a lot of things I have to do.
Mary: Yeah. What happens when you are a little kid . . . be at home. . . . What happens when you say, "*I am mad at a lot of things I have to do*"?
Lee: I never said it.
Mary: Mmmhmm.
Lee: I was always angry and couldn't show it.
Mary: Be there.
Lee: I am angry at you, Mother. For having your eye on Joe. Telling always how good he is. How great he is for eating the goddamned Lithuanian garbage we had to eat. It disgusted me, dandelion greens, onion tops, whatever shit . . . there you are, saying, "*You can eat everything, Joe. Lee, why can't you eat everything? Why aren't you like Joe?*"

Mary: Answer her.

Lee: Shit, Maw, I'd like you to see me as me and not just someone who ought to be like Joe. (*Still adaptive, pleading*)

Mary: OK, we'll come back to Maw and Joe in a minute. Right now, see that examining committee and say to them what you said to Maw.

Lee: I'd like you board members to see me like me, not like Joe. (*This time he is firm, not placating.*)

Group Member: You sounded really good.

(*Applause*)

Mary: Now will you understand that it is all right for Abe and Art and Ann and you to present differently . . . that the board is not Maw and you are not little Lee.

Lee: I am realizing that perfection isn't Joe and Maw. That's where it is . . . it all is. Being perfect has been. . . . I have to be like Joe and I couldn't achieve that.

Bob: Perfection is eating Lithuanian garbage.

(*Loud laughter*)

Lee: Fantastic! I am not eating anyone's garbage anymore!

Mary: Great! Tell the examining board.

Lee: I am not eating garbage. I am not! I am not Joe. I am me. I AM ME.

Lee presents himself to the board; this time he does a fine energized job.

A change to a different scene is indicated if the client suddenly becomes aware of an important time of early decision. Jim Heenan,[5] our associate, is the therapist:

Lynda: I have this dream . . . nightmare. I would like to stop having it.

Jim: Hmmm. You dreamed this more than once?

Lynda: All the time.

Jim: *All* the time? (*With surprise*)

Lynda: Every week or two—I've always had it.

Jim: Even when you were a little tiny baby?

Lynda: No—since I was four or five—I can't see it clearly.

Jim: Can't see it clearly. (*Reflection*)

Lynda: Well—like a blur—sorta murky—don't know exactly.

Jim: Is that "blur" like your dream?

Lynda: Yes. (*Nods*)

Jim: When did you last dream this dream?

Lynda: Last night.

Jim: Be there—in your dream—and tell it like you're there now.

Lynda: I am in bed and there's a loud noise. I jump up. I'm running down a long dark hall. I'm scared. There's a light at the end and a phone is hanging on the wall. There's a voice screaming over the phone. I wake up. It's screaming, "*Lynda, Lynda,*" over and over.

Jim: So you wake up scared?

Lynda: (*Looking wide-eyed and scared*) Yes.

Jim: Be that hall. Tell the dream as the hall.

Lynda: I am a long hall. I have a light on one end of me and a phone on my wall. There is a little girl running in me. She looks scared.

Jim: Be the hall and finish telling the dream as the hall.

Lynda: My phone is screaming, "*Lynda, Lynda.*"

Jim: Be the voice on the phone.

Lynda: I am a voice on the phone. I am screaming, "*Lynda, Lynda.*"

Jim: Do it.

Lynda: Lynda, Lynda (*Hysterically. At this moment she collapses forward and begins to sob. After a few moments she speaks in a little girl voice*) It's the night my Daddy died. (*Shifts to Adult voice*) He had a heart attack in the shower and fell through the glass door. I ran in the hall. He was calling, "*Lynda, Lynda.*"

Jim: What's happening?

Lynda: My mom is telling me that it's just a bad dream and to go back to bed. (*Sobs*)

Jim: How old are you?

Lynda: I'm four and a half.

Jim: So you're out of your dream and remembering an experience. Do you want to do some more with *that* experience?

Lynda: Yes.

Jim: Be back in your bed after Mom tells you to go to bed. Be there!

Lynda: I'm in bed. I'm scared. (*Cries softly*)

Jim: What are you saying to yourself?

Lynda: I'm having a bad dream—It's not a dream!

Jim: (*Places chair in front of Lynda*) Say *that* to your Mom.

Lynda: It's *not* a dream. I did hear it. I did! I'm not making it up. I did hear it. It isn't a dream.

Jim: Be Mom. What do you want to say, Mom?

Lynda: (*As Mom*) I'm scared.

Jim: Tell little Lynda.

Lynda: (*As Mom*) I'm scared too. I'm sorry. You didn't make it up. *I* wanted it to be a dream. My name is Lynda, too. Your father was calling me.

Jim: Be little Lynda.

Lynda: (*As self*) My eyes and ears do too work—I know a dream and *I* know the difference! (*Looks at Jim and nods*)

Jim: (*Nods and smiles*) Say that to some folks here.

Lynda: (*Looks around the group*) I'm not crazy. I know the difference! (*Smiles*)

Jim: Where are you now?

Lynda: I'm through. I feel excited . . . and a little sad.

Jim: Finished with Mom?

Lynda: Yes for now. Thanks.

Jim: Thank little Lynda, too!

She finished saying goodbye to father at another session and six months later reports she no longer has the dream.

We are often asked how we know which type of scene to use. We guide ourselves by the following breakable rules: 1) We move from fantasy to reality whenever the reality is more important, as Jim did in working with Lynda's dream. 2) We use a scene that interests both the client and us, and in which the client is most likely to experience free Child energy. 3) If the client does not make a redecision, we move to a different scene the next time the client works. After the redecision, we probably shift back to the first scene for confirmation of the redecision. 4) We switch types of scenes as we move from client to client, to avoid repetition and stereotyped, adapted performances. If one client redecides in an early scene, the next work will be in a recent, present, or imaginary scene. 5) If a client regularly works in a particular type of scene, we suggest he experiment with a different modality. 6) When either of us has a "brainstorm," that takes precedence. If the so-called "brainstorm" turns out to a dud, we reinstate the rules.

CONTEXT, OTHER, AND CLIENT

Clients learn easily to create real, remembered, and fantasied scenes and to experience themselves in their Child ego states within these scenes. If that is all that happens, the results are grossly antitherapeutic. The client reexperiences the same scenes, the same beliefs, the same emotions, over and over—reinforcing pathology rather than changing. Mary remembers a workshop client who did a lovely, touching "goodbye to Auntie" scene and ended by saying, "This is my last goodbye to you." Mary asked when her other "goodbyes" had taken place. "Oh, I said goodbye at Esalen with Fritz Perls and in New York and. . . ." She listed half a dozen prominent therapists with whom she had performed. In order to redecide rather than perform, the client must integrate some new insight into her Child—insight that is sufficiently powerful for the Child to use it as a permission to change.

Our role as therapists is to listen and watch every second of every scene for the "missing something" that will turn the scene from tragedy to a drama that ends well. We are focused exclusively on what the client needs in order to renounce victimhood. To do this, we divide each scene, mentally, into three components, the self (or client), the context of the scene in which the client operates, and the other characters within the scene. We make ourselves aware of what specific facts, thoughts, behaviors, or feelings the client is suppressing about self, other, or context, in order to remain a victim of the old decision.

All people are selectively attentive and inattentive. When reading, Mary doesn't hear. To get her attention, Bob carries on a silly monologue, "Hey, Mary, aren't those elephants dancing on the front lawn? Why, I believe they are! And notice that there are monkeys climbing the palm trees." Eventually she hears. Eric Berne sometimes didn't see. Although he and Bob shared an office building and met often, a year after Bob shaved off his beard, Eric asked, "When did you stop wearing your beard?" A child plays happily all afternoon without noticing he is feverish or has an earache. In therapy we are interested in the client's general areas of inattention.

Virginia Satir[6] writes that clients are consistent in their inattention to self, context, or others. The blamer is inattentive to the needs and wants of others, as he discounts and blames them. The placator discounts himself. The rational person discounts both self and others, as he quests for "facts." The irrational discounts in all areas. To Virginia's list, we add the "flower child," who ignores context and thereby fails to solve reality problems.

When the blamer blocks redecision, he is usually waiting for the other to change, saying in effect, "I won't give up until that person does something for me." Redecision is possible as soon as he is willing to see the other in a different light and to recognize that the other does not make him feel.

The placator remains at an impasse when he does not let himself experience himself, his needs and wants and emotions. He must stand up to the others in his past, recognizing that he is not responsible for them and did not "make" them feel.

The rational does not recognize emotions in self and others, thereby making it very difficult for himself to experience himself in his Child. We stroke him for creating scenes and daring to feel while in them. We are careful not to push him to be dramatic, knowing that his redecisions, often barely expressed, will be as meaningful to him as the redecisions that others make with more obvious feeling.

The irrational (psychotic) first makes Adult decisions only. He decides while examining present and recent scenes. If he returns to the past, it is as Adult reporter rather than as child. When he becomes irrational in a scene, we stop the scene immediately. *"Hey, move off your chair and come sit here in the observer's chair. Be my consultant. What went wrong that the client . . . you . . . decided to act crazy?"* We interrupt in the service of reestablishing Adult functioning. Only when the client demonstrates firm Adult control, can he safely begin to do Child work.

The "flower child" seems to redecide so easily that sometimes therapists believe the client has done major work only to learn at the next session that no implementation took place. He is adept at understanding self and others, and at recreating emotion. Unless the therapist remains eminently practical, the client will give touching performances and not change. After each redecision, the "flower child" must be asked precisely what he is going to do differently as a result of the redecision he has made.

Context

Within the context of the scene, we continue to ask ourselves what the client is ignoring in order to justify old injunctions and decisions. What does the client need to know about the context of the scene so that she can fulfill her contract?

Pat, who is raising two small children alone, contracts to find ways to enjoy and improve her present life instead of feeling "ground down by everything." Her primary injunctions are *"Don't be a child"* and *"Don't succeed."* Her rackets are sadness in the present and anxiety about the future.

Pat returns to a childhood scene. She is told that she cannot take a lead part in a school play. Instead, she has to keep working in the family's tiny, New York City candy store. She says, *"What does it matter? Whether I can be in the play or not, everything is always so miserable. There's no way to be happy in our life."* Hearing this, we drop the issue of the school play, which later may be a vehicle for re-deciding to succeed, if she is willing to insist on her rights to "stardom." Instead, we focus on her early decision that there is no way to be happy unless the context of life is different.

She describes her home and the candy store and then we give the assignment: *"Pretend that you are in the same place . . . the candy store. Only difference, pretend that the day you were born a good fairy flew into the room and sprinkled you with happy powder. Be there and find a way to be happy IN SPITE OF!"* She does this, and recognizes that the candy store provided a background that had potential for joy or misery. Her family colored it miserable and she had accepted their feelings as the only possible reaction to the context of life. This fantasy experience freed her to look for happiness in her current life, while also making changes in her environment today.

Ned also concentrates on what is wrong in the context of his life. His contract is to decide either to live happily at home or happily away from home. He has twice separated from his wife and they are now temporarily reconciled. His primary injunction is *"Don't be close."* He is remembering the one happy period in his life, when he lived on a farm with his grandmother, before he was forced to join his parents in Chicago and attend the "miserable, sadistic Chicago schools." There are many obvious choices in terms of early scenes. Someday he'll need to say goodbye to grandma and tell her and his parents that he has decided to be close to people even though he might again be sent away. However, there are only 15 minutes left in the therapy session so we want him to work in a scene that can be completed quickly. Goodbyes may take more time.

Mary: Go to the grade school in Chicago. What do you see?
Ned: A bunch of sadistic boys fighting.
Mary: Look around carefully. Go into the school and walk around.

Ned reports on the dilapidated, dirty classrooms, the crowded conditions, the crabby teachers, and the boys who are fighting.

Mary: Good for you. You have great ability to put yourself back into the scene. Now go on the playground. See the boys fighting?
Ned: Yeah. (*He describes the scene*)
Mary: Are all the boys fighting?
Ned: Well, not exactly. Some kids are throwing the ball around.
Mary: Interesting. What is Ned doing?
Ned: Just sitting there on a bench. Sad.
Mary: Are there other kids sitting on benches?
Ned: Yeah.
Mary: I wonder why Ned doesn't make friends with them.
Ned: I don't know. He just doesn't. It's a huge school. I do remember one kid like me. . . . lived in the same building. I didn't play with him much. I don't know. I was sad.
Bob: Be Ned. On the bench. And say, "I'm going to stay sad until. . . ."
Ned: I'm going to stay sad until. . . . until. . . . until I get back to Grandma's. (*Weeps briefly*) I never got back.
Bob: Yeah. Now see your wife and say, "*I'm going to stay sad with you until I get back to grandmother.*"
Ned: For Christ's sake! (*Laughs*)

José, son of a Chicano farmworker, discounts the malignancy of his early school environment. Although he knows the prejudice of his teachers toward Spanish-speaking children, he believes that his "stupidity" was the major problem. He insists that if he had not been of low IQ, he could have overcome his problems. During previous sessions, he has been stroked by the group for his intelligent observations of their problems and he has done a double-chair experiment between his "smart" self and his "dumb" self. He also understands his game, in which he makes inappropriate remarks, is criticized, and thereby reinforces his belief that he is stupid.

We ask him to revisit his grade schools in fantasy. As he does this, he sobs with the pain of the experience. He can't make the teacher understand that he needs to go to the bathroom, is slapped with rulers for speaking in Spanish, is given the ragged textbooks instead of the new ones given to Anglo children, and is put into classes for "slow learners." For 30 minutes he guides himself through his terrible school years; by the time he finishes, most of the group is weeping. We ask him to be his grown-up self and tell little José how bright he must have been to learn to read and write English and to graduate from high school in spite of what was done to him. At the end of this scene he is claiming his true intelligence.

Others

Within the scene the important others in the client's life will play their roles as the client remembers or imagines the roles to be. The others are *not* to be changed. If father gave no evidence of being loving, we will not condone a scene in which father is changed into a loving person. The client may understand her non-loving father, fight back against him, tell him that she has found loving people in her life today, and change *herself* in any way in terms of her relationship to him. She may not change him. This is essential because most clients maintain their unhappiness in order to get parents to change; now they learn they are responsible for themselves no matter what the rest of their world is like.

José, recognizing the lethal quality of his school environment, next deals with his first teacher. He remembers her, has her play her part, does not change her, and does change himself.

José: Miss Jones, I am only nine years old when I come to your class. You are my first teacher. I had never gone to school before. The rest of the kids have been in school three years. They can read and write and speak some English. Of course they speak English. I am not stupid when I don't understand English.

Bob: Tell her, "You are stupid, Miss Jones...."

José: Yes, you *are* stupid! Stupid and mean ... very stupid. If you'd been smart, you would have known I was not stupid. I just didn't know English.

Bob: How long does it take you to understand English in her class?

José: I think longer than it should take. You see, we kids, the Mexican ones, talked to ourselves.... not in English. And my parents never learned English. My older brothers never really learned English. So ... maybe a whole year.

Bob: How many Mexican-American kids in the class?

José: About a third. We were all called stupid and I was the most stupid. That's what she thought.

Bob: OK, so Miss Jones is exposed to Spanish every day at school and you are exposed to English every day in school. You learn English in one year? How long does it take Miss Jones to learn Spanish?

José: She never learned.

Bob: So who's stupid?

(*José and the group laugh delightedly*)

Early in treatment we focus on the past shortcomings of others, particularly parents and older siblings, in order to clarify injunction-decisions or to defuse an explosive current situation. If husband and wife have constant uproar, they are more amenable to treatment when they recognize that he was taught by his father to argue in order to avoid non-sexual intimacy and she was taught by her mother to argue in order to avoid sexual intimacy. A suicidal client makes the first step in contracting when he recognizes that his suicidal impulses are not primarily in response to his current situation but instead are in response to very old messages about himself that he accepted.

Mitch, early in treatment, needed to be in touch with his father's harshness and perfectionism. Mitch was depressed and suicidal, and blamed himself for his predicament. As he goes into an early scene with his father, he recognizes that his father does not stroke him positively either for being or doing. If Mitch does well, father requires that he do better next time. Recognizing this, Mitch mobilizes his early, suppressed anger to fight back. He screams, *"I am loveable, damn you! I am loveable! It's your fault, not mine, that you didn't know how to love me!"* This is his first redecision. Later, in another scene, he redecides, *"I do not have to be perfect in order to stay alive! I won't kill myself if I don't live up to your expectations!"*

Some clients defend their parents, refusing to look at the parents' pathology, and thereby block themselves from needed redecisions. When this occurs, we often ask the person to remove self from the scene in order to understand it:

Mary: Hey, come over here and sit beside me. See little Cora and her father. Pretend you are the therapist.

or

Mary: Gosh, if I were a little kid in that family, I'd sure feel bad. I bet Cora just doesn't want the other kids to know how bad she feels.

or

Mary: I know your family isn't supposed to let the neighbors know what's going on. Be a neighbor and find out what the neighbor knows.

or

Bob: I bet your mission in life was to protect your father. When you were little, how did you protect him?

or

Mary: Yeah, so you tried to make your mother happy? Was she happy before you were born?
Jeb: No. Her mother died when she was young.
Mary: And no substitute mother made her happy? Is she happy now?
Jeb: No.
Mary: So, all her long life after her mother died, no one succeeded

in making her happy. How about that? Tell her, *"No one suc-ceeds in making you happy."*

Hugh wants to be more successful as a family therapist. He brings a tape of a family session in which everyone is working well until mother bursts into sobs. All work stops, as Hugh and the husband attempt to placate her. The older daughter joins in the placating, the younger daughter withdraws physically by needing to go to the bathroom, and the son begins to act irrelevantly.

We shut off the tape.

Bob: How does all this fit your own early life?
Hugh: I don't see that it does. I . . . my father was the manipulator. Mother was the strong one who held us together.
Mary: Well, it fits somehow. See your mother or father crying and experience you as helpless. All you can do is comfort.

Hugh begins to weep, as he tells of occasions when his mother, desperate about her marriage, would come into Hugh's bedroom and sit all night, rocking and sobbing. Hugh would attempt to comfort her. We continue to work with Hugh until he begins to experience some irritation with his mother for disturbing his sleep. He finishes his work by saying, *"Ma, I am sorry that you are so sad. There is really nothing I can do about your relationship to Dad. There are things you and he can do. In the meantime, I am a young boy who deserves to sleep. Pick up your rocker and take it out of my room."* Now Hugh is learning to differentiate, in dealing with his clients, what is his responsibility and what is theirs.

The client also looks at positives about his parents. Mitch, after redeciding to live even though father did not appreciate him, continues to feel cheated by his father.

Bob: What do you know of your father, when he was little?
Mitch: Not much. He grew up in China.
Bob: Be your father as a boy in China.
Mitch: (*As father*) I'm about . . . oh . . . any age. I started working in the rice fields almost as soon as I could walk.
Bob: Experience what it was like.

Mitch imagines a life of hard work and no money.

Mary: Such a little boy to work so hard. Tell me, who praises you for working so hard?

Mitch: (*As father*) No one. You have to work to eat. No one has . . . has time for praise. (*Mitch cries softly, face in his hands, then leaves "father's chair" to return to his own seat*) Yeah, I expect too much from him.

Mary: Yeah, you do.

Bob: Let me tell you a story, I am going to tell you a story. My father didn't praise either. He supported us and gave good messages about work. A few years ago, when he was still alive, I realized that I hadn't praised him much, either. So when I was visiting him, I said, "*You were a good father. I remember how you'd take me to Yankee Stadium and we'd watch Babe Ruth play. Those were fun times with you.*" Well, he just grunted. Later in the afternoon I lay down to take a nap. He came into the bedroom and grabbed my big toe. That's as much touching as I guess he felt safe with. And he said, "*You were a pretty good son, too,*" and then turned and walked out of the room.

Mitch understood, and planned to begin stroking his father even if father did not return the strokes. His redecision was to drop his bitterness and thereby become more human. The sequence of Mitch's understanding was crucial to his recovery. If we had begun with a "forgiveness" scene, Mitch might have kept his anger buried and his recovery from depression would have been delayed.

Before clients terminate therapy, we like them to recognize that their parents have strengths and weaknesses, and are no longer in any way responsible for the psychological health of their grown offspring.

José did not blame his parents for his poor school performance, but was sad as he recognized their limitations.

José: It wasn't just the school. No one uses words very much at home. In my family. I remember when I was in the fields with my father. He never talks. He sees. . . . if he sees a rabbit in the field, he doesn't say, "*Look, there is a rabbit.*" He nudges me with his elbow and points.

Bob: Yeah. Well, he sees the rabbit. And he shares it with you. Some fathers don't even see rabbbits and don't share them with their sons.

José: (*Smiles*) Right on, Bob. Thank you.

An advantage in family therapy is that children and parents make their redecisions together. Ruth McClendon and Les Kadis,[7] our associates, treat a family who came to them because of the "violent behavior" of their 10-year-old son. In the sixth session, father relives a childhood scene in which he recognizes how frightened he was in his non-responsive, perhaps psychotic household. Within the early scene he affirms his right to be alive. Returning to the present, he tells his family, "*I have a right to be alive in this family.*" Then, "*I am alive in this family and nothing anyone does will affect my right to be alive.*" He turns to his son, "*I love you and want you. You have a right to be alive in our family, too, and I am protecting your right to be alive. From now on you are not going to attack anyone in the family. And no one is going to attack you. Everyone is going to be safe in our family.*" At the next session, the boy announced, "*I like my family and I am not hurting anyone anymore.*" That weekend he organized a garage sale. . . . and sold all his toy guns.

Client

In redecision therapy the client is the star and the drama is carefully plotted to end victoriously. It is not coincidence or fakery that so many of the transcripts in this book end with the client laughing delightedly or saying, "Wow!" That is how redecision scenes almost *have* to end, inasmuch as the redecision is made by the free Child.

The therapist is director of the drama, writer of some of the lines, and occasionally interpreter. The participants are sometimes the "others" in the drama, sometimes co-therapists, and always the enthusiastic audience. The scene and the others are background for the change and growth of the star, the client. If the drama ends successfully, the star is the winner. We do not want to produce tragedies— we are interested in positive endings. Therefore, we would not encourage Lee to re-enact scene after scene in which he portrays himself a victim to pretty girls or mothers who serve Lithuanian garbage.

Pat, of the candy store, came to our workshop ready to recreate an infinite number of tragedies; in fact, had we been interested in her tragedies, she could have recreated 5,000 years of ancestral tragedy all the way back to Moses.

Instead, we begin planning the happy ending even before we know the scene. We know in what ways a client wants to change and in general we know what she has to do to make the changes. Lee, obviously, needed to be defiant in some Child way if he was to break through the impasse between the Parent who tells him to be polite and say "Yes" to others and the Child who wants to say "No."

A client may begin a scene in any ego state, though she will probably experience adapted Child, since that is the part that made the original decision. The adapted Child is a victim—and often a very boring one. Contrast Lee's "My inclination is to be somewhat intimidated and want to please" with his gusty "I WILL YELL WHEN I WANT TO AND I WILL GO TO THE BEACH!" Zoe was most easily overlooked as she stood shyly by the door, waiting and hoping someone would let her in. If the person first experiences her adaptation, then the redecision is especially powerful. Zoe now knows in her muscles the difference between hanging back and blowing her horn! This will be helpful to her at any time when she might be tempted to play the old, timid role.

When the client has established her adapted role (and sometimes even before), we point out every move, gesture, tone, and word that is designed by the client to perpetuate her remaining a victim. We underline the gallows laugh, the "wishes" and "hopes," the tilted heads, the tiny, high voices in grown women, the ways of playing out the accepted attributes, and especially we attack the notion that anyone or anything can make the client feel.

Then we look for a specific way that the client can be a victor, a star in the scene. Perhaps she'll do this by recognizing a new facet in others in the scene or recognize something new in the situation. She *must* find something new, some new hidden power, in herself. As Edith worked to get rid of her block, she might have been considered a difficult client, in that she would deconfuse herself and then almost immediately confuse herself again.

Edith: (*Laughs*) Yeah. I don't need you. I'm going to push you off.

Bob: What's happening?
Edith: It evaporated before I had time to push.

This "it" statement means that Edith believes she did nothing. She is not acclaiming her victory. There are many options. Bob might have had her be the block again to see how "it" evaporated itself. Instead, he tests out giving her autonomous words, as a shortcut to victory if Edith accepts them from free Child. She doesn't.

Bob: You are so powerful, you didn't need to push it? Instead, you just evaporated it.
Edith: I did?

Edith is back at "square one" . . . or so it appears. Mary exaggerates Edith's helplessness, which is often a successful technique to stimulate the free Child to fight back.

Mary: Nope, you didn't. Bob really did it. I saw him evaporate it with his secret anti-block ray gun. Didn't you see him? And now he's trying to pretend that helpless little you did it.
Edith: I'm. . . . oh, boy, my head is so clear. I am so clear. I am owning my own anti-block ray gun and you can't take it away from me. I hardly ever feel this clear. I can think. . . . I am thinking.

Her last statement is absolutely clear. . . . and she ends a star!

If the client doesn't end as a "star," doesn't make a redecision, we know that she will during another session. This time, she may not have experienced herself in her free Child, may have found that the scene somehow didn't fit, or perhaps she and the therapist were not tuning in well to what she needed. Whatever the reason, she or the therapist will decide to stop *without blame*. This is most important. We have heard therapists describe clients as "not wanting to change," or "wanting to be miserable"; that simply is not true. Clients are also described as too passive, too symbiotic, or too resistive, all words used to explain unsuccessful work. We believe that clients want to change and that sometimes neither the client nor the therapist know how to effect the change.

We know that our clients who do not redecide today will redecide tomorrow—if they are not blamed or threatened.

Redecision work is fast, often fun, and curative. Lee stands up for himself and growls his importance, and then at another session drops his self-effacing insecurity as he laughs at the "Lithuanian garbage." Philippe knows in his Child what his Adult has always known, that he does not have to be first to be worthwhile. Troy stops his headache. Zoe toots her horn. Edith imagines her secret ray gun and zaps away adapted Child confusions. Pat finds that a candy store could have been fun and sets about enjoying her present life. A minister imagines Heaven in order to redecide about happiness on earth. A woman builds a door in her wall. Arda frees herself from parents' pain. Ned gives up waiting for grandmother to release him from Chicago schools. José recognizes his intelligence. Mitch decides to live and then forgives his father. A young boy sells his toy guns.

CHAPTER 9

The Curing
of Depression

In this chapter we will discuss the treatment and cure of a number of behavorial, feeling, and thinking disorders that we see as connected. These do not all correspond to the generally accepted views on depression; they include suicidal patients, patients who are depressed but not at this time actively suicidal, and patients who are killing themselves with overwork, dangerous activities, addictions, and other manifestations of suicidal drives which are not entirely within their awareness.

Earlier we described injunctions given from the Child ego state of the parent. Most important of these, in terms of morbidity, is "Don't be." Our position is that in response to the injunction "Don't be" the child may make one or more of a number of early decisions that, if not changed, lead to depression, suicide, or "accidental" suicide:

1. *If things get too bad, I'll kill myself.*
2. *If you don't change, I'll kill myself.*
3. *I'll kill myself and then you'll be sorry (or love me).*
4. *I'll almost die and then you'll be sorry (or love me).*
5. *I'll get you to kill me.*
6. *I'll show you even if it kills me.*
7. *I'll get you even if it kills me.*

Each of the decisions may be allied to a number of different systems of behavior, feeling, and thinking that we consider as depression *even though the patient may not appear outwardly depressed.* When diagnosing the classically depressed, we do not make a distinction between endogenous and reactive depressions. Endogenous depressions supposedly originate from within the psyche, while reactive depressions originate outside the psyche. We believe that some people have been depressed since early childhood and therefore are labeled endogenous. They made early decisions to kill themselves if life doesn't get better. Their general feeling racket is sadness. They set up their lives so as to stay in their depressed scripts. Theirs is a third-degree impasse, in that they believe they have always been depressed.

Others blame outside forces for "making" them depressed or react to a new life situation with depression because depression is their chronic reactive process. They may only show their depression when something happens in their lives. Some, for instance, suffer from "menopausal depression" because during that period in their lives they are reacting to internal and external stress with depression. To the same stress, impending or actual climacteric, other people react in a host of different ways—with anger, anxiety, or joy! The depressed person reacts with depression. When we search for previous episodes of depression, as we always do, we find that the person has often in the past reacted to stress with depression, sadness, loss of self-esteem, and feelings of being overwhelmed and unable to cope.

We are also uninterested in another favorite topic during grand rounds and clinical conferences: Is a patient actually suicidal and how severe is the suicidal impulse? We are not interested in discussing, outside the patient's presence, whether the patient really "means it" when he says he is suicidal. Instead, when we see a patient who is depressed or who is managing some aspect of his life in such a way that he might die prematurely, we ask *him* for an Adult statement that he will not kill himself. Sometimes the patents says, *"I'm not depressed. Why should I decide not to kill myself. The thought never entered my mind."* We say, *"Fine! If you are not suicidal, then it shouldn't be difficult for you to decide not to kill yourself accidentally or on purpose. We want to hear you make that statement."*

A patient may not be congruent when making the statement. He may end in a questioning tone of voice, shake his head "yes" when saying "no," or use indefinite words such as *"I think I can say. . . ."* We then ask the patient to take both sides, *"I will kill myself"* and *"I won't kill myself"* until he has resolved the issue and contracted not to kill himself. A patient may attach conditions to staying alive. One psychiatrist, who was having an affair and whose wife was threatening divorce, said, "I won't kill myself unless my wife leaves me." Obviously, he was pushing her to leave, at which point he would become depressed and suicidal.

THIS IS IMPERATIVE. In our opinion no depression can be cured until after the patient makes an Adult contract with himself, and with us as witnesses, that he will not kill himself. (See Chapter 3 on "No-Suicide Contracts.") We recognize that some patients, who are severely depressed and suicidal, may not be willing at first contact to make a contract never to kill self. Instead, they make a temporal contract. In a one-week or four-week workshop our depressed clients make a contract not to kill self for the duration of the workshop. When this statement has been made, we are no longer concerned about the possibility of a client killing self, and we can devote our energies, and he his energies, to the cure. If he is struggling daily with a suicide decision, obviously he has far less energy available with which to work.

The Adult contract, then, is the prelude to redecision. It is not a redecision. The redecision is the ultimate, gut level statement from the free Child, "I will never kill myself." It is not a promise; it is a fact and a belief that is sufficient for the Child to break out of a lifetime suicidal script.

In this redecision work, environment is important. We think it is more difficult to do redecision work when the patient is surrounded by the same stresses from family, job, social and cultural milieu in which he usually exists.

Between the time of contract and redecision, the depressed person in one of our workshops enjoys an environment that is both nurturing and stimulating. Our property is beautiful, our staff cares about the participants, our chef creates fine food. Best of all, the other participants rapidly become a close, supporting group. They refuse to persecute "Kick me" players and instead cheer each gain the individual makes. We think that our environment, with few stresses and much support of change, is particularly helpful in setting the stage for redecision. However, the same work can be done when the patient lives at home and attends ongoing groups; usually the work takes longer.

IF THINGS GET TOO BAD, I'LL KILL MYSELF

Nan is a client in a four-week workshop. We recognize immediately that she is severely depressed. Her face is rigidly sad, her body tight, her voice strained, and she moves slowly, as if weighted down. During the first contract session, we ask if she is suicidal and she responds that she is. She says that she made a no-suicide contract with her therapist at home—she will not kill herself before her 40th birthday, which is two months off. She feels worthless, and states that she has no value except when she works. She believes she has always been worthless. She experiences life as "too painful" and does not want to live. She came to this workshop on the advice of her therapist, but has little hope that she'll change.

We hear her, and do not push her or struggle with her. She does minor therapy work during the first two and a half weeks, while we and the others stroke her for every small change she makes. The group involves her as much as possible in their activities during non-working periods. She begins to sing with the group—and to join them in the hot tub.

Slowly she begins to relax a little, laugh a little, and have a little fun. She begins to lose the strained look on her face and to let her muscles relax. We remind her from time to time that she has important redecision work to do when she is ready. At the end of the third week, she asks for help to get the important work done.

We ask her to sit in another chair and talk from her worthless self. This she does with ease. Then we ask her to take still another chair and talk from her worthwhile self. She has great difficulty expressing any worthwhileness from her free Child or even from her Adult. Finally, we asked her to si back in her original chair and imagine that she is looking at herself, just born, lying in a bassinet on the floor. When she says that she has the scene fantasized, we ask her to lean over, pick herself up as a child and hold herself. She bends over, pretends to pick up a child and cradles the imaginary child in her arms. *"Talk to your child,"* Bob says. She starts to talk:

Nan: I will love you.
Bob: I do love you. (*It is important to be in the present tense here.*)
Nan: I love you, I do love you, oh I do love you, and I will take care of you. I will never hurt you, I will never kill you, I will be good to you.

Her eyes brim with tears, as do the eyes of others in the room. She continues to cradle the baby in her arms, rocking her and crooning to her. After she experiences this for a time, we ask her to sit in the free Child chair and see what she feels. (In this piece of work, although deciding to nurture, she has not, so far as we can tell, made a redecision from her Child.)

Nan: I feel differently now. I feel more like living than I ever have. I feel some kind of end to a struggle, that I have never felt before.
Bob: Good. Say it to your Mother. Put her in this chair. (*Brings up another chair*)
Nan: I feel different. Yeah. No matter what you want, I'm not going to kill myself. I am free from you, from your not wanting me.
Bob: Now move to the adapted chair, and see what you do there.
Nan: I don't feel anything left over here. I don't feel like dying. I feel strong here too.
Bob: I feel finished. Do you?
Nan: YEAH!

The group gathered around Nan to hug her and tell her their pleasure in her redecision. Her work is done.

There are some unusual angles to this cure. Nan had had a very destructive mother, who she believed wanted her dead from birth. Whether this is true is not important so long as she *believes* it is true, so long as this is the way she remembered. Her early decision was, "If it gets any worse around here, I'll run away." In later childhood she decided, "If things get too bad, I'll kill myself." She experienced, as a child, that Mother wanted her dead, and her parent (P_1) in her Child ego state, therefore, was saying, "Don't be." In addition, she didn't experience much nurturing from mother and had little nurturing Parent in her own Parent ego state.

Thus, her work had to include some kind of reparenting in order to modify the lethal parent in both Parent and Child ego states. We don't believe that it is as effective for *us* to reparent as it is for the patient to find her own new parenting from her present-day experiences. In the work, therefore, she decided from *Child* to stay alive and from P_1 and P_2 to nurture herself, take care of herself. In her experience after the redecision work, she looked for ways to take better care of herself. Four months later she wrote Bob a virtual book outlining what she was doing to nurture and care for herself. She fed herself better, stopped drinking, put on her seat belt when driving, stopped smoking, allowed herself to play more, didn't work so hard in order to feel worthwhile, bought herself more and prettier clothes and, in general, increased substantially her self-nurturing. She did much of this from her Adult, of course, but the introjection of her new behavior was certainly also in Parent.

Patients like Nan are often hospitalized, given antidepressant drugs, and worried about. We see a supporting and nurturing atmosphere as far more essential than drugs. If we had ever given her antidepressants, she (and we, also) would have credited the drugs with at least some of her improvement, and she would not have felt as autonomous. Granted that all psychotherapists do not have the kind of facilities we afford our professionals who also are patients, the issue is, why not? It cost her $1200.00 for the month here; how much would it have cost her if she had been in a psychiatric hospital? And what would the outcome have been?

If we were hospitalizing patients, we would undertake to keep them in the same kind of regime: isolation from family, friends and stresses; many strokes; a good six-hour-a-day treatment program; support for change; and considerable involvement with an active group. We would not prescribe drugs unless the patients: 1) failed to respond in any way to the treatment program, and 2) were *physiologically* depressed—great loss of appetite, loss of weight, early morning awakening, lowered metabolic signs, and other evidence that they were depressing themselves to the point where drug stimulation might be advisable. We would not shock anyone with electro-convulsive therapy.

IF YOU DON'T CHANGE, I'LL KILL MYSELF

Nina is a participant in a three-day workshop in another city. Mary is the therapist. Twenty clients are working with Mary from 9 a.m. to 5 p.m. each day, and return to their own homes in the evening. They were referred by their own therapists, all of whom attend the marathon as observers or participants.

First session: Mary gets the facts: Nina has made four suicide attempts in the past six months and almost died from the last attempt. In her ongoing therapy, she refused to make a no-suicide contract, and was referred to this workshop for that reason. She says she will not attempt suicide during the workshop. Her dark hair, lack of makeup, and expressionless face give her the appearance of wearing a death mask.

She tells of her present life. She is successful professionally but claims she has "never" been happy. She is extremely depressed about her brothers' lack of success. Her parents were neglectful and abusive toward all the children.

Second session:

Mary: For how long have you been responsible for your brothers?
Nina: All my life. Since they were born.
Mary: I don't understand. You were three when Joe was born, four when Mike was born, and five when Cecil was born. Give a scene that shows your responsibility.
Nina: I was always responsible.

Mary: Willing to find a typical scene? Tell it as if it is happening right now.

Nina: I'm seven years old. (*She describes a scene where Father is angry at Joe and threatening to beat him. Mother argues ineffectually against the beating, and Nina rushes Joe and the babies out of the room. Mother and Father continue to fight, and later verbally attack Nina for defending Joe. They say she "causes all the trouble." She is very sad and also pleased that she is able to rescue the boys*)

Mary: OK. Now to age 14. What is going on?

Nina: (*Describes an almost identical scene. She is still rescuing the boys from Father. Mother is more vehemently angry at Nina and in this scene sounds psychotic.*)

Mary: You were very brave, beautiful and brave to save your brothers when you were only seven. They couldn't have saved themselves. Now I want you to give 14-year-old Nina something new to say to the boys: "*I defended you when I was seven.*" Say it from your 14-year-old position.

Nina: Yes, I did. I defended you.

Mary: "*And now that I am 14, and you are 11, 10, and 9, you are older than I was at seven. You are old enough to defend yourselves.*"

Nina: Possibly. (*Begins to weep*)

Mary: Tell them.

Nina: No.

Mary: They are old enough. (*Long pause*)

Mary: And now that Cecil is 25, he is assuredly old enough.

There are two other suicidal clients in the workshop and Nina listens silently to their work. One bursts into joyous relief when he decides he likes the child he was and will not kill him. Bouncing with energy, he asks for hugs from many group members. Nina sits impassively and does not congratulate him.

Third session:

Mary: Where are you?

Nina: I don't know. The same.

Mary: Suicidal?

Nina: I don't know. I have no desire to live. I have nothing to live for. I want an end. I can't live with my family and there is no other way.

Mary: I can see three options other than murdering you. One is to go on as you have, continuing to try to save your brothers. That is sad for you. Another is to divorce yourself from your brothers. And another is to give yourself time, in therapy, to learn to have contact with your brothers without being affected by their behavior.

Nina: I'll think about it.

Fourth session:

Nina: I want to work.

Mary: OK. Did you ever think of suicide before? *(Mary asks her to trace back the history of her suicidal impulses and she remembers first wanting to kill herself when she was eight years old.)*

Mary: Be eight. What's going on?

Nina: Mother is accusing me of something I did not do. *(Describes scene)*

Mary: OK. As an experiment, tell Mother, *"If you don't stop, I'll kill myself."*

Nina: If you don't stop, I'll kill myself. That's true, Mary.

Mary: No, it's not true. Because you didn't kill yourself when you were eight. Now be eight and tell her, *"No matter what you do, I won't kill myself."*

Nina: I can't say that.

Mary: Yes, you can. Because it is true. You did not kill yourself, no matter what she did.

Nina: I don't know how.

Mary: All eight-year-olds know how to kill themselves—jump off roofs, jump in front of cars. You chose not to kill yourself. It's very important for you to understand this.

Nina: That is true. No matter what you say to me, I'm not killing myself.

Mary: True?

Nina: Then, yes. I am feeling it now.

Mary: Now, still at eight, tell father. (*Nina does.*)

Mary: Now your brothers, one at a time.

Nina: When I am eight, I stay alive for you. I am not going to kill myself for you. (*She tells each one, calling each by name.*)

Mary: (*Mary asks her to go to age 14, and do the same. She does, weeping.*)

Mary: Now be you, today. See your father. Experiment with, "*If you don't change, I'll kill myself.*"

Nina: He won't change, and I don't care. I don't care.

Mary: So experiment with, "*No matter what you do, I won't kill myself.*"

Long pause, then:

Mary: Where are you?

Nina: You don't matter. I'll never kill myself because of what you do.

Mary: Now mother. No matter what. . . .

Nina: (*Weeping hysterically*) I'll kill myself for you. That's what you always wanted.

Mary: I'll kill myself for you and then you'll. . . .

Nina: She won't be sorry. She'll be glad. She blames me for everything. For everything that went wrong.

Mary: Nina, do you recognize that your mother is crazy?

Nina: That's what my therapist said. She says my mother is paranoid.

Mary: I'll kill myself because you are mentally ill. Because you don't know reality from fantasy.

Nina: (*Long pause*) No!

Mary: Then?

Nina: I don't know. (*For 15 minutes she vacillates, experiencing rage, sorrow, and then reality-testing that she is sane and did not cause mother's psychosis. Then, in a low voice*) What you do is not important. Whatever you do, I won't kill myself.

Mary: Is that true?

Nina: Partly. Mostly.

Mary: Take the other side. I'll kill myself for you. (*When there is still some ambivalence, taking the other side allows people to recognize the absurdity and redecide*)

Nina: No. You are not important. I don't care what you do. I'll not kill myself.

Mary: True?

Nina: I think so.

Mary: Say it again and see.

Nina: (*Says it again several times, before she says it is true.*)

Mary: Now your brothers, one at a time. Start with Joe.

Nina: I don't care . . . I can't say that! I care what happens to you. I love you.

Mary: Then say, I care what you do. I care what you become. And whatever you do or become, I won't kill myself.

Nina takes both sides, "*I will kill myself*" and "*I won't kill myself*," and finally knows and feels she won't kill herself because of Joe. She has the same dialogue with Mike and then with Cecil.

Nina: (*Sobbing*) Cecil, you had it worst. They were crazier and crazier and you had it worse. I wanted to save you. I want so much to save you. (*She sobs for almost five minutes*) Cecil, I care so much. But whatever you do, I'll always love you. And whatever you do, I'll not kill myself.

Mary: True?

Nina: Yes. For all of you, I . . . . I love you. And whatever you do, whatever you become, I won't kill myself. I will live, no matter what you do.

Mary: Anyone else you need to tell this to?

Nina: Yes. I don't want to explain.

Mary: OK. Just tell the person.

Nina: Whatever you do, I won't commit suicide.

Mary: Anyone else?

Nina: No.

Mary: Now you. No matter what I've done or will do. . . .

Nina: Yes. I will not kill myself. For anyone. Because of anyone. Including me. No matter what I do or what I become. I will not kill myself. (*Long pause*)

Mary: What are you experiencing?

Nina: The loneliest I have ever felt in my entire life. I am totally alone. Totally sad. And I will not kill myself.

Mary: I'm glad you won't. You know the book *I Never Promised You a Rose Garden?* That's what the title is all about. Deciding to live can be very sad and lonely. But you have a base now. A base for growing. A time for learning and finding new people to be close to. And learning how to be happy. And when you've ¹earned how to be close and happy, you may find a new closeness with your brothers or you may not. I can't promise you about that either.

Nina: I understand.

Nina and her therapist talk together. The therapist had been weeping during Nina's work, and now tells her how happy she is that Nina is not going to kill herself. They agree to continue therapy and Nina says that if she has the impulse to kill herself, she will not act on it but instead will tell the therapist at their next meeting.

Unlike many "If you don't change I'll kill myself" clients, Nina never attempted to blackmail her brothers into changing. She worked hard at mothering them . . . and depressed herself when she judged herself a failure. She did not ask them to be guilty.

In Sager and Kaplan's *Progress in Group and Family Therapy,*¹ Bob wrote of a blackmailing woman who demanded that Bob be her therapist, even though she knew that he no longer treated private patients. One day she came to his office and threatened to commit suicide if he wouldn't see her. Bob talked to her for a few minutes and learned that she was depressed because her ex-husband had married again. Bob then asked her when she first used sadness to get what she wanted.

She remembered when she had wanted a particular doll for Christmas, had not gotten it, and had become depressed. Then her parents bought the doll. She was still using the same "hysterical" technique.

Bob asked her to say again to him that she would kill herself if he didn't see her. She did so. Then Bob asked her to be five years old and tell her parents that she would kill herself if she didn't get the doll she wanted. She said she wouldn't do that. *"OK,"* Bob said. *"Then tell them that you won't kill yourself just because they didn't get you the right doll."* This she did, laughing. *"OK, now tell your ex-husband whatever feels right to you."*

She said *"Joe, if you don't divorce your present wife and come back to me, I'll kill myself."* Then, looking at Bob, she started to giggle. *"That is pretty silly, isn't it? I really wouldn't have killed myself if I hadn't gotten that doll, and I won't kill myself if I don't get back that doll of a husband. Besides, he wasn't such a doll anyway!"* This was not, of course, the end of her work, but it was certainly a dramatic shift from where she had been. She proceeded to get well in therapy with our partners.

Patients like her are often the ones that the staff has conferences about: Do they really intend to kill themselves, or are they "just threatening"? We are convinced that such an argument is futile. The first choice in therapy is to get patients to make a serious contract not to kill themselves or else put them in a hospital where they can't. They may not "mean" to do it, but they make mistakes sometimes and do it anyway. They must be protected from themselves until they learn not to use extortion and learn *"the only person you can guarantee will be with you the rest of your life is you."* No amount of blackmail will keep another person around; it is designed only to keep the blackmailer depressed and suicidal.

As mentioned, these patients are not easy to treat. At a professional meeting a few years ago, a well-known psychiatrist made the statement that no suicidal patient could really be "cured." He then demonstrated his technique for dealing with suicidal patients, presenting to the meeting a videotape of the care of a person who had been admitted to his service after a serious suicidal attempt. The tape demonstrated the techniques used by the team to save the girl's life. He explained that he had brought the parents in and shown them the rescue procedure tape. He then played back for the professional viewers the interview with the parents and the girl.. He asked her "What *made* you try to kill yourself?" (The italics are the authors' to underline our belief that no one can *make* anyone do anything.) She admitted that she made the suicide attempt when her parents wouldn't let her do something she wanted to do. At the end, after all the tears have been shed, the therapist turns to the parents and says, "And how does that *make* you feel?" (Again, the italics are ours.) These people were locked in a family system in which each blackmailed the other with crying, suicide threats, and actual suicide attempts in order to get someone to give someone else his or her way. The therapist must not play into this system, but must tease out of each member of the family the recognition that each is autonomous and cannot be blackmailed into feeling bad, feeling as if he or she is responsible. This therapist's question, *"How does that make you feel?"* provoked the family's staying in the script, letting the girl know that the way to get anything out of the parents was to threaten suicide. What the parents said, under these conditions, was, *"We feel terrible; we didn't know you felt so strongly; of course you can do what you want to do."* From now on for the rest of her life, or until she changes, either spontaneously or under other treatment, this girl will consider suicide as a viable choice.

I'LL KILL MYSELF AND THEN YOU'LL BE SORRY (OR LOVE ME)

The secret belief, which must be exposed, is that death is not death. Mommy and Daddy will love him after he is dead and somehow he can watch their sorrow or proclamation of love. "Big deal," we say. We make fun of this fantasy in order to get through the patient's refusal to understand, from his Child, that when he is dead, what they do or feel will be irrelevant. He's the one who'll be dead.

Some clients have a variation of this theme, when they want to die to be reunited with a dead parent. A young high school girl, Yvonne, whose mother had died, was not eating and was diagnosed as having anorexia nervosa, having gone from 110 to 65 pounds. Her fantasy was that if she died and joined mother, finally mother would love her. Some parents, as well as some ministers and others, foster the delusion that Heaven is a real place where all will be well. Maybe it is . . . we aren't arguing religion . . . but a Child who is told "You'll see Granny in Heaven" believes Heaven to be down the road a piece. The Child's delusion must be dealt with.

Bob worked with Yvonne to accept that mother was dead . . . dead . . . dead. Father, whose only strokes for Yvonne were his concerned encouragement that she eat, was asked by Bob to hold her on his lap during an interview. Bob taught him to give up asking her to eat and to find other ways of stroking. Yvonne's minister was persuaded to stop talking to her about "What would your mother in Heaven think of your not eating," because this supported the girl's delusion. The most important leverage was Yvonne's contracting and then deciding not to kill herself. She got well and regained her weight rapidly.

I'LL ALMOST DIE AND THEN YOU'LL BE SORRY (OR LOVE ME)

This decision is somewhat like *"I'll kill myself and then you'll be sorry,"* except that the client does not consider himself depressed nor does he think he is suicidal. Typically, the early decision is made when the child experiences a dramatic shift from neglect or negative stroking to great caring in times of illness. Sometimes one or both parents are physicians, who don't do much stroking until the child is ill. In other cases, the child may be one of many children, whose parents simply don't have time or energy for stroking any one child. However, when the child becomes ill, he learns that the whole family will take time to care about him. Although often there is a *"Don't be"* message, we don't believe that this is a prerequisite for a child's making this decision, *"I'll almost die. . . ."* We know one son of physicians, himself a physician, who as a preschool youngster had a series of ear infections. When he was sick, mother would rearrange her schedule to stay home with him. Later, he had a puncture wound, received a tetanus anti-toxin shot (not simply a tetanus booster) and had a severe anaphylactic reaction in which he almost did die. He was given intracardiac adrenalin, artificial respiration and other heroic measures necessary to save his life. This is one of the sharpest memories of his childhood. He developed severe hives after being returned from the emergency room, and both mother and father stayed home and took care of him. Since then, he has had other infections, one of which would have probably killed him if penicillin had not then just become available. Again, he almost died.

He tells hilarious stories about almost being killed in a parachute jump, of twice almost being killed when his forestry service planes caught on fire. He "barely avoided" being killed when the Army Air Force rejected him shortly before Pearl Harbor while all his buddies were being sent to Guadalcanal, where all were killed. His life is full of such adventures or misadventures, and his stories never fail to elicit gallows laughter. Although he no longer tells stories of almost dying, he has not quit smoking and probably is still in his script despite "heroic" efforts to get out.

These cases are particularly difficult because the patients are being asked to give up (for the Child) many positive strokes for almost dying. It is *true* that people loved them when they "almost died"; this is no delusion. The Child naturally asks, *"What's in it for me if I give up this position? What's the use of living if I can't get my warm, loving strokes?"* Although the grown-up patient *knows* that he can find other ways of getting such strokes, the Child fights to the— literally—last gasp. That is why it is so important, therapeutically, to build into therapy a way for the client's Child to be richly rewarded for living rather than almost dying.

I'LL GET YOU TO KILL ME

This is a position of despair, typical of victims of child abuse. These young people become so despairing, as they suffer the pain of abuse, that the only viable choice seems to be to wish to be dead . . . just as victims of terminal cancer wish to cut short their misery. A psychologist, who was a victim of child abuse, still lived out the "I'll get you to kill me" script by walking alone at night on danger- ous streets and by starting fights in bars. In therapy he recognized that his behavior was designed to get himself killed, and then went back into an early scene, in which his mother was throwing him against the wall. He reexperienced goading her on by refusing to cry or admit he was wrong; he remembered thinking that she was killing him and that he'd soon be dead. In his redecision he affirmed that he had not been killed, that he eventually escaped from her, then spontaneously affirmed that he would never again seek out another person to hurt him.

The first step in such therapy is to set the stage so that the client recognizes that he is attempting to get himself killed. Many deny this. The therapist needs to pick up the clues that this is where they are. For instance, one therapist/patient was on the patio talking to Bob when our former cook came roaring up our road on his motor- cycle without a helmet. Bob roared at him, *"Get your damn helmet on,"* and the therapist laughed. When Bob asked what was funny, he answered that he rode a "hawg" too, and *never* wore a helmet. He then proudly and "humorously" told of the number of times his stallion tried to kill him. Bob said he could see nothing funny about getting killed, and asked when the therapist was ready to do some work to protect himself from being killed by others, including horses. The therapist at first denied his suicidal position, but later did the work to get out of his lethal life script. Bob sometimes makes a nuisance of himself outside the therapy time when he confronts people at the meal table or in the swimming pool if he hears a gallows laugh. The shock value of the confrontation, however, is well worth the nuisance resentment. Otherwise, such persons may get past us, as they have gotten past others all their lives.

Bob adds this personal note: "It's OK with me to confront hard gallows laughter even when I have no therapeutic contract. Everybody who knows me at all well knows that I have a very strong persuasion that in a sense I *am* my brother's keeper, and that as a physician I have just as much responsibility to confront a death script as I have to brush a black widow spider off someone's neck."

I'LL SHOW YOU EVEN IF IT KILLS ME

These people can be divided into two groups: those who attempt to "show the parents of the world" by striving for greater and greater success, and those who strive to "show *up* the parents of the world" by smoking, drinking, and taking drugs. Defiantly, the latter may get hooked on addictive substances. All addicts do not start with a defiant decision, but many do, and these, we think, use anger to mask what otherwise would be a depression.

The first group—the over-achievers, the strivers, Friedman's Type A people,[2]—decide *"I'll show you, even if it kills me."* To decide *"I'll show you"* seems to be an OK decision; it's the rest of the sentence that gets people into trouble. The psychotherapeutic world is full of such people: striving and striving for recognition, getting degree after degree, achieving advancement after advancement, spending years in psychoanalytic training—and then not knowing where to go next and developing ulcers, hypertension, coronary artery disease, coronary occlusions, or finally becoming depressed and suicidal because no one notices or there is no place else to go. Bob was doing a demonstration workshop for one of the psychotherapy organizations a number of years ago, and one of the participants challenged him to arm wrestle. Ordinarily, we avoid such encounters, but this time Bob accepted. After the match, the participant commented that he had recently recovered from a coronary occlusion. He was still "showing them" by over-extending himself physically to the point where another coronary occlusion would have been highly possible. Another psychotherapist had also been in the hospital with an occlusion. Following his discharge, he went skiing and had a severe anginal attack while on the slopes. *Then* he came to a workshop, where he still was over-doing physically. He was still "showing them, even if it killed him." It almost did. He worked hard (of course) at the workshop, went into an early scene at five years of age when his father had discounted him and told him he wasn't manly (manly at five?). He screwed up his face and his fists and shouted at father, *"I'll show you even if it kills me."* Thus, this stubborn, brave little five-year-old was still running part of his life. He heard these words, experienced his anger, and then recognized an undercurrent of sadness that father didn't seem to like him as much as his older brother. Then he went ahead while still in the scene and told his father, *"You're nuts, Dad. I'm a neat guy and it's your fault if you don't see it. I'm not going to kill myself just to show you I'm a neat guy. I don't have to prove anything to you or anyone."* After this work, he began to slacken off, to work less, run less, have more fun, and to enjoy life instead of "showing them."

"I'll show you even if it kills me" people have two early decisions to overcome. First, they must redecide to live, and then they must redecide that they are important, uniquely important, no matter what they do or don't do. They have been striving for recognition for their deeds and getting conditional strokes instead of unconditional strokes. It is very hard for a person in this position to accept unconditional strokes, but once he has decided on his own importance it becomes easier. Usually it is essential to get this patient into an archaic scene in which he can both: 1) tell his parents he is going to live, and 2) tell them of his own intrinsic importance. Sometimes the impasse is such that a third degree impasse breakthrough is needed, since this person has *never* felt important just because he exists.

The most important step leading to cure is, again, the therapist's recognition of the impasse. The *"I'll show you even if it kills me"* people seldom look depressed and don't sound suicidal unless they come to us at the end of the script. To pick up the striver early is important, before he develops his tissue damage. One of Bob's first analysts told him that he (the analyst) had finally made it in life— good practice, beautiful home, new Cadillac convertible, all that he had ever wanted—and he had nowhere else to go, except to die. He did, shortly thereafter, of a coronary, and he was no older than Bob!

The second group of *"I'll show you if it kills me"* people are addicted to alcohol, food, drugs, nicotine, and use these substances to kill themselves slowly. They start out depressed and understroked, use anger to cover depression, and then start self-destruction to "show them." (Again, others with self-destructive habits may be responding to other messages, such as *"If you don't change I may as well kill myself with food,"* or *"I'll almost die from tobacco, but I won't really die, and then you'll love me."*) The rebellious are fighting back against Parent ego state messages, such as *"Be good," "Be clean," "Be reverent,"* while obeying the injunction, *"Don't be."*

One client, for example, said, "I remember when I started smoking. I picked up a cigarette from my mother's pack on the coffee table and defiantly lit it while no one was in the house. I have forgotten why I was angry, but I remember being very angry and believing that my mother was totally unfair toward me. I started drinking when I was angry about not getting funds to go to my third year of college, and recognized that they could have given me something without any hardship to them. I still sometimes light a cigarette angrily or take a drink angrily, even though I know many other ways of dealing with my anger."

The first treatment step is, again, to help the client make a decision to stop killing himself with alcohol, food, smoking, or drug addiction.

Jon, for example, said he wanted to quit smoking. Bob asked if he had quit yet. When he said he had not, Bob said he was willing to work with him after he had not smoked for 72 hours. This is a common ploy of ours in order to get the addict *first* to stop taking in the poison. If he is not willing to do this, then we are dealing with a Parent contract, which the client does not intend to keep.

If the patient agrees and comes back in three days to work, we will set up a dialogue. Bob did so with Jon:

Bob: Set out two chairs in front of you. OK. Now, in the first chair, you are your lungs. You have been assaulted by this guy with smoke for years. Talk to him.

Lungs: Hey, man, what are you doing to me? You are killing me.

Bob: No, you are the lungs, lungs. What is Jon doing to *you*, lungs?

Lungs: Oh, you are filling me up with junk, man. I can't let enough air in to give you enough oxygen to live on. Man, stop this jazz.

Jon: (*Switches chairs*) Oh come on, lungs, you are not hurting that much.

Lungs: Enough is enough, man. I can't function like this anymore.

Jon: Huh. (*Stops, doesn't seem to be willing to break the impasse*)

Bob: Be your lungs, in the other chair, 10 years from now, if Jon keeps smoking.

Lungs: I won't be around 10 years from now. I'll be in the coffin.

Bob: Tell that to Jon, pretend you are not quite in the coffin.

Lungs: See what you did! You are about dead because I have been tarred, heated, drowned in all that smoke you have been pushing in me. For God's—no, for *your* sake, quit already before we are all dead—heart, me the lungs, all of us.

Jon: I'm sorry, man; I'll quit.

Bob: Ten years from now, or now?

Jon: I'm quitting.

Bob: When?

Jon: Right now.

Bob: Tell your lungs that.

Jon: OK, lungs, you win. Hey, I win too.

Bob: OK. Now be your lungs 10 years from now when Jon hasn't shoving all the smoke down you.

Lungs: Yeah. Hey, Jon, thanks a lot. I really feel good now. I'm getting pinker, and hold lots more air.

The intensity of this experience is almost always quite remarkable. Patients do usually get into the experience of their tarred lungs. If they don't seem to be doing so, we work with them to describe themselves (as lungs) fully, adding words from our own pathological information if they profess not to have that information. We also give a great deal of information about smoking that we have learned from others: the craving each time usually lasts only a few minutes; breathing gets much better in 72 hours because of the decrease in carbon monoxide hemoglobin and with the increase in oxygen being carried by the hemoglobin. We urge people to give themselves goodies (not sugar) and force sugar-free fluids during the first 72 to 96 hours to move out the toxins faster and to replace the smoke with something tasty.

Foodaholics, alcoholics, and drug addicts can be reached in the same general way. A fat person, for example, may establish a dialogue between her fat and her mouth, or between her body 10 years from now if she continues to overeat and her body if she eats sensibly. Whatever the dialogue, the purpose is for the client to feel the severity and the sadness of what he is doing to himself. Then we go to the no-suicide redecision.

The following example concerns a patient who is a food addict. His name is Joe, and he opens up late one afternoon.

Joe: I want to stop eating when I am not hungry. And I want to stop kicking myself if I do eat.

Bob: Whew, I have really worked this afternoon and I'm not sure I want to work more—but go on a little more, and let me decide after I hear. (*It is really OK for a therapist to decide not to take on a contract, just as it is OK for a therapist to make mistakes from time to time. One of the biggest problems young, inexperienced (or old, too experienced) therapists have is they do not refuse to work or to "try" to be perfect. One of the marks of a good therapist is the willingness to risk making a mistake and then to deal with whatever happens as a result of that mistake.*)

Joe: Sometimes it will be meal time and I'll eat; I won't feel like eating anything, but I'll eat until I really hurt and am very uncomfortable.

Bob: What is your archaic background around food? What is it like around the house, and who is there? (*Already Bob is moving into present tense, in order to facilitate Child ego state work if possible.*)

Joe: Well, I go back to my grandmother's house. When I was in high school and I'd come from living with an aunt. She fed you just enough to maintain your calories.

Bob: Who did? (*Bob gave up on present tense work—a mistake.*)

Joe: The aunt did. And then I was moved to my grandmother. And if you didn't act like a garbage disposal, you were sick. (*At this point Bob should have worked with the "you," which is a parent introject, but again he gave up. Bob was tired, and it might have been better if he had refused to work.*)

Mary: Where was your mother?

Joe: My parents were divorced when I was five. I first went to live with my aunt and then my grandmother.

Mary: Your mother crazy or sick or something?

Joe: Yeah. She was crazy.

Mary: Hospitalized?

Joe: (*sadly*) The deal with my grandmother was, my mother was never around enough for long segments. She was a nurse. She worked from 3 to 11 and never got up in the morning, so whenever we wanted something to eat we would have peanut butter and toast. We wouldn't see her for five days at a time.

Mary: How old were you? (*Mary has apparently given up on present tense work too.*)

Joe: Nine.

Mary: So you mothered yourself, and then you got a woman who won't give more than a minimum for life, and then you got grandma. So no wonder you overfeed you.

Joe: Yeah. And I also overeat when it is not meal time and I'm stressed. Like if I have something to do and I'm not sure how to go about it.

Mary: How else do you nurture you?

Joe: I take baths.

Mary: You married?

Joe: Yes.

Mary: You have a wife who nurtures you, and vice versa?

Joe: Yeah. We're doing better at that. And my wife is sort of like my grandmother. If I say I want a sandwich because I am going someplace, I get a whole bagful.

Bob doesn't want to work anymore. It appears to him that we are allowing Joe to *talk about* rather than *be in* scenes. We are getting a history but no opportunity to work, and Bob decides he will ask Joe to do an assignment and *then* work later, when there is more chance of getting a Child redecision.

Bob: Some homework for you. This week will you put on your plate what you think you want to eat and will you stop and leave it on your plate when you have had enough? No matter what food you might waste. You can't waste here anyway, because the dogs or the ducks or the horses or the steer or something will eat everything!

Joe: Yeah.

Bob: Just stop and see what happens. An experiment.

Mary: I'm also hearing a tremendous issue around nurturing. You're not depressed?

Joe: Not now.

Bob: When were you last suicidal?

Joe: A couple of years ago.

Bob: Ever do anything about it?

Joe: Yes, I made a contract that I'd find another way to solve the problem, and I did. That's when I started overeating again.

Mary: Are you in therapy now?

Joe: No.

Mary: Are you willing to have a contract this week to gain the goal of both deciding to live and enjoying living?

Joe: Yeah.

Group member: How did you get to the suicide issue? I didn't hear anything.

Mary: (*Saying her answer to the patient, not to the other member, for emphasis—we don't like to talk* about *people, only to* them.) You were brought up without enough nurturing. Brought up by a mother who, for whatever reason, didn't want you. She passed you off to various others and she didn't care for you when you were with her. Nurses can pick better shifts than always 3 to 11 if they want to.

Bob: So, indirectly at least, you received a *"Don't be"* injunction.

Mary: And your aunt doesn't want you enough to feed you well. Sounds like a lot of people didn't realize what a cute kid you were.

Additional important points surface in the dialogue. The part of the Little Professor is tricky. When Joe made a *contract* not to kill himself, but not a redecision, the "little kid" starts eating more, as a way of suborning the implicit contract. And the message, if read back, was *"If you don't eat, you are sick."* So the way the little kid can con everyone is to say, *"See, I'm just doing what they told me!"* It would have been better if the former therapist had gotten to a no-suicide redecision, in addition to the contract; that might have kept Joe from starting to kill himself by overeating.

The other issues: Fat people can learn to eat only those foods that seem to hum to them and to avoid any food that doesn't hum. Sooner or later the body does protect one, if this is maintained. Secondly, most fats clean their plate, as part of their subservience to old voices. By asking them not to clean their plate, we are giving them some new messages, which they can first hear with their Adult and later incorporate in their Parent. By giving Joe this experience, this experiment, we are giving him the opportunity to restructure his Parent.

As for asking Joe about suicide, we were not reading minds. Any time we hear any evidence that there was neglect, we wonder about suicide and ask about it. Then we are less likely to miss the obvious, or even the hidden.

I'LL GET YOU EVEN IF IT KILLS ME

These patients appear angry rather than outwardly depressed, but they are headed for an early death just as surely as the obviously suicidal patient, the despairing patient, the "work hard to show you" patient, or the addict.

Think of the 100 mile-an-hour chases down the freeway, as the cops chase the robbers. Think of the robbers who carry firearms, who engage in armed robbery, who go to prison, and who keep their anger in prison, stabbing other prisoners, killing guards. Brought up in angry households, these individuals maintain their anger as they grow up. When they get themselves killed in their script to get others, they are just as dead as the outwardly depressed patient who kills himself. The advanced *"I'll get you even if it kills me"* patient is the paranoid who even makes up his enemies.

We have been training the California Youth Authority staff now for 14 years. These great people deal every day with angry young crooks who, underneath their anger, their "shine them on" attitude, are terribly depressed. One of the ways that the CYA staff gets to these young people is by doing a script checklist early in the encounter between staff and ward. When the ward discovers, as the checklist is developed, that he is planning to be dead by the time he is 25, he may begin to become interested in serious therapy. He discovers that *he* is in charge of his own destruction, that the world is not out to get him except as he sets up the world to get him, and gradually he learns to value himself sufficiently to want to stay alive.

The adult offender is in the same place. Martin Groder, formerly at Marion Federal Penitentiary, set up an outstanding program for adult offenders, many of whom were lifers in for murder, without possibility of parole. At a three-day workshop we did there some years ago, one of the prisoners was ruminating about an escape plan, in which he was almost bound to kill and be killed. The therapeutic choice was for him to decide not to be killed, to give up his *"I'll get you even if it kills me"* script. The movement that Groder and others started was highly successful in turning criminals into therapists who could deal skillfully with other prisoners (as well as with some people outside prison). Groder used a combination of TA, gestalt, primal scream, Synanon games and other approaches.

SUMMARY

At least four steps are essential in depression redecision:

1. The Adult no-suicide contract.
2. The Child second degree impasse work, in which the Child fights back against the injunction and redecides to live.
3. The Child third degree impasse work, in which the adapted Child

gives up his self-concept of worthlessness and insignificance, and the free Child acknowledges his own intrinsic value and declares himself worthy of living.

4. The *self*-reparenting, in which the new Parent loves and cares for the Child.

CHAPTER 10

Obsession-Compulsion: A Case History

Zach is a very special client. Working with great courage, he permanently stopped his obsessive-compulsive behavior in a three-day workshop. We don't suggest that every person with a 10-year history of handwashing, retracing steps, and constant obsessing and doubting can become well in three days. Since much of the literature suggest that clients like Zach are virtually incurable, we include his work to demonstrate that cure is possible.

On Friday morning we begin the workshop with introductions. There are 14 participants, half of whom are therapists. Sixteen therapists, attending this month's four-week workshop, are observing. After introductions, we ask for contracts. *"Pretend it is now Sunday afternoon and the workshop has ended. You are driving away from*

Mt. Madonna. You've accomplished what you came here to accomplish. How are you different as you drive away?" Zach is the fifth participant to respond:

Zach: I am not an obsessive-compulsive anymore. (*As he speaks, he wrings his hands as if he were washing them, and he stares fixedly at the floor. He's blonde, handsome, and appears younger than his age, 22; in another way, however, he seems older because of his obvious tension.*)

Bob: What does obsessive-compulsive mean to you? How are you different, driving off?

Zach: I am not worrying that I ran over somebody even though I know I didn't. I am not stopping to turn around and drive back to be sure I didn't run over somebody. (*He tells of other obsessive-compulsive behavior, such as washing his hands repeatedly and checking light switches.*)

Bob: OK. During this workshop, will you do no compulsive behavior?

Zach: Yes, I understand that is a rule. Dr. Y. explained that to me. (*Dr. Y. has seen Zach twice, on referral from Zach's employer, then referred Zach to us for this weekend workshop. Zach will be returning to therapy with Dr. Y.*)

Bob: When you want to do an obsessive-compulsive act, instead of choosing to do it, will you choose to have a sexual fantasy instead?

The most important work of the weekend has already been accomplished: Zach has agreed to alter his *behavior* and, in agreeing, must recognize that he is in control of his symptoms. We had told his therapist we would not accept Zach without that prior agreement.

Bob's suggestion of a "sexual fantasy" is also dramatically important. Bob suggests that Zach has the ability to choose his *thoughts*. Bob asked him to have sexual fantasies because, in our experience, obsessive thoughts and compulsive behavior are very often used by the adapted Child as a defense against forbidden sexual thoughts and feelings. This assignment cuts through the early prohibitions and places us on the side of the free Child. If the client doesn't accept, we know this is a crucial issue for future work. If he says he "can't," we will look for ways for him to demonstrate to himself that he "can" take charge of his thoughts. If he does permit himself sexual fantasies, this may lead to a redecision to be sexual and to drop his obsessions and compulsions.

Zach: I don't know what you mean.
Bob: Instead of choosing to obsess and compulse, want to have a sexual fantasy instead?
Zach: Oh, no! No, that isn't what I wanted. I want to not obsess and not think about anything really. I wasn't wanting. . . . (*He is confused, believing he is being accused by Bob of desiring sexual fantasies.*)
Bob: Are you willing to do an experiment? For the rest of this day, are you willing to give yourself a sexual fantasy whenever you think about a compulsive activity? Instead of doing the activity or worrying about doing it?
Zach: I don't know what you mean.
Bob: Fantasize about sex instead of obsessing and compulsing.

Usually, we would not repeat ourselves and instead would ask a client what he thought he heard or would "stroke the rebel Child" by saying, for instance, "*Wow, I'll bet you knew how to get your parents to climb the wall. I'll bet whenever you didn't want to do something, you did a fantastic job of pretending not to understand!*" Zach is different. He is frightened and needs the calm reiteration that Bob is giving. This time Zach lets himself understand the assignment.

Zach: If I do that, I would feel guilty. (*Again, he wrings his hands and appears agitated.*)
Bob: That's the problem. That's what I am talking about. Will you go ahead and have a sexual fantasy instead of obsessing and compulsing?
Zach: (*Wringing his hands*) Are there special fantasies? With my wife or with other women?
Bob: Your pick, man. Not mine. They're your fantasies.
Zach: (*Long pause*) I am not sure I understand.
Mary: I've got a hunch that when you were a little kid you were

never allowed to say "no." (*Mary finds a "kind" way to confront his resistance.*)

Zach: There was always, you know, what has to be done.

Mary: So you were allowed to say only *"I will" or "I can't."*

Zach: Mostly *"I will."*

Mary: So, would you play around here, during the marathon, with saying *"I won't"* whenever you don't like what someone tells you to do?

Zach: That's very hard for me.

Mary: I know. So far you have not said *"No"* to Bob's suggestion about sexual fantasies . . . and you haven't said *"Yes."* And you haven't said *"Yes"* or *"No"* to what I suggested.

Zach: (*Long pause. He wrings his hands and doesn't answer.*)

Bob: What else do you want from the weekend?

Zach: When I get my job back, if I get my job back, I can perform . . . not really outstandingly . . . I don't really want that. But I can perform without being stagnant because of obsessive-compulsive behavior.

Mary: What's your job?

Zach explains that he is a draftsman and has been promoted to supervisory rank. He has taken this so seriously that he rereads everything and has not OK'd any of the work done by his subordinates. *"What if it is wrong in some way?"* His anxiety is extreme. The entire group appears concerned. The participants are leaning forward, watching us closely, and the man beside Zach keeps reaching toward him and then pulling back. No one makes a sound. Zach explains that he has been asked to resign, but hopes to be cured and to keep his job.

Zach: And now what I think is that everything is kind of bleak. I won't have a job and my wife is having a baby. I am going to have to go home and work for Dad, if I lose my job. I'll have to work on my Dad's farm and I don't like working on the farm. That's why I went to college. I had hoped to do well.

Mary: Are you depressed?

Zach: I don't think you'd call it a depression. It's more a horror. An anxiety and helplessness, you could say. I want to be able to do something. My psychiatrist didn't say anything about depression. He said it was obsession-compulsion.

We ask about suicide and he establishes that he will not kill himself, even if he is fired and/or doesn't drop his symptoms.

Zach: You see, I am very much opposed to suicide. My mother tried to kill herself and she ... often ... suggests she will kill herself.
Mary: When she is threatening suicide, first, how old are you?
Zach: Eleven, I think.

We ask more details and learn his Child decisions:

Zach: What I said to myself kinda was I had to be perfect. If I do everything right for her, she won't kill herself.
Bob: Now I understand! If you do anything wrong, your mother may kill herself. No wonder you don't commit yourself to sexual fantasies or saying "No" to me or Mary. No wonder everything seems like a horror for you. Anything you do, you'd have to do perfectly or your mother might kill herself. No wonder you think you have to be so careful to do everything right and check again and again.
Zach: Yes. I'd like to go out of here and not worry about making mistakes.
Bob: OK, Zach. I hear you. I want to stop at this point. (*Bob is stopping because he and Zach have made a direct contact. Also, Bob's interpretation is very important and he wants Zach to think about it.*)

In the next session, Zach asks to work.

Zach: I feel a lot like Al, I think, when he talks about worrying all the time. That's all I do. It seems like I worry 24 hours a day. I can't conceive of my life without worrying.
Bob: Had any sexual fantasies since this morning?
Zach: No, sir. I tried. In here I tried three times. I was afraid ... I'd start crying. I felt a lot of anxiety.
Bob: Worrying about having sexual fantasies?

Zach: Just thinking about it. I felt . . . kind of all tight.

Bob: And then?

Zach: And then I'd say to myself, you are getting all tight because you've been thinking of having sexual fantasies and there is no reason to be uptight. Then I wouldn't think of it anymore. *(Zach pauses, then launches into a frenzied account of his job experiences. He believes that his constant worrying helped him become the best employee in his group and that this led to his rapid promotion. After his promotion, he slept little, worried constantly, and increased his symptoms.)* I'm supposed to approve their work . . . what if one of the others doesn't do it right? Someone could die. If I approve the blueprint and it's wrong and someone dies, I am a murderer! This kind of problem broke me down. *(He sits with head in hands.)*

Mary: So at this point are you ready to concede that your worries are excessive and led to your stopping your own productivity?

Zach: Yes. That is when I went to the psychiatrist.

Mary: I'd like to know more about you. What did you worry about five years ago, if you are willing to say?

Zach: About not getting good enough grades. About not learning enough. About having to wash my hands a hundred times and never feeling clean enough. I've always worried about that.

Mary: Always?

Zach: Since I was about 11. Always worried about locking doors. *(Pause)* Always worried about masturbating. I don't masturbate anymore. But up until I saw the psychiatrist, I worried I was a homosexual because I used to masturbate. Then I learned from Dr. Y. . . . that masturbation and homosexuality don't go together. I worried about. . . . I lock the doors five times and turn off the light switch six times and worry if I really did it.

Mary: And you were about 11 when your mother was threatening suicide?

Zach: About 11.

Mary: Everything crashed down at once, huh?

Zach: Yeah. And I started what you could call sexual feelings then too.

Mary: Of course. And nobody told you that proved you were normal.

Zach: No, nobody told me. About sex. No. And I started masturbating.

Bob: Of course.

Mary: And nobody told you that was normal.

Zach: Oh, no! My grandmother said it was shameful. She found my underpants in my drawer and she said, *"Don't you ever do that again! I'm tired of washing your filthy underpants."*

Mary: So there was no one who told you that your growing up and becoming a man was great.

Zach: No, I didn't have anyone to talk to. My parents were breaking up and my mother was going to kill herself and that was more important.

Bob: They were more important than you?

Zach: I thought they were more important. I wish I . . . I would have . . . could have had more attention.

Bob: What did they say about your checking light switches six times and locking doors five times.

Zach: They didn't know. For about a year. Because I lived in a room away from the house and I'd do all those things out there.

Mary: You were separated from your family! (*Mary is amazed, remembering a young obsessive-compulsive she'd treated years ago, who grew up in a cabin behind the family home.*)

Zach: A little room with a bathroom and closet. And bed. There weren't enough bedrooms in the house. My grandmother had one, my sisters had one, and my parents had one. I'd be out there two or three hours a day, showering and checking things.

Bob: Pretend you are there right now. Be in your room. How do you explain to yourself, 11-year-old Zach, why you are showering and checking things?

Zach: I am very cautious about being dirty. I have to make sure I am clean. I'm worried . . . if I have any germs and someone else gets them, they might die. Or get very sick. I had hepatitis and that put me up for a month and maybe that's where I got the germ idea.

Mary: There you are . . . what are you saying about hepatitis . . . or about germs. Be there.

Zach: I'm . . . I think I got it from a dirty kid. A dirty kid who lives next door. I don't know. I honestly never even touched him but

I figure I must have gotten it from him and I am very sick. He was dirty. I wore clean clothes. Our family is cleaner. He wore dirty clothes and told dirty jokes.

Bob: So that's where he's dirty. He thinks about sex.

Zach: He knew more about sex.

Bob: See him there and tell him whether sex and germs are the same?

Zach: I am not sure what you mean. People who are dirty, who don't wash, can be like that kid and also be dirty in their minds.

Bob: See the kid there in front of you, pretend he is there, and tell him, *"Germs come from thoughts"* or *"Germs don't come from thoughts."*

Zach: No, germs don't come from thoughts.

Mary: You are sure?

Zach: Yes. They are not the same even if the same people have them. Even if a kid doesn't keep clean and also tells dirty jokes.

Bob: Right on, pal!

They continue to work until Zach concedes that no one gets physically ill from having sexual thoughts and fantasies. Zach smiles for the first time during the marathon.

We divide the group, including the observers, into triads, that will meet for 45 minutes. Within the triads they take turns being therapist and clients and continue to work.

When the late afternoon session begins, Zach asks to work.

Zach: My triad thinks I should tell you. . . . When I was 12 or 13, I knew something was wrong with me. When I was . . . after awhile . . . I figured I couldn't go on like this. So finally I went to my Dad and . . . well . . . told him about washing and everything. I told him I wanted to see a psychiatrist. My father said, *"You shouldn't worry about things like that. You're making a mountain out of a molehill."* And last month I told him I was going to see a psychiatrist and he was upset. He said, *"Don't see a psychiatrist. I worry about things, too. I'm real cautious and I don't see anything wrong with that."*

Bob: Sure hard to get heard in your house.

Zach: Yes. There wasn't much motion either way. (*Long pause*)

Bob: Would you be willing to consider that a great deal of your obsessive-compulsive thinking and behavior has to do with avoiding sexual thoughts and fantasies? Now that you've separated dirt from dirt, one of the quickest ways you can cure yourself is to go ahead and have sexual fantasies.

Zach: I am kinda locked in another thing just now. It's my religion. It's Catholic. And it's another thing that comes with that . . . not wanting people to die because of me. It's a mortal sin. You go to hell for causing someone's death.

Mary: I don't understand how you can cause someone's death by enjoying sexual fantasies. What's the connection?

Zach: Christ. Christ died for our sins. To sin is like causing His death. It's taboo, you know, to think about sex. To think about a boy and girl . . . situation.

Mary: Well, Zach, a lot of Catholics do it. They'd have died out, that first generation, if they hadn't thought about sex and then gone and done it. (*Group laughs.*)

Bob: Hell of a lot of Catholics in the world and they only got here one way. Somebody screwed somebody.

Zach: You think I should think about sex?

Bob: Every time you start obsessing, have a sexual fantasy instead. For today only. To see what you do with it.

Zach: What about my religion?

Mary: Well, by luck, you came to the right place. (*Laughs*) You'll never believe this. There are three priests and two nuns in this room.

Zach: (*Looking around*) I . . . really?

Mary: You all willing to introduce yourselves? (*During morning introductions, they had simply said that they were counselors.*)

All five introduce themselves to Zach.

Zach: I thought of talking to a priest. Even recently. I asked my psychiatrist and he told me not to, because they are biased and . . . wouldn't be good for me.

Jay: Well, you and I are in the same triad. And so is Joe. You didn't know you've already been talking to two priests.

Zach laughs. Several talk at once.

Group member: If you want a really unbiased opinion from one of the world's greatest sex-fantasying Catholics, just ask me!
Nun: Your psychoanalyst doesn't know about the new theological understandings.

The group spends about 15 minutes discussing sex and theology. Everyone tells him that sexual fantasies are fine.

Mary: Hey, Zach, your parents must have been very frightened of sex. And Granny, too. They didn't give you support for growing up. I don't think it matters all that much what the Church says. If your parents had been loving and warm and happy about sex and about each other, you'd have paid little attention to the anti-sexual-thoughts part of your religion. You'd have used your Catholicism differently.
Priest: I'd like to say one thing about that. Every time the Church has committed heresy in its history, it's always had to do with the degradation of the human body. The body is to be cherished and enjoyed.
Bob: Will you enjoy your sexual fantasies?
Zach: I will.

Before dinner Zach and one of the nuns have a long conversation during which Mary heard her say to Zach, *"You want to be well, don't you? If you want to be well, you must do as the doctor says. If he gave you penicillin, you'd take it. Just the same way, you should have sexual fantasies!"* The group had coalesced around Zach. Everyone liked him. Bob thought of him as an ailing but favorite quarterback who the whole community was determined must be well for the Big Game.

Friday evening Zach works again briefly:

Zach: I found out my anxiety makes my life completely miserable.
Bob: Claim that. I make me anxious and I make my life miserable.
Zach: I don't know. I don't feel I make myself miserable with my anxiety. I feel my anxiety makes me miserable.

Bob: Whose anxiety is it?

Zach: Not mine.

Mary: Then whose?

Zach: Other people's. My anxiety is not caused by me, though. It's caused by looking around at situations and . . .

Mary: You look at situations and decide to be anxious about them.

Zach: No, the situations give me anxiety.

Mary: Again. It's absolutely essential that you become aware that you are the one who reacts with anxiety. Nobody gives you anxiety.

Zach: (*Long pause*) I feel my anxiety has control over everything I do. And that it can drive me to do any ridiculous thing.

Mary: I am sure that is how you feel. You were an anxious kid. And you still make yourself anxious.

Bob: Are you willing to keep your mind open that you are in charge of your own anxiety?

Zach: It's very hard to control.

Bob: I know. Right now I'm not talking about getting your feelings under control. Are you willing to keep your mind open that you are in charge of your anxiety and ɔobody else is?

Zach: I'll keep my mind open.

Bob: I'd like to leave you with that.

Saturday morning:

Zach: I am feeling responsible for some of the people here. We talked a long time last night and I know they want me to get over my symptoms. I am worried that I could let them down. If I don't get well, they might worry and it would be my fault.

Bob: Tell them personally.

Zach: Especially you, Jay. I know you want me to be over all my symptoms and if I don't. . . . You're a priest . . . will it hurt you in some way?

Jay: No . . .

Mary: Wait, Jay, don't answer yet. Zach, sit here in this chair and pretend you are Jay. Answer what you would answer if you were Jay.

Zach: I would be praying for you and if my prayers didn't come true

I would believe that it was my fault. I'd done something wrong.

Mary: Say more. Exaggerate. Start with, *"I am a priest and therefore I am totally in charge of curing everybody."*

Zach: I am a priest and if anything goes wrong it is my fault.

Mary: No one would ever die or have a disaster except when I do something wrong.

Zach: That isn't true. Not entirely true.

Mary: Stay with it. Tell Zach, priest, exactly what your responsibilities are in how Zach runs his life.

Zach: (*Long pause*) I have responsibility . . . no, I have no responsibility. I can't control what you do.

Bob: Great! I think you've got it! Now, see your mother, and tell her the same thing. *"I have no responsibility. I can't control what you do."*

Zach: Mother, I have no responsibility. I can't control what you do. I really can't. (*He begins to sob.*) I'm not feeling bad. I am . . . relieved. (*Jay holds Zach, as he weeps.*)

Saturday afternoon Zach does some very brief third degree impasse work between his autonomous self and his helpless self. He accepts that he creates his anxiety by his beliefs.

Saturday evening Zach reports that his triad wants him to realize that he is a nice person.

Jay: I said "loveable." I didn't say "nice person." You are a nice person, too.

Mary: Great idea. Zach, are you willing to pretend you are the part of you that loves you? And say what is loveable and what is nice about you?

Zach: I don't have a clear idea of why I am in this world.

Bob: Because your father's sperm joined your mother's egg.

Zach: (*laughs*) This is a very strange experience here. You say things people are not supposed to say. And I am getting well. I mean, I don't know if I can say I am valuable without knowing why.

Mary: When will your baby be born? (*Zach answers.*) OK, pretend your baby is born and tell the baby whether or not the baby's valuable.

Zach: To me he seems very valuable. Or she. Yes, you are valuable.

I don't know why. You are valuable. I want a baby very much.

Mary: (*Goes to tape recorder and plays back his words.*) Say these same words about yourself.

Zach: *I seem to be very valuable. I don't know why. I am valuable. I want me very much.* I understand. You are saying I can feel the same way about me as I do about my wife and baby. That will take some practice.

Bob: Practice away! You'll have fun practicing.

Sunday morning, Zach brings up his job problems and resolves that he is not totally responsible there, either. He still feels some responsibility.

Mary: Some, yes. But listen to your grandiosity. You have in the past acted as if the world was full of nincompoops about to kill themselves or others. And you are the only one in charge of everything. Would you let the rest of them assume a little bit of charge of their own lives?

Zach: Yeah, I will. But what about careless people?

Mary: Fire them. (*Zach laughs.*)

Mary: You've been suckered. Suckered into thinking you have to push all the right buttons for everyone. I'll show you. Come over here and sit. (*Mary describes a giant switchboard in front of him.*) Now let yourself be very busy trying to plug everyone in. Move your hands . . . that's it . . . keep that switchboard going. You've got the idea. Now, Zach, let's walk around behind the machine. Look . . . all your work, and none of the wires are connected.

Zach: Whew. Yes. I understand. I make up the connections.

Bob: (*Goes to the board and draws a script matrix.* See Figure 24) From your Parent: *"Be perfect. Do everything right. Work hard."* And from here, the injunction, *"DON'T MAKE IT, ZACH. DON'T BE SUCCESSFUL."* (*Bob adds the other injunctions*). I want you to think about *"Don't be successful."* In the service of this injunction, you were compulsive, obsessive, and therefore unproductive. That's what you've done on the job so far. The compulsive things you have done are in the

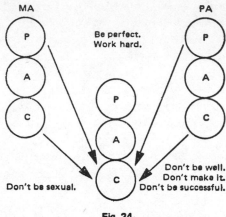

Fig. 24

service of not making it. Not the other way around. Should you stay obsessive and compulsive, there is not a possibility in the world that you'll have a successful life.

Zach: I don't think anyone told me not to be successful.

Bob: Your father tells you not to get rid of the symptoms that cause you to be unsuccessful. My hunch is he told you in other ways, too. Being critical . . . not listening . . . however.

Zach: He's critical all right. I really don't want to work for him. I'd never do anything right by his standards. I see what you mean. If I use his standards, I am never successful. Yes. He has the same problems. He worries all the time. Income tax, putting down every penny he earned. He's always afraid he forgot a dollar somewhere and he really doesn't have any money anyway. I know the IRS isn't watching him, for goodness sake.

Bob: Will you see your father and tell him the differences between you.

Zach: Well, I am weaker physically . . . shorter, lighter, not muscular. I am . . . smarter. Yes, by golly, I am smarter. And I am not worrying half as much today. I believe I am getting well.

Bob: I am curing myself. I see when something is wrong with me and I do something about it.

Zach: That is absolutely true. I used to listen to you. That's why it took me 10 years to see a psychiatrist. I am not listening to you. I think for myself.

Bob: Good! Now, will you tell him that you masturbated and that is OK. That you have sexual fantasies and that is OK. That you have sex with your wife and that is OK.

Zach: I can't tell him that. He has never once mentioned sex to me.

Bob: So that's another way you'll be different.

Zach: Whew! I . . . before I married my wife, I used to masturbate. And that was OK for a boy to do. I still do not believe it is OK for a married man.

Bob: OK. You've a right to figure out your own beliefs. So long as you allow yourself to think and to be flexible.

Zach: Yes. I used to masturbate and that was OK. I . . . I found out here that practically everyone masturbates and has sexual fantasies. Even . . . people I didn't think did that. I have sexual fantasies and now I enjoy them. And I never used to enjoy sex with my wife until two weeks ago when my psychiatrist gave me a book about sex in marriage and I learned a great deal and so did my wife. I enjoy sex with my wife and that is all right.

Bob: Now tell your mother.

Zach: OK. She would be shocked. Mother, I have sexual fantasies, I used to masturbate, and I have sex with with my wife. All of that is all right.

Bob: When I do these things, I am all right.

Zach: I am all right! And I don't feel guilty . . . even with sexual fantasies!

The group cheers and many of them rush up to hug Zach. For several minutes participants congratulate him. He is smiling and laughing.

During "goodbyes," Zach collects addresses and promises to keep in touch with various participants. He is laughing and crying and reports that he has never been this happy in the past. He agrees to continue his "no obsessive-compulsive behavior" contract with his therapist on his return from the marathon.

The following week Zach's therapist phoned with great enthusiasm for the gains Zach had made. Zach remained in therapy for several months. When he learned that his employers decided to fire him, in spite of his changes, he looked for and found a comparable job. His son was born and he phoned us with the news.

Two years later Zach came with his wife to a marathon. We didn't even recognize him until Saturday morning, when he talked of his previous symptoms. He was self-assured, very much liked his family and his work, and had come to the marathon primarily, we guessed, to show us his successes. He and his wife worked on some minor problems and this time Zach let himself experience his rage at his parents. At the end of the marathon, he recognized that he is now sufficiently intact to protect himself and his son from their pathology. His wife, in telling participants about his previous experience, said, *"I was so scared. I thought they had given him a special, new kind of drug, because he came home so happy and relaxed. I kept thinking it would wear off . . . but it never did. He was a whole new person."*

During the next three years, we received occasional letters and phone calls from Zach and his wife. At last report, they were doing well.

In treating obsessive-compulsives, we have some rules:

1) The first contract is that the client stop performing compulsive acts, no matter how difficult this may seem. Without this contract, therapist and client support the magic that the client "can't" control his behavior and therefore "can't" get well. This is similar to agreeing to treat a kleptomaniac who continues to steal.

2) Because the client may be very anxious when he stops obsessive-compulsive behavior, we offer at least once-daily sessions and prefer that the client be treated in a workshop. If the client can't afford intensive treatment, we refer the client to public agencies for part of the treatment, making certain that the therapists involved are all knowledgeable about our rules. These extra sessions would be for specific goals, such as learning to give and receive strokes.

3) We offer short-term rather than long-term treatment. Therapists and clients alike must be clear about a termination date, so that they do not become involved in "forever" therapy.

4) We offer group treatment, because obsessive-compulsive clients are isolates who are helped greatly by group support and encouragement. Also, because they are isolates, they need friends.

5) Whenever a client uses religion to support pathology rather

than health, we like assistance from willing clergy. If this is not available, we focus back to the family injunctions, as Mary did when she said, *"Your parents and Granny must have been very frightened of sex."*

6) From the beginning we stress the autonomy of the individual. The individual chooses his behavior, thoughts, and emotions. Therefore, he can make new choices. As soon as Zach began to understand that he made himself anxious, he became less anxious.

7) The compulsive clients we have known have all hated themselves. The therapist and group must love them in order for them to learn to love themselves.

8) Compulsive acts are designed by the adapted Child to ward off disaster by magic rituals. The client's magic is confronted as soon as the therapist hears it. However, the entire magical belief system does not have to be understood before the client stops being compulsive. When the client drops one piece of magic, as Zach did when he differentiated between dirt and "dirt," he is on his way to health. Nor does the therapist need to know all the underlying feelings and thoughts that the client guards against by being compulsive. Zach's rage at his parents, an extremely important aspect of his pathology, remained buried for two years after his therapy work was finished. We urge that therapists be willing to work quickly rather than thoroughly. An obsessive-compulsive client does *not* do well with an obsessive therapist.

9) *"Have a sexual fantasy"* is a fine way to start.

CHAPTER 11

Phobias: One Wednesday Afternoon

In each four-week workshop, we set aside a specific time for treating phobic clients. This Wednesday afternoon we list the participants and their fears on the blackboard and then begin.

Mary: I want to start with the Japanese mouse. That sounds fun. OK, Aiko?
Aiko: I don't think they are fun. I'd like to start.
Mary: It will be fun. First, I know American mice and Mexican mice. But I've never met a Japanese mouse. What's it look like?

Mary is setting the stage for a comedy, because we have found that clients desensitize themselves much more easily while playing and enjoying than they do when we use the more classical desensitization methods that require relaxation and calm. Mary asks for a description of the mouse so that both she and Aiko will be seeing the same creature.

Aiko: It's three inches long and its tail is another three inches. It's ugly. It's brown and furry and has beady black eyes.

Mary: Kinda cute. Anything about it that is actually harmful or dangerous.

Aiko: Yes, it carries germs.

Bob: Like your fingers and your neighbor's fingers . . . and mouths. . . .

Aiko: (*laughs*) It gets in the food.

Mary: OK. Everything has to eat. So . . . pretend right now that I am holding a Japanese mouse, and I'm putting a lovely gold collar around its neck. It's a brown mouse, three inches long plus a three-inch tail . . . beady eyes.

Aiko: Can it get loose? (*Obviously Aiko is actively in the scene when she asks this.*)

Mary: No way! The collar is very firm and it's fastened to a two-foot-long fine gold chain. And fastened to the chain is a pin. I am going to stick the pin into the rug and the mouse can only move on a two-foot radius. Where should I stick the pin . . . how far away from you?

Aiko: There. (*About 15 feet from her chair*)

Mary: OK. See it there? It's running around in its circle. Tell it what you are experiencing?

Aiko: It gives me the creeps.

Mary: Tell it how come you think it is in charge of your creeps.

Aiko: (*laughs*) By darting around without forewarning.

Mary: OK, you see it darting around with the chain still pinned to the rug. You willing to tell it that you scare yourself, give yourself the creeps, when you see it?

Aiko: Yeah. I do scare myself.

Mary: Aware that is so?

Aiko: Yeah.

Mary: Tell it some more.

Aiko: I remember when I got so scared. It was the time that my father was in the hospital. I was staying with him, taking care of him, and I was getting out fresh clothes for him . . . to dress him . . . and there was a dead mouse in the clothes. (*trembles visibly*)

Mary: Oh, so you scared yourself about a dead one?

Aiko: Right. And I feel as if he sent all the mice in Tokyo to retaliate . . . I am seeing mice all over and I am afraid of the live ones.

Mary: Want to work with this live one first or with a dead one?

Aiko: Live.

Mary: OK, tell it what you are feeling now.

Aiko: I'm OK. It isn't paying any attention to me.

Mary: And what are you experiencing?

Aiko: That my fear is reaching out to it, attracting its attention. I have this feeling that if any animal sees you're afraid, he'll attack.

Mary: Yeah, that's an old belief. And what would he do if he attacked? What would happen?

Aiko: I don't know. I'm afraid . . . He might crawl on me or I might accidentally step on him and kill him. (*shudders*)

Mary: I am hearing that you are afraid of his crawling on you, but you sounded more afraid at the thought of you as the killer of the mouse.

Aiko: I'd never thought of that. I think it is true.

We prefer to keep phobia work very simple . . . with one scene at a time. Now we suddenly have many issues complicating the work.

Mary: Aiko, I hear several places to go. There's your father in the hospital and there's your fear of killing mice and your fear of dead mice and your fear of live mice. There are too many things to deal with. Are you willing to deal only with the live mouse now because we started with that . . . and save the other issues for later?

Aiko: I think that is a good idea. Yes. And I know I have work to do about my father.

Mary: OK, back to this mouse. I'm going to pick him up and give him to Bob to keep for us. (*Does this in pantomime*)

Bob: What am I supposed to do with it? I'll put it in this little box. It'll be safe there.

Mary: Fine. Now, Aiko, I want you to come over here and sit on the floor and be a nice Japanese mouse . . . and describe yourself. Willing?

Aiko: (*laughing and crawling about*) I move very fast and I can crawl under anything. I know my way around and I know how to get what I want.

Group Member: Right on!

Aiko: (*smiling*) That's true. I move fast, know my way around, and know how to get what I want. (*She is owning these qualities in herself. The group members cheer and applaud, because they agree with this description of Aiko, who is very intelligent and successful.*)

Mary: Fine! Now go back to your seat. I'm bringing the mouse back and putting it right where it was. (*Bob pantomimes taking it out of the box and handing it to Mary, who pantomimes sticking the pin in the carpet and putting the mouse down.*)

At this point we usually move the feared object closer to the client, a few inches at a time, as the client says she is comfortable and wants it closer. Whenever she feels any fear, we move it back and ask the client to tell the mouse what fantasy she is using to scare herself. Before we could suggest moving Aiko's mouse nearer to her, Aiko came to sit beside the fantasied mouse. She pretends to pick it up and strokes with her other hand.

Aiko: It's not really scary. It's not moving. It's soft.

Mary: You've got a Japanese mouse who likes a massage.

Aiko: (*laughs*)

Mary: You all right with it? Even if it moves?

Aiko: I don't want it to move. Well, when I let go, it will move. I don't want it to run toward me.

Mary: You willing to use your hands to push it away, if it does such a strange, unmouselike thing as run TO you?

Aiko: Yes. (*She lets go of the mouse and pretends to push it away.*) I am not ready yet to deal with killing it.

Mary: Another time?

Aiko: Yes. I'm fine. I'm not afraid. Thank you.

Mary: If you want to, you can see how you are with a live one. Jacob (*a boy who lives nearby*) has a mouse or rat in a cage. I can't remember which.

Aiko: I would like to experiment. I'll do that. (*She does, and at the next session reports that she was not at all afraid as she held the rat.*)

The next client, afraid of butterflies and moths, imagines a brightly colored butterfly in a tiny silver cage. She tells the butterfly she is afraid of its fluttering and afraid *"You might fly in my hair or in my ears or down my neck."* (Her voice is very young.)

Mary: OK. Now say it again. Say, *"You might fly in my hair or in my ears or down my neck and I am such a tiny little girl that I can't stop you."*

Rea: I'm such a . . . that's nonsense. I'd have to be less than a year old.

Mary: Then say what is true.

Rea tells the butterfly that she, Rea, can and will protect herself. To finish her desensitization, she pretends to hold the fluttering butterfly.

Mary: It's fluttering. On your hand. What does your hand experience?

Rea: It feels light. A little bit tickly.

Mary: Is that an all right feeling?

Rea: Yes. Yes, it is.

Bob: A little bit sexy, isn't it?

Rea: I'm not sure. (*giggles*) But I'm not a bit afraid.

The third client on Wednesday afternoon wanted to stop being afraid of birds. Since we had already worked in two imaginary scenes, Bob asked for an early experience with birds. Rosemary remembered a scene when she was five years old. A sparrow flies into their house and mother traps it in the bathroom, shutting the door so that the bird cannot get into the rest of the house. Mother remains sob-

bing and hysterical until father comes home to free the bird. Bob
asks Rosemary to be there and talk to the bird through the closed
door. *"I am afraid of you because . . .,"* Rosemary begins, but finds
no reason to be afraid. She says, *"The bird can't hurt me."* She opens
the door just enough to peek inside. She reports that the bird is flying wildly about the bathroom. She says, *"Little bird, you are the
only one who could get hurt."* Feeling very young, she weeps for the
bird and then Bob asks if there is anything she is willing to do for
the bird. She allows herself to imagine darting into the bathroom to
open the window so that the bird can fly away. She tells her mother
that she is no longer accepting mother's fears. Later in the afternoon, she goes, in reality, into our large pheasant coop and feeds the
pheasants. The next day she feeds the chickens and ducks and even
pets them. She lets herself enjoy watching the many species of wild
birds on our property and is not afraid.

After the mouse, butterfly, and bird, Bob announces that there is
time left this afternoon only for height phobias and swimming
phobias.

Bob: Everyone who has a height phobia please sit here on the floor
in front of me where you can see that ladder across the driveway leaning against the roof. (*Nine people gather together on
the floor, where they can look out the door to the driveway.*)
Mary: Wow, what a lot of phobias in one group. Weed yourself out
of the group if you are not afraid of climbing the ladder to the
roof; we'll take other kinds of height phobias later.
Bob: If you are at all scared and are climbing counter-phobically, get
back in. Now, what I want to do is to have you fantasize some
things, and every time you feel scared, even the slightest bit,
raise your left hand. At that point I'll stop, even if only one
hand is raised. This is your choice. You don't have to climb any
ladder anywhere—there is no pressure. (*So often, children who
are scared do it anyway, because of parental or peer pressure;
we want to do this from free, not adapted, Child.*) I do not
want anyone scaring self. Just do what feels perfectly fine. OK.
Fantasize you are opening the glass doors and walking across
the driveway. Walk step by step until you arrive at the foot of
the ladder. This tripod ladder is very steady and, in addition,

all your friends at the workshop will be holding it. They are grabbing hold and they hold it very firmly, so there is no possibility that the ladder will slip in any direction. Got it? I want you to look at the ladder and not close your eyes; some of you have your eyes closed, and it is dangerous to climb a ladder with closed eyes. (*group laughs*) You don't go climbing ladders with your eyes closed. I don't go climbing ladders with my eyes closed (*the YOU sounded as if Bob were coming from his Parent, so he changed it*). You are going to learn how to climb a ladder safely. Each of you pretend you are the first one to climb the ladder. So, grab ahold of either side of the ladder, grab with *both* hands, or grab a rung if you prefer to hold onto rungs—either way is safe. And your friends are standing around holding the ladder. Put one foot on the bottom rung. Stand there with one foot on the bottom rung and one foot on the driveway. You are firmly gripping the ladder so there is no chance that you will fall (*we don't say "of falling" or "slipping" because these words tend to be passive. Falls don't "happen" to people; people fall*). Be sure you have shoes that will grip firmly, and if you are wearing slippery shoes, get off the ladder, take them off, and go barefoot, or go get better shoes from your room. OK. Your feet are very secure—very, very secure. There is no chance that your feet will slip. Now, as you have your first foot on the bottom rung of the ladder, bring your second foot up and stand steadily on the first rung with both feet. And what are you all experiencing?

Ann: I experience anxiety for the future.

Bob: Back up. If you are in the future instead of the present, go back to the ground. Any other anxieties? Everyone else comfortable? The rest of you for the moment—pretend you are on another ladder, while I talk to these others. What are your anxieties about?

Ann: I might . . . fall off.

Bob: How are you going to fall off with a firm grip on the ladder and your feet planted firmly on the rung?

Ann: Only if I scare myself.

Bob: Even if you scare yourself more, how are you going to accomplish falling off?

Ann: True, I'm not.

Bob: Then would you say, *"There is no way I can fall off this ladder if I hold on"?*

Ann: That's right. There is no way since I'm holding tight.

Bob: OK. Will you see your mother and father down there in the audience and tell them, *"I'm not going to fall off or jump off this ladder"?* (*This is the beginning of the REDECISION; we are asking her to claim her own power in her Child.*)

Ann: I'm not going to fall off or jump off this ladder.

Bob: What does your mother do?

Ann: She's nervous.

Bob: Respond to her nervousness.

Ann: Be as nervous as you like. I'm not going to jump or fall. (*Many childhood fears are based on Episcripting,[1] or the Hot Potato Syndrome; parents scare children because they are afraid and thus pass on their fears to their offspring.*)

Bob: OK. What does your father do or say?

Ann: He's proud of me.

Bob: Good. What does he say?

Ann: Right on.

Bob: OK. Beth, what are you scaring yourself about?

Beth: I'm scared of switching from the ladder to the roof.

Bob: You are on the first step, not the top. Stay on the first rung, see your mother and father, and tell them you are not going to jump or fall. (*Many phobias are maintained by going into the future, instead of staying in the present, where there is actually nothing to be afraid of.*)

Beth: I'm not going to jump or fall.

Bob: Good. What does your mother say?

Beth: Get off that ladder right now. You might hurt yourself.

Bob: Answer her.

Beth: That's a lot of baloney. I'm only on the first rung.

Bob: Tell her again, *I'm not going to hurt myself.*

Beth: I'm not going to hurt myself.

Bob: What does your father say.

Beth: I don't know.

Bob: Guess.

Beth: You won't hurt yourself.

Bob: Great, take him along in fantasy to offset your mother, OK?

Beth: Yeah.

Bob: Willing to put your feet back on the first rung, Ann and Beth? (*They nod.*) OK. Put one foot on the rung, then bring the other up slowly, firmly, and plant it on the rung. Stand there firmly. What are you experiencing?

Ann and Beth: OK.

Bob: The rest of you still on the first rung? OK. Will you reach up and grab ahold above where your hands are, one hand at a time. Get a good grip. Now bring your feet up to the second rung, one foot at a time. Move one foot, then the other. You are now on the second rung. If you are nervous, raise your left hand. (*No one does, this time.*) OK. Look all around, see your mother and father down there, and will you all tell your mother and father, "*I'm not going to fall off or jump off this fucking ladder*"? (*All do this and laugh.*)

The profanity we use is not accidental. We are doing whatever we can to elicit free Child, and one of the ways is to use profanity. All little kids at some time enjoy using profanity, and using it here encourages the phobics to stop listening to Parental injunctions, to be non-adaptive.

Bob: Do any of you have any response from your mothers?

Beth: (*as her mother*) Get off that ladder, I told you.

Bob: Answer her back.

Beth: No way. (*laughter*)

Bob: Any other responses?

Al: Mine doesn't mind my climbing but is having such a fit that I said, "*Fuck.*"

Cindy: Mine says, "*You are making me nervous.*"

Bob: Answer.

Cindy: (*not audible*)

Bob: Yell so she can hear!

Cindy: *I* am not nervous!

Brad: Mine says, "*Be careful!*"

Mary: What does that mean? Answer her.

Brad: It just means . . . you know . . . take good care of yourself and hang on tight or you'll fall.

Mary: Respond.

Brad: Don't worry, I'll hang on tight.

Mary: Find a way to respond that is safe and not compliant.

Brad: I will take care of myself.

Bob: Any other mothers have anything to say?

Dee: Mine sits and smiles and says, *"You think you are brave. Wait until you get higher. The ladder will slip."*

Bob: Answer that. First, ask your friends if they are holding the ladder tightly or will they push it over when you get higher?

Dee: Will you push it over?

Group: NO.

Bob: Believe them?

Dee: Absolutely.

Beth: I am climbing fine. My mother is warning me about dizzy spells.

Bob: Answer.

Beth: I am strong, and I am not sick, and I never had a dizzy spell in my entire life in spite of all your talk about dizzy spells. I am perfectly safe. Hey that's true. All my life I have been phobic because of your damn fake dizzy spells. And you . . . you, mother, never had dizzy spells either. You faked dizzy spells to get your way. Heh, I am not scared anymore. I am very happy about that.

Bob: Any fathers have anything else to say?

Al: My father wants me to go faster.

Bob: Answer.

Al: I am enjoying myself, and I don't have to go faster. I'll take my time.

Bob: Ready for the third rung? OK. The hand moves higher on the ladder. (*realizing his switch from the imperative*) Move up the second hand, get a firm grip, move up one foot to the next rung, get well balanced, now move up your second foot. Is anybody scared?

Cindy: I am.

Bob: Go back to the second rung. What do you experience?

Cindy: My stomach gets fluttery and I feel breathless.

Bob: You flutter your stomach and hold your breath. Tell your mother that. *"When I get this high I flutter my stomach and hold my breath."*

Cindy tells mother that.

Bob: What does she say?

Cindy: Of course, because you are scared!

Bob: Answer.

Cindy: I don't want to do that. I want to get to the top.

Bob: Don't want to. (*Bob is reminding her of the difference between want and autonomy; people can "want" forever, and not "do" anything.*)

Cindy: I am breathing easier now, and I am not fluttering my stomach. I am not scaring myself.

Bob: Tell your mother: I'm not going to fall or jump off.

Cindy: I'm not going to fall or jump off, and that ladder is not going to break down under me.

Bob: Has she any response?

Cindy: No, but she doesn't believe I'm safe.

Bob: Will you tell her, *I don't give a fuck whether you believe me or not?*

Cindy: I don't. I don't give a fuck whether you believe me or not. That's your problem.

Bob: Want to go to the third step now?

Cindy: Yeah.

Bob: What do you experience?

Cindy: This time I'm fine.

Bob: (*to group*) Any other trouble on the third rung?

Ann: I feel proud of myself, and I am pounding my heart. . . .

Bob: What are you saying inside your head? To get you to beat your heart faster.

Ann: I might fall off and kill myself.

Bob: Will you take the other side: I WON'T fall off . . .

Ann: I don't know.

Bob: Who is in charge of your falling?

Ann: I am. I WON'T fall. I won't kill myself.

Bob: Say it again.

Ann: I won't fall. I won't kill myself. I see mother running out of the room, and hiding her face in a pillow, while my father is cheering.

Bob: What does he say?

Ann: He says you are a really good girl to climb when you are scared.

Bob: Tell him you are a woman, not a girl, and whether or not you are scaring yourself *now*.

Ann: I'm great now. I am a woman, and I am not scaring myself.

Bob: True? (*not sure about her*) (*She nods.*) Great. Everybody OK? Anybody not feeling good? (*looks around*) OK, will you look down on this gang helping you by holding the ladder and tell them, *"I can see further than you can, down there on the ground."*

All speak at once, some pretty quietly.

Bob: Come on, say it with enthusiasm. (*laughing*) (*Group does, laughing too.*) OK. Now will you climb up to the fourth rung. in the same manner you did before, holding the ladder firmly. Now look around. Everyone on the fourth rung? Everybody OK? What's wrong, Brad? (*He had held up his hand.*)

Brad: I am beginning to find anxiety. (*Bob decides not to quibble with the word "find," as finding a black cloud, or a case of measles!*)

Bob: OK, go back to the third rung. How are you scaring yourself?

Brad: I might fall. I feel ashamed, but the truth is I've never climbed this high on a ladder before in reality, and I might fall.

The reader is asked to remember at this point that we are still in the conference room: the participants are still sitting on the floor looking out the glass doors at the ladder. No one is actually on the ladder. This is how true to life this fantasy has become.

Bob: How are you going to fall?

Brad: I don't know.

Bob: Will you let go and fall backwards?

Brad: Of course not.

Bob: Of course, so tell your mother—of course I won't fall.

Brad: Of course I won't fall.

Bob: What do your parents say?

Brad: My father says, *"Go ahead."* My mother *"Pay attention."*

Bob: Answer her in German. *(German is this client's first language.)*

Brad: (Speaks in German. His friend, also from Germany, translates: *"You don't have to worry about me, I'm grown up."*)

Bob: OK now? *(Brad nods)* OK. Everybody comfortable on the fourth rung? OK. Now to the fifth rung and see how much more you can see than when you were lower. You can see the pond and the ducks and the horse and the cattle and our lovely plum trees in full bloom in the pasture. See all that? Everybody comfortable? Good. Take more time . . . maybe you can see the hawk soaring . . . maybe you can see further up the hill. See all the new things you can see that you missed, standing on the ground. Let yourself really enjoy. Everybody OK?

Brad: I am scared.

Bob: Go back to the fourth rung. How are you, there?

Brad: I am OK there.

Bob: OK, explain to your mother and father what the difference is between the fourth and the fifth rung.

Brad: Well, there's no big difference between the fourth and the fifth rung. I am moving up. I feel OK this time.

Bob: Great. What do you see?

Brad: I see birds flying, trees, I feel a breeze on my face. And all these people's faces looking up at me. I feel good.

One of the purposes of the work is to facilitate people's getting out of their scare by concentrating on the "here and now" fun things, rather than the projection into the future of what might happen. Hence, we bring in anything that we think of to switch the attention of the client to the present—birds, cattle, views, etc. One of the easiest ways for *anyone* to move out of bad feelings, ordinarily, is to learn to be aware of what is happening in his environment—see the hawks soaring, the plum trees in bloom, hear the ducks quack, the whippoorwill sing, feel the breeze on the skin, the warmth of the sun.

Dee: I'm bored with the ladder and don't think it's worth going up anymore.

Mary: Then don't. If it's not dramatic, it's not worth anything. (*Dee is a spoiler, and we don't want her spoiling this trip for others.*)

Bob: You are out of the trip. (*Highhanded of Bob, but he can always go back and work with her later, and it is important to find out what she feels when she sets herself up to get rejected, and teach her how she does it to herself.*)

Beth: I am not scared, and I want to say something to my parents right now. Because in my fantasy my father came out and is arguing with my mother and saying, "*For heaven's sake, let her be. She is enjoying it.*" And my mother is saying something to him to put him down. And to frighten everybody.

Mary: You are trying to change your mother.

Beth: OK, but what I am saying to her is, *I'm not listening to you anymore.*

Mary: Great. Fine.

Bob: Anyone else have anything to say to anybody?

Al: Yes, to my mother. You have been nervous all your life, and you'll continue to be nervous, and that's *your* bag. (*cheers*)

Fran: I'm going to say, Mother, you used to climb trees, and you used to tell me how you climbed to the top of trees, and I was always afraid to do it. Well, today I am climbing and I'm not going to fall and break my neck.

Mary: Tell your mother that it's OK for you to be a good tree climber even if it is her specialty.

Fran: I am going to climb as good as you climb.

Mary: Even though she may not like that? (*Mary has picked up that the real fear is of competing with a jealous mother, who says, in effect, "Don't compete with me."*)

Fran: Even though. I am doing it for me. Even though you did it first.

Bob: Anyone else? OK. Now up to the sixth. I am on the roof, waiting for you. Everybody OK?

Cindy: I feel a long way from the people holding the ladder.

Bob: And you are closer to me. (*After Bob says this, he thinks that it may have been a mistake and is encouraging a transference he doesn't want, but he decides to wait and see if this gets in the way of the real ladder climbing later. This is still the fantasy trip.*)

Cindy: True. *(laughs)*

Ev: I'm afraid. It is almost time for me to go from the ladder to the roof, and I hear my father saying that the ladder may go over.

Bob: I guarantee you that nothing will happen to the ladder. (*This may seem presumptuous, but in terms of both experience and statistics it won't. The ladder is very safe, and so are the people when they hold it.*) The ladder is very safe, and the roof is safe. It cannot fall over.

Ev: My father is worried that. . . .

Mary: In real life, does your father do your thinking for you?

Ev: Well, yes.

Mary: Will you tell him that you can test out situations for yourself . . . or tell him you need his brain. Whichever is true.

Ev: Hmmm. Dad, you sure do a lot of thinking for me.

Mary: Dad, I let you do a lot of thinking for me.

Ev: You like to do a lot of thinking for me. I can think for myself. *(cheers from the crowd)*

Bob: OK. One more rung to go. Now everybody spit . . . see who can spit farthest.

Participant: I am not going to hold the ladder if everybody is going to spit on me. *(laughter from all)*

Bob: Just this trip. Next trip we spit from the roof, downwind from the ladder holders. *(Everyone laughs again.)*

Bob: Now, move your right leg to the roof. Now your left leg. Let go of the ladder and you are on the roof. Is everyone on the roof?

Brad: I was frightened for a moment . . . when I . . . when you said to let go. I thought of waiting . . . then I let go. I think I'm OK, but I will find out on the real test.

Bob: Fine! Everybody who's ready for the real test, come on outside. And everyone else, too . . . the rest of you hold the ladder.

Group member: Wait . . . I have to get my camera.

Several run off to collect cameras and some of the climbers exchange tennis shoes for the sandals they had been wearing. Bob climbs the ladder and gets on the roof.

Bob: OK. One at a time. Who's first?

Several climb quickly and easily. As they reach the roof, the crowd below cheers, claps, and takes pictures. When Brad reaches the top, he is smiling and laughing.

Brad: I did it, I did it! I AM NOT AFRAID!

The rest, even rebellious Dee, scramble up the ladder to the roof. They stand on the sloping roof and look around.

We are on the side of one of the Santa Cruz mountains, Mt. Madonna, and we can see other slopes dotted with green pastures, live oak and redwood trees. The Monterey Bay is to the South and across the bay we can see Monterey Penninsula, with the Big Sur mountains in the background. The view is beautiful. Below us, in our pasture, is our "lake," and on the lake are ducks. The groups quacks at them and they quack back, and all laugh. Bob checks out each of them (the clients, not the ducks) to make sure they are not disguising or repressing some remnant of fear. One of the group is still afraid of getting back on the ladder to climb down. Bob asks her to holler down at her fantasized parents and tell them she is not going to fall off or jump off; then she gets on and off the ladder several times. The group below cheers, she waves to them, and goes on down the ladder. One of the participants has been taking Polaroid pictures, and gives each ex-phobic client a picture of the group on the roof. We ask them to continue going up and down the ladder during the remainder of the workshop.

Some of them request additional desensitization for other height phobias and some find that this single desensitization is sufficient. During the weekend, some go to Big Sur to climb on the rocks, some ride the outside elevators in San Francisco, and the following Wednesday a large group, including Ev, Brad, Cindy, and Al, ride the ferris wheel and roller coaster at the Santa Cruz Beach Amusement Park.

Next we go to the swimming pool, which is kept at 85 to 90 degrees for work with phobic clients, because they relax more easily in warm water. Bob takes the participants to the side of the pool and asks them to sit on the steps with their feet in the water. The others, who are again a cheering section, sit on the deep water side.

Bob asks each person to describe his fears exactly. *"Are you afraid of water in your nose?" "Your mouth?" 'Your throat?" "Your lungs?"* After hearing their fears, he invites them to come into the shallow water with him. All but Joe do. One at a time, they put their faces in the water and "blow bubbles." Bob demonstrates for them, making great, whale-like noises. They laugh and duplicate his actions. They have noise battles with each other and with Bob. This is fun, funny, and exciting, and already each Child is beginning to be less afraid. After they have been blowing at each other for a few minutes, Bob goes to Joe.

Bob: How long are you willing to put your head under the water?
Joe: Not at all.
Bob: Tell that to the water.
Joe: Water, I'm not going to put my head in you.
Bob: Tell the water you're afraid it will drown you.
Joe: Water, you may drown me.
Bob: Tell the water how.
Joe: You may get in my lungs and drown me.
Bob: Tell the water you are helpless in keeping it out.
Joe: (*laughing*) That's bullshit.
Bob: Yeah, tell the water that.
Joe: I can keep you out of my lungs, water.
Bob: Tell the water you are not going to let it drown you.
Joe: Water, I won't let you drown me.
Bob: Now tell that to your father and mother.
Joe: No, it's my brother. He threw me in.
Bob: OK. Tell your brother.
Joe: Pete, I am not going to let you drown me. You were bigger than me then, but you are not now. I WON'T LET YOU DROWN ME!
Bob: OK, now put your head under the water.

Joe does, at first just for a few seconds, and then, after a time, he is willing to play the noise game with the rest. The observers cheer.

Sometimes Bob gets the stopwatch and desensitizes one or two seconds at a time. Sometimes he uses fantasy first, having the client fantasize putting his head under water in increasingly longer periods of time, while he uses the stopwatch. This time, that wasn't necessary. As Joe talked to the water he began to be in touch with his original fear. Another client remembered an early scene in which father didn't catch her, as he had promised, at the bottom of a slide. She enters the scene with father and redecides, recognizing that she no longer needs him to catch her. Thus Bob combines redecision work with desensitization.

Bob asks if anyone has any lingering fear of water. One person is afraid of getting water in her throat and choking, so Bob has her take water in her mouth, put her head back, and gargle. She opens her mouth underwater and recognizes that she can suck in and spit out without choking. One man is afraid of water getting up his nose and Bob asks him to deliberately try to suck water up his nose. This is very difficult to do and those who succeed sometimes complain that it stings. Bob asks if he wants to drop his fear of water and swim, or if he is going to let a little stinging stop him. Bob picks up water in his hand and lets it run into his nose, and then blows it out.

All participants are now happily ducking their heads, blowing bubbles, and spitting streams of water at each other. They are ready to move on. Bob asks them to sit on the edge of the pool and watch him float. He demonstrates how easily he floats, lying in the water on his back with his arms outstretched above his head, relaxed, allowing the water to hold up his body, legs, arms, head. He shows how, when he moves his hands to his sides, his feet go down, but he still remains afloat, with just his head out of the water. (Most people, except for skinny children and very skinny men and women, can float. Bob has met only three non-floaters, who can't learn to float. He encouraged them to wear a padded belt for safety.)

Bob now demonstrates that he sinks as he lets the water out of his lungs. He reminds them, while floating, that *they* are also in charge of their own breathing, and that if they inspire deeply and then blow out only enough air to stay afloat and then inspire again, they will *not* sink. He demonstrates this, breathing out enough air to stay afloat, but not enough for his head to go under. Then he asks for volunteers to learn to float first.

Joe volunteers first.

Bob: OK, I am going to ask you to lie down in the water, as I have been doing, and I am going to hold you up with my hands, so that you can't sink. I absolutely guarantee you that I will not trick you in any way; I will ask your permission for each thing I do, as you begin to realize that you can float. I will *not* surprise you in any way. I will support you less and less as you begin to float. Do you believe me?

Joe: Yes. I know you won't trick me.

Bob: OK. Lie down on my hands. Put your hands well above your head, as I was doing a few minutes ago. (*Joe does this, but like most frightened clients, he keeps his hands out of the water, as if trying to hold on to the air. His body is rigid.*)

Bob: Let your hands relax in the water. You need all your skin surface to float, and if you pull your hands or arms out you have less skin for the water to support. The water will hold you up if you let it. Let your hands float. (*Bob is shouting so that Joe, whose ears are under water, can hear him.*)

Bob: Your hands are still out of the water. Put them back in. Let your elbows and your forearms relax, and let your hands just lie in the water. (*Joe does.*) That's better. Now, breathe more deeply, and see if you can rise off my hands. There. You almost got off. Cheer, you characters! (*The group cheers.*)

Bob: I am going to hold you with only one hand, so that I can use my other. OK? (*Joe agrees.*) Now, let your hands relax again. You are holding them out. (*Bob takes each hand, shakes it from the wrist, while continuing to hold him afloat with his other hand. Joe relaxes his arms*) . That's better. Breathe deeply, see if you can rise off my hand. That's it, you were off for a second. (*cheers*) Do you feel how light you are as you ride off my hand? (*Joe grins.*) Now, are you ready for me to just hold you with four fingers? (*Joe nods.*) OK, four fingers. Rise off. Relax your arms, you are holding your hands out again. Put them back. Let your legs go, you are holding them tight. (*Bob moves his left hand down and shakes Joe's legs.*) Don't try to push into the water like you are. Then the water gives. Let the water hold you. The water will hold you up if you let it. (*Notices that Joe has relaxed his legs, but now is holding his neck stiff, so changes hands again.*) Let your head lie in the water. If I cut it off and threw it away, it would float. (*Group laughs, Joe laughs, as Bob moves Joe's head up and down with his hand.*) That's better, just let it lie there. Your brains are much lighter than the water, your head is hollow, just let it lie there. (*Joe does.*)

Bob: OK. Now I am going to hold you with just three fingers, and see if you can rise off my fingers. Fine, you were off for a second. (*Group cheers again.*) Now that you are almost floating, take a deeper breath. Breathe deeply. Breathe from here. (*Puts hand on Joe's belly.*) Suck air way down here. Open your eyes, you can't see where you are going if you close your eyes. Let your head relax and take a deep breath, get off my fingers. That's it, you were off again. Did you feel that? (*Joe nods.*) OK, get off again. Wow, that's great. (*Group cheers again.*) OK, now two fingers. Are you ready? Joe, you are doing great. You are almost ready to float. Two fingers now? (*Joe nods.*) I can't hear you. Answer me. (*Joe says yes, he's ready.*) OK. Two fingers. Rise off, Joe. Take a deep breath, and rise off. (*Joe does, completely off.*) Wow, that's great. You're great. Do it again. (*Group cheers and applauds.*) OK. Now only one finger, you don't even need that, though. Feel yourself rise off. Do you feel your body rising up as you breathe? (*Joe nods.*) OK, now rise off that one finger, and then I will pull it away, and you just breathe and float, breathe and float. Are you ready? (*Joe grins again.*) There, you made it. You are floating. (*Bob raises both his hands in the air over Joe's face, and the group cheers and whistles and applauds with a great deal of noise.*) Wow, great, great. You are floating, you are floating. Just lie there for a minute and float all by yourself, then we will rest.

Joe lies there on the water, floating, with a huge smile on his face. Bob then shows him how to lower his legs and stand.

Bob: How do you feel, Joe.

Joe: Great. I feel great. I am great.

Bob repeats this exercise with each one. Joe was not difficult, but he was a little more scared to start with than the others. The others know this and each floats very easily. The crowd stays around watching and cheering each movement, each victory, as all six learn how to float.

Bob: OK. Now you are all doing great, floating, I want you now to lie on your backs and float, and then take your hands and make small movements with your hands, like this. (*Demonstrates lying on his back and propelling his body with small hand movements, keeping his arms up over his head, floating on the water. All of them do so, some more easily than others, but in two or three minutes all are swimming on their backs, while Bob says with great gusto*) : You're swimming, you're swimming. (*Group cheers.*) Practice that a while, while I rest. (*They do while Bob watches and yells encouragement.*)

Bob: Now it is time to learn another exercise, and then we will quit for the day. Who volunteers? (*Joe volunteers again.*) OK, Joe, I want you to go over to the wall and do like this. (*Bob demonstrates lying face down in the water, pushing off against the wall, and floating face downward out to the middle of the shallow water, where he executes a turn, so that he is now floating on his back, and breathing.*) OK, I want each one of you to do that. Here at Mt. Madonna we do NOT call that the Dead Man's Float. Not at Mt. Madonna. (*All laugh. Bob knows that everywhere they teach swimming, that float is called the Dead Man's Float, which doesn't exactly inspire enthusiasm in the novice or the phobic. Bob wants to verbalize this fear, that most non-swimmers have, so that they can deal with it overtly. The laugh does it. Then they, at their own speed, do the exercise, some better than others, some with great difficulty.*)

Bob: OK, I want to quit now. Some of you did it very well, you all did it some. It is not difficult, but it takes practice, like anything else. You may be inclined to harass yourself if you don't do it perfectly. Don't do that! Realize that all of you, less than an hour ago, were afraid to go into the water, and now you have all swum, all floated. You are great, and you will all learn to swim several strokes before the month is over. Practice tonight, after we are through, with each other. Practice floating first, then practice turning. Remember, you already have your arms out in front of you, so leave one arm out there, and bring the other around as you turn. That way you have one arm already there to help hold you up. Do it like this. *(Executes another turn, very slowly, showing them how to do it with one arm stretched out throughout the whole turn.)* OK, let's quit, and practice later. *(Bob then does a fast four or five laps Australian crawl and backstroke, while the group cheers him, now. After he comes out of the water, he says with a grin)* : Pretty good for a 60-year-young man, huh?

The next day, and for several days after that, Bob works with them in the water. They learn to turn from front to back, so they all have the choice, anytime they are in deep water and get tired, to rest by floating on their backs. This is a survival technique that all swimmers need.

When people have learned to relax and float, so that their very cells understand that floating is possible, they stop being afraid and are ready to learn strokes. Bob teaches backstroke, breast stroke and sometimes side stroke. He's not interested in making them skillful swimmers of the Australian crawl and won't even teach the crawl until they can do the other strokes well enough to be competent in the water. In all these strokes they can swim with their heads out of the water, breathe easily, and gain confidence in themselves. When they are confident, they move to the deep end, a short distance at a time, holding onto the side of the pool, and then swim back to shallow water. They then practice turning from front to back and floating in deep water. Finally, they are swimmers, confident and competent in deep water.

This is exciting work. Creating an environment in which people cure themselves is exciting. Enjoy!

CHAPTER 12

After Redecision

Redecision is a beginning rather than an ending. After redecision, the person begins to think, feel, and behave in new ways. At this point he may decide to terminate therapy. We applaud this choice. Our philosophy of treatment is that therapy should be as condensed and quick as possible and that termination is a triumph, like graduation. Whenever possible, we prefer that clients practice their redecisions without additional therapy and return to therapy only if they encounter difficulties. We also tell clients that they don't have to find difficulties in order to be in contact with us. We like telephone calls and letters telling of their triumphs and we encourage them to visit us.

Because we prefer short-term treatment, we have been very satisfied with the treatment format we have evolved for weekend, one-week, two-week, and four-week workshops. When the workshop ends, the work is over. We recognize that this is not treatment of choice for some clients, and also that most therapists do practice primarily ongoing therapy. Whatever the treatment format, we believe that the client should be encouraged to terminate when he has made the personal changes he wants to make, and should be welcomed back if he encounters difficulties he doesn't know how to solve on his own. This minimizes dependency and transference problems.

When a client is ready to terminate, we ask him to shut his eyes and pretend he is in his own home. *"Concentrate on yourself. Remind yourself of the redecisions you have made. How are you putting them into effect? How are you different? Bring your family into your scene if you like . . or remain alone. Either way, notice the changes you are making in the way you feel . . . the way you think . . . the way you behave."* We then ask him to imagine himself at the family dinner table with the entire family present. *"See the others in your family? How are you and they interacting? Do they notice changes in you? Do you imagine them to be pleased or displeased? If the changes that you imagine they notice are not the changes you want them to notice, how will you demonstrate the changes you want them to notice? Don't tell them your changes, show them!"* The person reports. *"Go back again to your home. See if there is any way . . . any way that you will let yourself or others persuade you to give up the gains you have made in therapy?"*

We then ask the client to fantasize himself at work and we offer the same questions about himself and others at work. If the client experiences difficulties in his fantasies, we re-contract and work with him to solve the difficulties. If the client fails to realize that the others might be displeased, we offer our opinions. For example, a woman who had depended on her mother for advice is now quite self-reliant; mother may be unhappy. If a client fails to report his solution to a problem known to us, we bring that fact to his attention:

Bob: I like your fantasy of the way you'll be. How about your son? You didn't mention him. How will you react if he comes home drunk and wants to borrow money?

Ord: I've worked on so many problems and done so much, I forgot to tell you about Ed. As you know, he's fine right now. If he drinks again and comes home . . . that's his problem. He knows . . . I've talked to him . . . he's welcome sober. And I have definitely given up being his ineffective alcohol counselor. Not drinking, he can ask for money and I may give it to him. The important part is, I'm not guilty about what he does with his life and I'm not responsible.

Bob: Fine!

Pat, who redecided while fantasizing that she was in her parents' candy store, believed that her parents would not react well to her changes.

Mary: Pat, I'm amazed by you. When you first came, you blemished so much of your life. And you were sort of a prickly pear. Now you are happy and loveable. How are you going to stay that way?

Pat: I've been thinking about that and I've got some ideas.

Mary: Great! Be at home and tell your ideas. Tell what you are doing and feeling that's different.

Pat: OK. I'm there. (*pause*) I'm OK. It's my parents. No, I'm OK even when my parents visit. They don't know they could have been happy in our store. When my father starts complaining about everything . . . about me . . . I silently . . . SILENTLY . . . pricker him when he prickers me. (*giggles*) When he is sarcastic, I'll pretend I'm sucking a raspberry lollypop. That was one thing I liked about where we lived . . . lollypops.

Sometimes Bob gives clients his "handy-dandy" formula for the modification of the behavior of parents or friends:

Bob: OK, I hear you are tired of her complaints. I'll tell you what to do if you'll promise not to say *yes, but*.

Dana: (*laughs*) OK.

Bob: First, when your mother starts to complain, ask her, "*Ma, what good happened today?*" If she continues to complain, ask her, "*So otherwise how are you?*" If that doesn't work, say, "*Good-bye.*" And leave. When she begins to learn to tell you what good happened, stroke the hell out of her.

We also warn clients against returning home to be the unpaid, unwanted family therapist:

Mary: You'll all be leaving in a couple of hours. I want to give you some advice. Don't therapize your family or your friends. Remember that while you were here having a great time and making great changes in yourselves, they were back home doing the same old dumb things. They are not going to be thrilled to learn from you that it's not *"can't"*—it's *"won't,"* or that nobody can make them feel. They will not change just because you draw them a diagram of the game they are playing. In fact, if any of you psych-out your family, you are playing the game which I call *"hostalysis"*—analysis with hostility as the underlying motive. *"It's not that I am angry at you, darling, but let me show you how sick you are!"* And you therapists tend to be the very worst offenders. Lord, it's bad enough to be a kid without being the son or daughter of a shrink! So *stop shrinking your families* and instead love them.
Bob: Yeah. I agree. *Don't burn up on reentry*.

For some problems, redecision is all that is necessary. This is particularly true of phobias. When a person gives up being afraid and tests herself successfully in a reality situation, she will remain unafraid. In ten years of curing phobics, none has reported experiencing the same phobia again. Many, once they have given up one phobia, proceed spontaneously to stop being afraid in other situations.

For some problems, the client will need practice after making a redecision. Obviously, giving up a fear of water is not very important until the person learns to swim well enough to enjoy being in water. Zoe, who enjoyed the birthday party and stopped being "timid," said that she needed to learn skills in order to deal more assertively with people. We referred her to an assertiveness group for women. Another client, with a similar problem, wanted to learn social skills. After her redecision, we referred her to Stéphen Karpman,[1] who leads ongoing therapy groups in which a client may learn what he calls TA for "social control, social options for change, and social openness." In his groups clients practice using their ego states to transact more successfully with others. He also does redecision therapy when that is necessary.

Edith, who gave herself the anti-confusion ray gun, is a welfare mother and has decided to become a physician. The road ahead will be long and as exciting as she permits it to be. She desires long-term group support in order to keep herself in her redecision to think clearly, plan clearly, and be a winner in the career of her choice. She is going to test various groups until she finds one that agrees with her belief in her own potentialities and which does not stroke for sadness or confusion. She's looking forward to the search for a healthy group run by a healthy therapist in a clinic that provides free therapy while she continues her schooling.

Clients who redecide to live may or may not need additional therapy after redecision. Usually they do in order to make other redecisions—to be close, successful, or fun-loving. Clients who have had problems trusting others and clients who have never experienced emotionally close relationships certainly benefit from additional therapy after the redecision to trust. However, the therapist must guard against their remaining in prolonged therapy in order to experience closeness from group members as a substitute for finding close relationships outside of the group.

Impulsive clients need practice changing destructive behaviors and finding adequate substitutes for the types of strokes they had been receiving. Chronically psychotic clients may elect to remain in groups over a long period of time, as they test out their new non-psychotic behaviors.

We predict to all clients that from time to time they'll play their former games and experience old, stereotyped emotions. They can harass themselves for not being perfect or congratulate themselves for recognizing games and dropping the payoffs more quickly than formerly.

Some clients find it difficult to maintain a redecision. A client whose spouse or friends are losers will probably get only negative strokes for becoming successful. Edith may find that even her welfare worker, if she's secretly jealous, will put up roadblocks to Edith's becoming a physician. Some clients will have to renounce certain goals. A female client, redeciding to trust and be close to men, may not find a man who wants to marry her, particularly if she is over 50 when she makes her redecision. She may then need to deal with the fact that a close, intimate life-style does not have to depend upon being married.

At various times of our lives, all of us face crises that seem unbearable. We believe that clients who have experienced the excitement and wonder of changing their own lives will be motivated to deal constructively with stress and to return to therapy if they choose.

Again, REDECISION is a beginning. There is no magic. The person discovers his ability to be autonomous and experiences his new, free self with enthusiasm, excitement and energy. He goes out in.o his world to practice changing and the practice is a continuous process. He looks upon the world through a different pair of glasses, a different pair of eyes, not coloring the world muddy and tainted by his original decision, but seeing clearly, sharply, as if the rain had washed away the smog.

NOTES

Chapter 1. Introduction to Redecision Therapy

1. Lieberman, Morton A., Irving D. Yalom and Matthews B. Miles, *Encounter Groups: First Facts,* New York: Basic Books, 1973.
2. Goulding, Mary McClure, Phobias, *Transactional Analysis Journal,* 7, 1, 47, 1977. Reprinted in *The Power is in the Patient,* with Robert Goulding, San Francisco: TA Press, 1978.

Chapter 2. Overview of Transactional Analysis

1. Berne, Eric, *What Do You Say After You Say Hello?* New York: Grove Press, 1970, p. 116.
2. Dusay, John, *Egograms,* New York: Harper and Row, 1977.
3. Stuntz, E. C., Multiple Chair Technique, *Transactional Analysis Journal,* 3, 2, 29-32, 1973.
4. Berne, Eric, *Principles of Group Treatment,* New York: Oxford University Press, 1966, and private communications in lectures, seminars.
5. Berne, Eric, *Transactional Analysis in Psychotherapy,* New York: Grove Press, 1961.
6. Berne, Eric, *Games People Play,* New York: Grove Press, 1964.

7. Kaufman, Jack, D.S.W., Madison, Wisconsin, personal communication to R. L. Goulding.

8. Karpman, Stephen, Fairy Tales and Script Drama Analysis, *TA Bulletin*, 7:26.

9. Goulding, Robert and Mary McClure Goulding, *The Power is in the Patient*, San Francisco: TA Press, 1978.

10. Kahler, Taibi and Hedges Capers, The Miniscript, *Transactional Analysis Journal*, 4, 1, 26-42, 1974.

11. George McClendon, MFC, is a family therapist in Aptos, California and a member of WIGFT faculty.

12. Holloway, William, *The Clinical Transactional Analysis with Use of the Life Script Questionnaire*, Ohio: Holloway Books, undated.

13. McCormick, Paul, *Guide for the Use of the Life Script Questionnaire*, San Francisco: Transactional Publications, ITAA, 1971.

Chapter 3. Impasses and Redecisions

1. Goulding, Robert, Thinking and Feeling in Psychotherapy: Three Impasses, *Voices*, 10, 1, 11-13, 1974. See Goulding, Robert and Mary McClure Goulding, *The Power is in the Patient*, San Francisco: TA Press, 1978.

Chapter 4. Contracts

1. Drye, Robert C., Stroking the Rebellious Child, *Transactional Analysis Journal*, 4, 3, 23-26, 1974. Bob Drye, M.D. psychiatrist and psychoanalyst, is on the faculty of the Western Institute of Group and Family Therapy (WIGFT) with offices in Seaside, CA.

Chapter 5. Stroking

1. Dusay, John M., *Egograms*, New York: Harper and Row, 1977.

2. Howard, John, M.D., psychiatrist in private practice, Little Rock, Ark.

Chapter 6. Emotions

1. Cupchik, Will, Ph.D., is a gestalt therapist in Toronto, Canada.

2. "My Melancholy Baby." Reprinted with permission of Jerry Vogel Music Company.

3. Shepherd, Irma Lee, Ph.D., and Joen Fagan, Ph.D., are editors of *Gestalt Therapy Now*, New York: Harper Colophon Books, 1971,

and are on the faculty, Psychology Department, Georgia State College in Atlanta.

Chapter 7. Goodbyes

1. Mary's favorite film of Fritz Perls' work is "Grief vs. Pseudo Grief," in which there is a comparison between racket emotion and a genuine goodbye.

Chapter 8. Redecisions

1. John McNeel, Ph.D., and Ellyn Bader, Ph.D., are members of WIGFT faculty, in Palo Alto, California.
2. Eugene Kerfoot, Ph.D., is in private practice in Seaside, Ca., and is on the faculty of WIGFT.
3. W. Graham Barnes, M.A., M.Div., founded the Southeast Institute, Chapel Hill, N.C., and is editor of *Transactional Analysis After Eric Berne*, New York: Harpers College Press, 1977.
4. George Thomson, Ph.D., practices in Palo Alto, Ca. and is a faculty member of WIGFT.
5. James E. Heenan, Ph.D., is in private practice in Palo Alto and is on the WIGFT faculty.
6. Satir, Virginia, *Peoplemaking*, Palo Alto: Science and Behavior Books, 1972.
7. Ruth McClendon, M.S.W., and Les Kadis, M.D., are family therapists and on the WIGFT faculty.

Chapter 9. The Curing of Depression

1. Goulding, Robert L., New Directions in Transactional Analysis: Creating an Environment for Redecision and Change. In Sager, C. S. and H. S. Kaplan (Eds.), *Progress in Group and Family Therapy*, New York: Brunner/Mazel, 1972, pp. 105-134.
2. Friedman, M. and R. H. Rosenman, *Type A Behavior and Your Heart*, New York: Knopf, 1974.

Chapter 10. Phobias: One Wednesday Afternoon

1. English, Fanita, Episcript and the Hot Potato Game, *Transactional Analysis Bulletin*, 8, 77-82, 1969.

Chapter 11. After Redecisions

1. Stephen B. Karpman, M.D., psychiatrist, is in private practice in San Francisco, CA.

GENERAL BIBLIOGRAPHY

Books by Eric Berne

1. Berne, Eric, *The Layman's Guide to Psychiatry and Psychoanalysis,* Simon and Schuster, New York, 1947, 1957, 1968.
2. Berne, Eric, *Transactional Analysis in Psychotherapy,* Grove Press, New York, 1961.
3. Berne, Eric, *Games People Play,* Grove Press, New York, 1964.
4. Berne, Eric, *The Structure and Dynamics of Organizations and Groups,* Grove Press, New York, 1966.
5. Berne, Eric, *Principles of Group Treatment,* Oxford University Press, New York, 1966.
6. Berne, Eric, *Sex in Human Loving,* Simon and Schuster, New York, 1970.
7. Berne, Eric, *What Do You Say After You Say Hello?* Grove Press, New York, 1972.
8. Berne, Eric, *Intuitions and Ego States: The Origins of Transactional Analysis,* TA Press, San Francisco, 1977.

*Other Transactional Analysis Books, Chapters in Books,
and Articles*

9. Abell, Richard, *Own Your Own Life*, McKay, New York, 1976.
10. Barnes, Graham (Ed.), *Transactional Analysis After Eric Berne*, Harpers College Press, New York, 1977.
11. Blakeney, Roger N. (Ed.), *Current Issues in Transactional Analysis*, Brunner/Mazel, New York, 1977.
12. Dusay, Jack, *Egograms*, Harper and Row, New York, 1977.
13. Ernst, Ken, *Games Students Play*, Celestial Arts Publications, Millbrae, Ca., 1972.
14. Forman, Louis, H., and Ramsburg, Janelle Smith, *Hello Sigmund, This is Eric!* Sheed Andrews and McMeel Inc. (Subsidiary of Universal Press Syndicate), Mission, Kansas, 1978.
15. Goulding, Robert, and Goulding, Mary, *The Power is in the Patient*, TA Press, San Francisco, 1978. (Collection of the Gouldings' articles, edited by Paul McCormick.)
16. Goulding, Robert, Four Models of Transactional Analysis, *International Journal of Group Psychotherapy*, XXVI:3, 385-392, July, 1976.
17. Goulding, Robert, Decisions in Script Formation, *Transactional Analysis Journal*, 2, 2, 62-63, April, 1972.
18. Haimowitz, Morris and Haimowitz, Natalie, *Suffering is Optional*, Haimowoods Press, Evanston, Ill., 1976.
19. Harris, Thomas, *I'm OK, You're OK*, Harper and Row, New York, 1967.
20. James, Muriel and Jongeward, Dorothy, *Born to Win*, Addison Wesley, Reading, MA., 1971.
21. James, Muriel, *The Power at the Bottom of the Well*, Collin Associates, New York, 1974.
22. James, Muriel, *Marriage is for Loving*, Addison Wesley, Reading, MA, 1979.
23. McCormick, Paul, *Ego States*, TA Publications, San Francisco, 1977.
24. McCormick Paul. *Guide for Use of a Life Script Questionnaire in Transactional Analysis*, Transactional Publications, San Francisco, 1971.
25. McCormick, Paul and Campos, Leonard, *Introduce Yourself to TA*, Transactional Publications, San Francisco, 1968.
26. McCormick, Paul, and Campos, Leonard, *Introduce Your Marriage to TA*, Transactional Publications, San Francisco, 1969.

27. Woollams, Stan and Brown, Michael, *Transactional Analysis*, Huron Valley Institute Press, Ann Arbor, MI, 1978.

Gestalt Books

28. Fagan, Joen and Shepherd, Irma, *Gestalt Therapy Verbatim*, Science and Behavior Books, Palo Alto, CA, 1970.
29. Hatcher, Chris, and Himelstein, Philip, *The Handbook of Gestalt Therapy*, Jason Aronson, New York, 1976.
30. Perls, Fritz, *Gestalt Therapy Verbatim*, Real People Press, Lafayette, CA, 1969.
31. Perls, Fritz, *Ego Hunger and Aggression*, Random House, New York, 1969.
32. Perls, Fritz, *In and Out the Garbage Pail*, Real People Press, Lafayette, CA, 1969.
33. Perls, Fritz, *The Gestalt Approach and Eyewitness to Therapy*, Science and Behavior Books, Palo Alto, CA, 1973.
34. Perls, Fritz, Hefferline, R. F. and Goodman, P., *Gestalt Therapy*, Julian Press, New York, 1951.
35. Polster, Erving and Polster, Miriam, *Gestalt Therapy Integrated*, Brunner/Mazel, New York, 1973.
36. Smith, Edward W. L. (Ed.), *The Growing Edge of Gestalt Therapy*, Brunner/Mazel, New York, 1976.

Others:

37. Bandler,, Richard, Grinder, John and Satir, Virginia, *Changing with Families*, Science and Behavior Books, Palo Alto, CA, 1976.
38. Jongeward, Dorothy, and Scott, Dru, *Women as Winners*, Addison Wesley, Reading, MA, 1976.
39. Keys, Margaret Frings, *The Inward Journey*, Celestial Arts, Millbrae, CA, 1974.

INDEX

Adult ego state
  contamination of, 23-25
  early, 13-15, 19. *See also* Little Professor
  and the ego, 23
  functions of, 12
Anger
  collecting of, as stamps, 121. *See also*
    Trading stamps
  as defense against injunctions, 127
  questions to ask when feeling, 121-122
  repression of, 147
Anxiety, 150-155. *See also* Phobias, treat-
    ment of
Autonomy
  and feelings, 5-6, 29, 227-228
  in redecision therapy, 5-6
  words that deny, 85-90, 111

Bader, Ellyn, 193-194
Barnes, Graham, 196
Berne, Eric, 4, 11, 12, 13, 15, 17, 21, 24, 26,
  27, 30, 31, 33, 38, 39, 42, 118, 202
Blame, 133-135
Body language, 93
Bridges, Harry, 169

Child abusers, 170
Child ego state
  adapted, 18-19
  contamination of, 24
  early, 12-13, 21
  free, 18-19
  functional division of, 15, 19
  structural division of, 15
Contracts
  changing of "forever," 80-81
  changing of "game," 78-80
  changing of "Parent," 71-75
  changing of "someone-else-must-change,"
    75-78
  clarifying of, 50-55
  confronting of ulterior, 85-93
  for no homicide, 55, 60-61
  for no psychosis, 61-69
  for no suicide, 55-60
  as patient's goal, 5
  with reluctant clients, 69-71
  working with no, 82-85
Counter-injunctions, 34, 38-39
Counter-phobias, 155-156
Cupchik, Will, 134

Decisions, early, 6, 18, 40-42, 45, 46, 191
    and depression, 215-216
    following "Don't be" injunction, 216
Depression
    endogenous v. reactive, 216
    steps in curing, 239-240
    use of drugs in treating, 220-221
Dream work, 148-150, 196-197, 199-201
Drivers, 38
Drye, Robert C., 74
Dusay, John M., 24, 104

Ego states, 12, 48. *See also* Parent, Adult,
    and Child ego states
    identification of, 25
Egograms, 24
Egograms, 104-109
    of "typical" therapists, 104-106
Episcripting (Hot Potato Syndrome), 265
Erikson, Erik, 34

Fagan, Joen, 160
Fear, 150-157. *See also* Phobias, treatment
    of
First con, 90-91
Freud, Sigmund, 34
Friedman, M., 231

Gallows laughter, 91-92
Games
    awareness in, 30, 31, 33, 80
    definition of, 30
    evidence of, 30
    formula of, 31
    payoffs of, 30, 31, 32, 33
    players in, 31
    rules of, 31
    transactions in, 27, 30
Games People Play, 4, 30
Goodbyes, saying of
    accepting facts in, 175-178
    completing unfinished business in, 178-
        179
    fantasizing ceremonies in, 179
    formula for, 175
    mourning after, 179
    saying hello to today after, 179
Goulding, Mary McClure, 19, 23, 31, 38,
    196, 202
Goulding, Mimi, 174-175
Goulding, Robert L., 15, 34, 45, 118, 167-
    168, 174-175, 210, 226, 230 passim, 274-
    279
Groder, Martin, 239

Group process, 49
Group therapy, advantages of, 7, 159
Guilt, 160-171

Happiness, 110-117
Heenan, James E., 199-201
Holloway, William, 8, 43
Hot Potato Syndrome (Episcripting), 265
Howard, John, 106-107

Impasses
    degrees of, 45-48
    resolution of, 6. 44-49
Injunctions
    acceptance of, 39, 40
    basic list of, 35-37
    decisions following "Don't be," 216
    definition of, 34
    givers of, 39, 40
    most morbid of all, 215
    and redecisions, 191-194
International Transactional Analysis As-
    sociation, 4

Kadis, Les, 211
Kahler, Taibi, 38
Kaplan, H. S., 226
Karpman, Stephen B., 31, 283
Karpman Drama Triangle, 31
Kaufman, Jack, 30
Kerfoot, Eugene, 196

Lieberman, Morton A., 6
Little Professor, 13, 15, 23, 45 passim

McClendon, George, 43
McClendon, Ruth, 211
McCormick, Paul, 43
McNeel, John, 193-194
Marion Federal Penitentiary, 71, 239
Miles, Matthew, 6
Mixed messages, 39, 41

Obsession-compulsion, rules in treatment
    of, 256-257

Parent ego state
    early, 16-18
    functional division of, 22-23
    internal and external components of, 23
    structural division of, 22-23
    structure of, 12
"Parent interview," 165, 192
Perls, Fritz, 118-119, 152, 175, 202

Phobias, treatment of
  of birds, 262-263
  of butterflies and moths, 262
  of heights, 263-273
  importance of redecision in, 283
  of Japanese mice, 258-262
  of water, 273-279
Principles of Group Treatment, 24
Progress in Group and Family Therapy,
  226

Rackets, 33, 113, 117, 143
Redecision therapy, 4, 8-10, 19. *See also*
  Redecisions
  adaptation in, 9
  affect and cognition in, 6-7, 25, 28
  with angry clients, 117-133
  with anxious clients, 150-155. *See also*
    with phobic clients
  with ashamed clients, 157-160
  autonomy in, 5-6
  with blaming clients, 133-135
  contracts in. *See* Contracts
  without contracts, 82-85
  creating environment for change in, 49,
    218
  diluted transactions in, 29
  direct transactions in, 28
  dreams in. *See* Dream work
  with fearful clients, 150-157. *See also*
    with phobic clients
  focus of, 104
  with food addict, 235-238
  goodbyes in. *See* Goodbyes, saying of
  group process in, 49
  group work in, 7
  with guilty clients, 160-171
  with phobic clients, 258-279, 283. *See
    also* with fearful clients
  redeciding in, 44-49
  with regretful clients, 171-173
  resolving impasses in, 6, 44-49
  rules for setting scenes in, 201-202
  with sad clients, 135-150
  setting scenes in, 9-10, 28-29, 45-47, 184-
    214
  with smokers, 233-235
  with suicidal clients, 215-240
  termination of, 280-285

  transference in, 49, 271, 281
  use of profanity in, 266
Redecisions. *See also* Redecision therapy
  as beginnings, 280-285
  description of, 8-10
  injunctions and, 191-194
  maintaining of, 284
  maker of, 19, 45, 211
Regret, 171-173

Sadness, 135-150
Sager, C. J., 226
Satir, Virginia, 203
Scripts
  checklists for, 42, 43
  fairy tales in, 42
  of families, 43
  matrix for, 253-254
Shame, 157-160
Shepherd, Irma, 160
Strokes
  definition of, 29
  importance of, in therapy, 96
  kinds of, 29, 94, 95, 96
  reasons for rejecting, 99-102
Stuntz, E. C., 24

Thomson, George, 197
Time structuring, ways of, 29
Trading stamps, 34, 121
Transactional analysis, 4, 11
  and psychoanalytic theory, 12, 33
Transactional Analysis Bulletin, 11
Transactional Analysis in Psychotherapy,
  30
Transactional Analysis Journal, 11
Transactions, kinds of, 26-29
Transference. *See* Redecision therapy,
  transference in

*Voices: Journal of the American Academy
  of Psychotherapists*, 11

Wall of trivia, 124-125
What Do You Say After You Say Hello?,
  17, 31

Yalom, Irving D., 6

Selected Grove Press Paperbacks

E732   ALLEN, DONALD M. & BUTTERICK, GEORGE F., eds. / The Postmoderns: The New American Poetry Revised 1945–1960 / $9.95

E609   ALLEN, DONALD M. and TALLMAN, WARREN, eds. / Poetics of the New American Poetry / $3.95

B445   ANONYMOUS / The Boudoir / $2.95

B334   ANONYMOUS / My Secret Life / $3.95

B415   ARDEN, JOHN / Plays: One (Serjeant Musgrave's Dance, The Workhouse Donkey, Armstrong's Last Goodnight) / $4.95

E711   ARENDT, HANNAH / The Jew As Pariah: Jewish Identity and Politics in the Modern Age, ed. by Ron Feldman / $6.95

E611   ARRABAL, FERNANDO / Garden of Delights / $2.95

B439   ARSAN, EMMANUELLE / Emmanuelle / $2.95

E127   ARTAUD, ANTONIN / The Theater and Its Double / $3.95

E425   BARAKA, IMAMU AMIRI (Leroi Jones) / The Baptism and The Toilet: Two Plays / $3.95

E670   BARAKA, IMAMU AMIRI (LeRoi Jones) / The System of Dante's Hell, The Dead Lecturer and Tales / $4.95

E96   BECKETT, SAMUEL / Endgame / $2.45

E692   BECKETT, SAMUEL / I Can't Go On, I'll Go On: A Selection from Samuel Beckett's Work, ed. by Richard Seaver / $6.95

E777   BECKETT, SAMUEL / Rockaby and Other Short Pieces / $3.95

B78   BECKETT, SAMUEL / Three Novels: Molloy, Malone Dies and The Unnamable / $3.95

E33   BECKETT, SAMUEL / Waiting for Godot / $2.95

E152   BECKETT, SAMUEL / Watt / $6.95

B411   BEHAN, BRENDAN / The Complete Plays (The Hostage, The Quare Fellow, Richard's Cork Leg, Three One Act Plays for Radio) / $4.95

E531   BERGMAN, INGMAR / Three Films by Ingmar Bergman (Through a Glass Darkly, Winter Light, The Silence) / $4.95

E331   BIELY, ANDREY / St. Petersburg / $6.95

E417   BIRCH, CYRIL and KEENE, DONALD, eds. / Anthology of Chinese Literature, Vol. I: From Early Times to the 14th Century / $8.95

E584   BIRCH, CYRIL, ed. / Anthology of Chinese Literature, Vol. II: From the 14th Century to the Present / $4.95

E368   BORGES, JORGE LUIS / Ficciones / $3.95

E472   BORGES, JORGE LUIS / A Personal Anthology / $3.95
B60   BRECHT, BERTOLT / Baal, A Man's A Man, The Elephant Calf / $1.95
B312   BRECHT, BERTOLT / The Caucasian Chalk Circle / $1.95
B414   BRECHT, BERTOLT / The Mother / $2.95
B108   BRECHT, BERTOLT / Mother Courage and Her Children / $1.95
E580   BRETON, ANDRE / Nadja / $3.95
E751   BROWN, DEENA, ed. / American Yoga / $9.95
B193   BULGAKOV, MIKHAIL / The Heart of a Dog / $2.95
B147   BULGAKOV, MIKHAIL / The Master and Margarita / $3.95
B115   BURROUGHS, WILLIAM / Naked Lunch / $2.95
B446   BURROUGHS, WILLIAM / The Soft Machine, Nova Express, The Wild Boys: Three Novels / $5.95
B164   BURROUGHS, WILLIAM / The Ticket That Exploded / $2.95
B440   CLEVE, JOHN / The Crusader: Books I and II / $2.95
E773   CLURMAN, HAROLD, ed. / Nine Plays of the Modern Theater (Waiting for Godot by Samuel Beckett, The Visit by Friedrich Dürrenmatt, Tango by Slawomir Mrozek, The Caucasian Chalk Circle by Bertolt Brecht, The Balcony by Jean Genet, Rhinoceros by Eugéne Ionesco, American Buffalo by David Mamet, The Birthday Party by Harold Pinter, and Rosencrantz and Guildenstern are Dead by Tom Stoppard) / $11.95
E771   COCTEAU, JEAN / Opium: The Diary of a Cure / $6.95
B405   CRAFTS, KATHY and HAUTHER, BRENDA / The Student's Guide to Good Grades / $2.45
E739   CROCKETT, JIM, ed. / The Guitar Player Book (Revised and Updated Edition) / $9.95
E190   CUMMINGS, E. E. / 100 Selected Poems / $1.95
E159   DELANEY, SHELAGH / A Taste of Honey / $3.95
E639   DOSS, MARGARET PATTERSON / San Francisco at Your Feet (Second Revised Edition) / $4.95
B412   DOYLE, RODGER and REDDING, JAMES / The Complete Food Handbook. Revised and Updated ed. / $2.95
B75   DURAS, MARGUERITE / Four Novels (The Afternoon of Mr. Andesmas, 10:30 On a Summer Night, Moderato Cantabile, The Square) / $3.95
E284   DURAS, MARGUERITE / Hiroshima Mon Amour. Text for the Film by Alain Resnais. Illus. / $3.95
E380   DURRENMATT, FRIEDRICH / The Physicists / $2.95

E344   DURRENMATT, FRIEDRICH / The Visit / $2.95
B179   FANON, FRANTZ / Black Skin, White Masks / $3.95
B342   FANON, FRANTZ / The Wretched of the Earth / $2.45
E772   FAWCETT, ANTHONY / John Lennon: One Day At A Time. A
       Personal Biography (Revised Edition) / $8.95
E671   FEUERSTEIN, GEORG / The Essence of Yoga / $3.95
E47   FROMM, ERICH / The Forgotten Language / $3.95
E223   GELBER, JACK / The Connection / $3.95
E577   GENET, JEAN / The Maids and Deathwatch: Two Plays / $3.95
B322   GENET, JEAN / The Miracle of the Rose / $3.95
B389   GENET, JEAN / Our Lady of the Flowers / $2.45
E760   GERVASI, TOM / Arsenal of Democracy II / $9.95
E702   GILLAN, PATRICIA and RICHARD / Sex Therapy Today / $4.95
E704   GINSBERG, ALLEN / Journals: Early Fifties Early Sixties, ed. by
       Gordon Ball / $6.95
B437   GIRODIAS, MAURICE, ed. / The Olympia Reader / $3.50
E720   GOMBROWICZ, WITOLD / Three Novels: Ferdydurke, Pornografia
       and Cosmos / $9.95
B448   GOVER, BOB / One Hundred Dollar Misunderstanding / $2.95
B376   GREENE, GERALD and CAROLINE / SM: The Last Taboo / $2.95
E71   H. D. / Selected Poems of H. D. / $2.95
B152   HARRIS, FRANK / My Life and Loves / $4.95
E695   HAYMAN, RONALD / How To Read A Play / $2.95
B205   HEDAYAT, SADEGH / The Blind Owl / $1.95
B306   HERNTON, CALVIN / Sex and Racism in America / $2.95
B154   HOCHUTH, ROLF / The Deputy / $3.95
B436   HODEIR, ANDRE / Jazz: Its Evolution and Essence / $3.95
E351   HUMPHREY, DORIS / The Art of Making Dances / $3.95
E456   IONESCO, EUGENE / Exit the King / $2.95
E101   IONESCO, EUGENE / Four Plays (The Bald Soprano, The Lesson
       The Chairs, Jack or The Submission) / $2.95
E614   IONESCO, EUGENE / Macbett / $2.95
E679   IONESCO, EUGENE / Man With Bags / $3.95
E387   IONESCO, EUGENE / Notes and Counternotes: Writings on the
       Theater / $3.95
B421   JAMES, HENRY / The Sacred Fount / $2.95
B418   JAMES, HENRY / Italian Hours / $2.95
E496   JARRY, ALFRED / The Ubu Plays (Ubu Rex, Ubu Cuckolded, Ubu
       Enchained) / $4.95

E9   KEENE, DONALD / Japanese Literature: An Introduction for Western Readers / $2.25
E216   KEENE, DONALD, ed. / Anthology of Japanese Literature: Earliest Era to Mid-19th Century / $7.95
E573   KEENE, DONALD, ed. / Modern Japanese Literature: An Anthology / $7.95
B253   KEROUAC, JACK / Lonesome Traveler / $2.95
B135   KEROUAC, JACK / Satori in Paris / $2.25
B454   KEROUAC, JACK / The Subterraneans / $3.50
E705   KERR, CARMEN / Sex For Women Who Want To Have Fun and Loving Relationships With Equals / $4.95
B413   LAVERTY, FRANK / The O.K. Way To Slim / $2.95
B9   LAWRENCE, D. H. / Lady Chatterley's Lover / $1.95
E748   LESSER, MICHAEL, M.D. / Nutrition and Vitamin Therapy / $7.95
B262   LESTER, JULIUS / Black Folktales / $2.95
E163   LEWIS, MATTHEW / The Monk / $5.95
E578   LINSSEN, ROBERT / Living Zen / $3.95
E54   LORCA, FEDERICO / Poet in New York. Bilingual ed. / $4.95
B373   LUCAS, GEORGE / American Graffiti / $1.75
E701   MALRAUX, ANDRE / The Conquerors / $3.95
E719   MALRAUX, ANDRE / Lazarus / $2.95
E697   MAMET, DAVID / American Buffalo / $3.95
E778   MAMET, DAVID / Lakeboat / $4.95
E709   MAMET, DAVID / A Life in the Theatre / $3.95
E716   MAMET, DAVID / The Water Engine and Mr. Happiness / $3.95
B61   MILLER, HENRY / Black Spring / $3.95
B326   MILLER, HENRY / Nexus / $3.95
B100   MILLER, HENRY / Plexus / $3.95
B325   MILLER, HENRY / Sexus / $4.95
B10   MILLER, HENRY / Tropic of Cancer / $2.50
B59   MILLER, HENRY / Tropic of Capricorn / $3.50
E583   MISHIMA, YUKIO / Sun and Steel / $4.95
E433   MROZEK, SLAWOMIR / Tango / $3.95
E568   MROZEK, SLAWOMIR / Vatzlav / $1.95
E636   NERUDA, PABLO / Five Decades: Poems 1925–1970. Bilingual ed. / $5.95
E364   NERUDA, PABLO / Selected Poems. Bilingual ed. / $5.95
E650   NICHOLS, PETER / The National Health / $3.95
B199   OE, KENZABURO / A Personal Matter / $3.95

E687	OE, KENZABURO / Teach Us To Outgrow Our Madness / $4.95
E413	O'HARA, FRANK / Meditations in an Emergency / $4.95
·E359	PAZ, OCTAVIO / The Labyrinth of Solitude: Life and Thought in Mexico / $3.95
B359	PAZ, OCTAVIO / The Other Mexico: Critique of the Pyramid / $2.45
E315	PINTER, HAROLD / The Birthday Party and The Room / $2.95
E299	PINTER, HAROLD / The Caretaker and The Dumb Waiter / $2.95
E411	PINTER, HAROLD / The Homecoming / $2.45
E764	PINTER, HAROLD / The Hothouse / $4.95
E690	PINTER, HAROLD / The Proust Screenplay / $3.95
E683	PUDOVKIN, V. I. / Film Technique and Film Acting / $6.95
E641	RAHULA, WALPOLA / What the Buddha Taught / $4.95
B438	REAGE, PAULINE / Story of O, Part II: Return to the Chateau / $2.25
B213	RECHY, JOHN / City of Night / $2.95
B171	RECHY, JOHN / Numbers / $2.95
E710	REED, ISHMAEL and YOUNG, AL, eds. / Yardbird Lives! / $5.95
B112	ROBBE-GRILLET, ALAIN / For A New Novel: Essays on Fiction / $2.25
E698	ROBBE-GRILLET, ALAIN / Topology of a Phantom City / $3.95
B69	ROBBE-GRILLET, ALAIN / Two Novels: Jealousy and In the Labyrinth / $4.95
B133	ROBBE-GRILLET, ALAIN / The Voyeur / $2.95
E759	ROBERTS, RANDY / Jack Dempsey: The Manassa Mauler / $6.95
E741	ROSSET, BARNEY, ed. / Evergreen Review Reader: 1962–1967 / $12.50
B207	RULFO, JUAN / Pedro Paramo / $1.95
B138	SADE, MARQUIS DE / The 120 Days of Sodom and Other Writings / $7.95
B148	SADE, MARQUIS DE / Justine, Philosophy in the Bedroom, Eugenie de Franval, and Other Writings / $7.95
B259	SCHNEEBAUM TOBIAS / Keep the River on Your Right / $3.45
B323	SCHUTZ, WILLIAM C. / Joy: Expanding Human Awareness / $1.95
E494	SCHWEBEL, MILTON / Who Can Be Educated? / $3.45
B313	SELBY, HUBERT, JR. / Last Exit to Brooklyn / $2.95
B363	SELBY, HUBERT, JR. / The Room / $1.95
B456	SINGH, KHUSHWANT / Train to Pakistan / $3.25
E618	SNOW, EDGAR / Red Star Over China / $8.95

E672   SOPA, GESHE LHUNDUP and HOPKINS, JEFFREY / The Practice and Theory of Tibetan Buddhism / $4.95

B433   SAUNERON, SERGE / The Priests of Ancient Egypt / $3.50

E395   SHATTUCK, ROGER, and TAYLOR, SIMON WATSON, eds. / Selected Works of Alfred Jarry / $6.95

E684   STOPPARD, TOM / Dirty Linen and New-Found-Land / $2.95

E703   STOPPARD, TOM / Every Good Boy Deserves Favor and Professional Foul: Two Plays / $3.95

E489   STOPPARD, TOM / The Real Inspector Hound and After Magritte: Two Plays / $3.95

B319   STOPPARD, TOM / Rosencrantz and Guildenstern Are Dead / $2.25

E341   SUZUKI, D. T. / Introduction to Zen Buddhism / $1.95

E231   SUZUKI, D. T. / Manual of Zen Buddhism / $3.95

E749   THELWELL, MICHAEL / The Harder They Come / $7.95

B432   TROCCHI, ALEXANDER / Cain's Book / $3.50

E658   TRUFFAUT, FRANCOIS / Day for Night / $3.95

B399   TRUFFAUT, FRANCOIS / Small Change / $1.95

B395   TRUFFAUT, FRANCOIS / The Story of Adele H / $2.45

E699   TURGENEV, IVAN / Virgin Soil / $3.95

E328   TUTUOLA, AMOS / The Palm-Wine Drunkard / $2.45

E559   TUTUOLA, AMOS / My Life in the Bush of Ghosts / $4.95

E746   VITHOULKAS, GEORGE / The Science of Homeopathy / $9.50

E209   WALEY, ARTHUR, JR. / The Book of Songs / $5.95

E84   WALEY, ARTHUR / The Way and Its Power: A Study of the Tao Te Ching and its Place in Chinese Thought / $4.95

E689   WALKENSTEIN, EILEEN / Don't Shrink to Fit! A Confrontation With Dehumanization in Psychiatry and Psychology / $3.95

E579   WARNER, LANGDON / The Enduring Art of Japan / $4.95

B365   WARNER, SAMUEL J. / Self Realization and Self Defeat / $2.95

E219   WATTS, ALAN W. / The Spirit of Zen / $2.95

E112   WU, CH'ENG-EN / Monkey / $4.95

E767   WYCKOFF, HOGIE / Solving Problems Together / $7.95

B106   YU, LI / Jou Pu Tuan / $1.95

GROVE PRESS, INC., 196 West Houston St., New York, N.Y. 10014